A-level Study Guide

English Literature

Revised and updated

Alan Gardiner

Revision Express

Acknowledgements

I would like to thank: my wife Marian; readers of the *English Language* and *English Language and Literature* books in the Revision Express series, whose kind words encouraged me to complete the trilogy; the football of Tottenham Hotspur (during the season 2005–06) and the music of the great Jerry Lee Lewis, both of which kept me going during the writing of this book. I hope the book helps as many students as possible to get the result they want.

The author and publishers are grateful to the following for permission to reproduce copyright material:

Cambridge University Press for an extract from 'Portrait of The Miller' taken from *The General Prologue to the Canterbury Tales* by Geoffrey Chaucer, edited by James Winny, published by Cambridge University Press 1965; Penguin Group (UK) for an extract from *A Passage to India* by E. M. Forster published by Penguin Books 1973, © The Provost and Scholars of King's College Cambridge, 1934, 1979; Methuen and New Directions Publishing Corporation for an extract from *A Streetcar Named Desire* by Tennessee Williams © 1947 by The University of the South; and Everyman's Library for an extract from *Edward II* by Christopher Marlowe.

In some instances we have been unable to trace the owners of copyright material and we would appreciate any information that would enable us to do so.

Series Consultants: Geoff Black and Stuart Wall
Pearson Education Limited
Edinburgh Gate, Harlow
Essex CM20 2JE, England
and Associated Companies throughout the world

© Pearson Education 2006

British Library Cataloguing-in-Publication Data
A catalogue entry for this title is available from the British Library.

ISBN-10: 0-582-77295-8
ISBN-13: 978-0-582-77295-3

First published 2006
Printed by Ashford Colour Press, Gosport, Hants

It's very likely that you studied English Literature at GCSE, and this introductory chapter begins by outlining the differences between GCSE and AS/A2. In some ways the courses are very similar: you'll be studying set texts (probably about four at AS and another four if you go on to A2), and reading a mixture of poetry, plays and prose. You'll also be looking at characters and themes, though obviously you'll be studying these aspects of your texts in more depth. A major difference from GCSE is that you'll be approaching texts from other directions as well – considering, for instance, how texts are influenced by their historical context (i.e. the time when they were written), and how readers' interpretations of them might differ. In the A2 year you also need to compare texts.

The marks you're given during the course (for coursework as well as for exams) are based on 'assessment objectives', and there's a section in this chapter explaining what this means and what the objectives are. Finally, there are two sections on some of the key terms and concepts you'll encounter during the course. In your essays and other written work you're expected to include relevant terminology, and you should try to get into the habit of using these terms from the outset.

Exam themes

→ Understanding the assessment objectives

→ Use of appropriate terminology

Topic checklist

AS ○ A2 ●	AQA/A	AQA/B	EDEXCEL	OCR	WJEC	CCEA
Moving up from GCSE	○	○	○	○	○	○
How you're assessed	○●	○●	○●	○●	○●	○●
Literary terms and concepts 1	○●	○●	○●	○●	○●	○●
Literary terms and concepts 2	○●	○●	○●	○●	○●	○●

Moving up from GCSE

This introductory section looks at the transition from GCSE to AS/A2. Your GCSE English course will have provided you with a good foundation for the AS course, but there are some important differences between the two levels of study, and these are explained here.

GCSE and AS/A2 – the differences

If you're studying AS or A2 English Literature, it's likely that you've already successfully taken GCSE English Literature. Alternatively, you might just have sat GCSE English, which in itself involves the study of a substantial number of literary texts. The examining boards try to ensure there is continuity between GCSE and AS/A2, and in some respects the differences are not that great. The main ones can be summarised as follows:

→ You'll probably find you're studying **more books** – a minimum of four at AS and another four at A2 – and when you study them you'll be looking at the whole text, not just selected extracts.

→ You'll study books in **more depth**, which means the essays you write will need to be longer and more detailed.

→ There is more emphasis than at GCSE on how books are influenced by their **contexts**, and on how different readers at different times have **interpreted** the texts (see 'Contexts' and 'Interpretations of texts' below).

→ You may be asked to undertake more **research** and **wider reading** – for example, knowing something about the historical background to a particular book might be important.

→ You'll still use terms such as *metaphor* and *simile*, but will also be introduced to a wider range of **literary terms and concepts**, which you can use when analysing texts.

→ Perhaps most importantly of all, you'll be encouraged to develop the skills of an **independent reader**, able to form your own opinions about the books you study, and to argue these opinions convincingly.

If this list sounds a bit daunting, remember these two things:

→ Some of your other AS/A2 subjects might be completely new to you – this is almost certainly not the case with English Literature.

→ Ideally, you've chosen the course because you enjoy reading and writing about what you've read. Taking your skills as an English literature student to another level should enable you to get *more* out of the books you read, giving you a new insight into how great books and great writers 'work' – an insight that you will never lose.

Links

Contexts and **interpretations** are also discussed in more detail on pages 148–59 and 160–5 respectively.

Links

Some relevant terms and concepts are explained on pages 8–11. There is also a list of terms and definitions in the **Glossary** at the back of the book (pages 184–8).

What you'll be studying

As mentioned above, a two-year AS/A2 course usually involves the study of eight or more set books. The specific books vary from one examining board to another, but national requirements mean that the course must include:

→ poetry, prose (usually novels or short stories) and plays;
→ Shakespeare;
→ at least one work written before 1770, and at least two other works written before 1900.

At A2, as well as studying individual texts you also **compare** two or more texts. Another feature of some of the A2 examinations is the analysis of **unseen** texts – that is, shorter texts (such as poems or prose extracts) that you have not studied before.

Contexts

An important part of the course is considering the effects of background influences – known collectively as **contexts** – on the books you are studying. For certain texts – your teacher will tell you which they are, or you can find out by checking the syllabus or specification – your understanding of contextual influences is especially important, as it is specifically assessed. The main types of contextual influence are:

→ **biographical** – aspects of the writer's life that are reflected in the work;
→ **cultural and literary** – the influence of other writers, artistic movements and the conventions and traditions associated with the work's genre;
→ **historical** – the influence of political and other events which occurred around the time the work was written;
→ **social** – how the society of the time influenced the work, or is reflected in it.

Interpretations of texts

Another important element is the consideration of alternative **interpretations** of texts. As with contexts, this will be of particular relevance to certain specified works. You will look at how **critics** from different historical periods or different **critical perspectives** have interpreted particular books. At the same time, it is important to show that you can think for yourself by comparing the views of others and justifying your own opinion.

Check the web

All of the AS/A2 English Literature specifications can be found on the relevant examining board websites. See page 171 for a list of website addresses.

Watch out!

In answers, only mention biographical factors which might have influenced the text in some way (don't simply tell the story of the author's life). And keep such references brief – the main focus should always be on the text itself.

Watch out!

The word **critic** as used here does not mean someone who necessarily has a negative view of a text. A critic is simply someone who comments on or interprets a text – any views expressed may be positive *or* negative.

Take note

An example of a **critical perspective** is **feminism**. A feminist critic would tend to focus on the attitudes towards women evident in a text.

Take note

You might for example have materials on Shakespeare that will be helpful.

Exam preparation

As explained above, there is some continuity between GCSE and A level, so if you still have them, it is worth collecting together your GCSE English notes and keeping them, as they might be of some use.

How you're assessed

This section outlines the structure of AS/A2 English literature courses, looking in particular at the seven official **assessment objectives**, which examiners use to calculate your marks.

Coursework and exams ●●●

Depending on the specification you're taking, and the options chosen by your school or college, you may be assessed by exam only or by a combination of exams and coursework. If the assessment is purely exam-based, you will sit three exam papers in your AS year and another three in your A2 year. If coursework is part of your assessment, you're likely to find that coursework assignments replace one AS paper and/or one A2 paper. Coursework (if taken) is worth 30% of the AS assessment and 30% of the A2 assessment, which means that when the marks are added together it is also worth 30% of the full A level.

Assessment objectives ●●●

Assessment objectives (**AOs**) identify the skills and knowledge you're expected to acquire during the course. Each module usually assesses a combination of between three and five objectives. Overall the objectives have a fairly equal weighting, but within individual modules the objectives will have varying degrees of importance.

Listed below are the seven assessment objectives for English Literature, with a brief explanation of what each one means. Unless indicated, they are tested at both AS and A2; the difference is that at A2 a higher standard is expected.

AO1

Communicate clearly the knowledge, understanding and insight appropriate to literary study, using appropriate terminology and accurate and coherent written expression.

This objective highlights your own writing skills (you need to *communicate clearly*), and also the need to know and use effectively relevant literary terms, such as 'metaphor', 'soliloquy' and so on.

AO2i (AS only)

Respond with knowledge and understanding to literary texts of different types and periods.

This objective indicates that you will study a range of literary genres (poetry, prose, plays), and texts from different historical periods. In writing about the books you study, you will need to show *knowledge and understanding*. 'Knowledge' implies offering clear evidence that you've read the books, in the form of quotations and detailed references. 'Understanding' implies something deeper – that you've grasped and can explain the themes and ideas present in texts, and the techniques writers have used to convey these.

AO2ii (A2 only)

Respond with knowledge and understanding to literary texts of different types and periods, exploring and commenting on relationships and comparisons between literary texts.

This extends AO2i: you also need to closely compare texts.

AO3

Show detailed understanding of the ways in which writers' choices of form, structure and language shape meanings.

You need to analyse closely the language of the writers you study. You also need to look at *form* and *structure*. Form is closely linked to genre: for example, some of the poems you study might take the form of sonnets, others might be odes or ballads. Structure refers more to a text's overall organisation, including for example how it starts and ends, and the sequence of ideas or events.

AO4

Articulate independent opinions and judgements, informed by different interpretations of literary texts by other readers.

You should express your own views of the texts you study, but also consider the views and interpretations of other readers.

AO5i (AS only)

Show understanding of the contexts in which literary texts are written and understood.

You will need to show an understanding of background influences on the texts that you study.

AO5ii (A2 only)

Evaluate the significance of cultural, historical and other contextual influences on literary texts and study.

This takes AO5i a stage further. You examine more closely how external factors have influenced texts and readers, and assess their importance.

Links

For more on **form, structure and language** see page 8.

Links

See pages 160–1 for advice on dealing with different interpretations of texts.

Take note

Contextual influences on a text might for instance include relevant aspects of the historical period when the text was written, or the historical period of the writer's life in which the text was written. See pages 148–59.

Exam preparation

Download the specification for your AS or A2 course (website addresses are on page 171), and check which assessment objectives are relevant to each of the units or modules you are studying.

Literary terms and concepts 1

The next two sections explain some of the main terms and concepts relevant to AS/A2 English Literature. Terms which are mainly of relevance to a specific genre (e.g. poetry or drama) are covered later in the book. At the back of the book (pages 184–8) there is also, for reference purposes, a **Glossary** listing terms and definitions.

Genre

A **genre** is a **type** of text. The three great literary genres are **prose**, **poetry** and **drama**. There are also 'genres within genres'. The prose genre, for example, includes novels and short stories. Novels can be subdivided further into other genres, such as romantic novels, historical novels, comic novels, science fiction and crime writing.

Form

Form refers to the overall shape or pattern of a text. Sometimes it means the same as 'genre': for example, you might refer to the 'sonnet form' in poetry. The term also includes other, smaller aspects of a text's organisation, such as the use in some poems of rhyming couplets.

Structure

The terms **structure** and **form** (see above) are often used interchangeably, though structure can also be seen as a broader term which includes not only form but also the **sequence** of ideas in a text. For example, this might include looking at how a text begins or ends, or at how an episode in one part of a novel or play echoes an episode in another part. There might also be identifiable patterns within a text – for instance, certain **symbols** or **images** (see below) might be repeated. **Prefiguring** occurs when something in a text anticipates (or **foreshadows**) a later part of the text. In Emily Bronte's *Wuthering Heights*, for example, the relationships involving the first generation of characters in many ways prefigure the relationships involving the second generation.

Language

Considering how writers use **language** essentially involves studying their use of **vocabulary** (that is, their choice of words), **grammar** (see page 10) and **sound** (see page 11). The terms discussed in the remainder of this section and on pages 10–11 are all relevant to language.

Imagery and symbolism

An important aspect of vocabulary is **imagery**. This term sometimes refers very broadly to writing which appeals to any of our five senses. Looked at in this way, there are five types of imagery, according to which of the senses is involved:

Links

Later in the book there are chapters on each of these three genres.

Take note

The main dramatic genres are tragedy and comedy. Poetic genres include sonnets, odes and elegies.

Examiner's secrets

Students tend to find commenting on what a text is about easier than analysing how it is written. Try your best to include in your answers points about form, structure and language.

visual imagery	sight
auditory imagery	hearing
tactile imagery	touch
olfactory imagery	smell
gustatory imagery	taste

Imagery also sometimes refers specifically to the use of **comparisons**. From this perspective, an **image** is usually a **simile** or **metaphor**. A **simile** is a comparison which involves the use of *like* or *as* (e.g. *She ran like the wind*). A **metaphor** fuses the two things being compared together, saying something that is not literally true (e.g. *the winds of change*). Imagery therefore often involves the use of **figurative language** – language that is not to be taken literally. Another related term is **personification**, which occurs when something inanimate is given human qualities (e.g. *The sun is smiling on us today*).

A **symbol** is something used in a literary text to represent something else. Often, a physical object is used to represent an abstract idea: for example, a locked door or window might symbolise the idea of emotional repression. In a literary text, important symbols are sometimes used repeatedly, emphasising and developing their significance.

Connotations

The **connotations** of a word or phrase are its **associations** – the ideas and feelings it suggests to a reader. Some words (e.g. *divine*) have connotations that are clearly **positive**, while other words (e.g. *serpent*) have connotations that are mostly **negative**. As well as describing connotations as positive or negative, you should try where you can to be precise about the **specific** connotations of words or phrases – for example, the word *divine* has connotations of purity and perfection, and religious associations. Connotations can vary according to how a word or phrase is used – the **context** is important.

Concrete and abstract vocabulary

Concrete vocabulary refers to things that physically exist, **abstract vocabulary** refers to things that do not. *Bread*, *butter*, *marmalade* are concrete words; *love*, *hate*, *fear* are abstract words. Look for how writers make use of these two kinds of vocabulary. If a writer's description of a room enables the reader to visualise it clearly, for example, one reason for this may be that a large number of concrete words has been used.

Take note

This table includes terms you may well not have encountered at GCSE. It illustrates how at AS/A2 you should try to make use of a broader range of terminology.

Take note

If a writer develops a metaphor over several lines of a text (or perhaps over a whole text), this is known as an **extended metaphor**.

Take note

Think about the **effects** of using concrete or abstract vocabulary.

Exam preparation

It is a good idea to keep your own list of terms that you encounter during the course, together with definitions and examples.

Literary terms and concepts 2

This section covers some more terms relevant to the **language** of literary texts.

Formality and informality

Formal language uses Standard English, often involves the use of **polysyllabic** words (words with several syllables) and tends to be complex and impersonal. **Informal language** is generally simpler, more relaxed and more familiar. It may involve the use of **colloquial language**, which is the language of everyday conversation. For example, if you described someone as *a good bloke* you would be using a **colloquialism**.

Watch out!

Not all language can be clearly identified as **formal** or **informal**. There are many different degrees (or **levels**) of formality. Sometimes a text only appears formal or informal in comparison to another text.

Ambiguity

Ambiguity occurs when language has two or more possible meanings or interpretations. The term might be applied to a single word, phrase or sentence, or more broadly to a larger portion of a text (e.g. we might say that a particular novel or play has an ambiguous ending).

Examiner's secrets

You should always be alert to the possibility of ambiguity; showing an awareness of alternative interpretations is an indicator of close attention to language and is rewarded by examiners.

Irony

Irony is a very broad term and it is used in a variety of ways. Usually it involves something being said that is, either knowingly or unknowingly, the opposite of the truth. Thus in Shakespeare's *Othello* it is ironic that the treacherous Iago is on several occasions described as *honest*. Ironic language is sometimes humorous – used in this way, irony is close to sarcasm. There can also be situations that are ironic: at the beginning of Shakespeare's *King Lear* it is ironic that Lear, who has three daughters, disowns the one who in reality loves him most.

  Dramatic irony is a particular kind of irony found in plays. It occurs when there is a disparity between what a character knows and what the audience knows, so that something the character says has a meaning that is understood by the audience but not by the character.

Example

For instance, in *Othello* Desdemona says she cannot get out of her head a song sung by her mother's maid just before she died. The audience recognises the dramatic irony here because we know that Othello plans to murder Desdemona.

Grammar and syntax

Grammar is a broad term for the rules that govern how we form words and combine them into sentences. For instance, one aspect of grammar is **tense**. If an action is happening now, we use the **present tense**: *He walks down the street*. If an action happened yesterday, we use the **past tense**: *He walked down the street*. If you comment on a writer's use of tense – for example, a poem might include a significant change of tense – you are commenting on grammar.

  Another important aspect of grammar is **person**. A novel might have a **first person** narrator (which means it uses pronouns such as *I* and *me*). A poem might use the **second person** (*you*) if it is addressed to somebody.

Take note

Writers sometimes use the **present tense** to create an impression of **immediacy**.

Syntax is a particular area of grammar and refers to the **structure of sentences**. Important elements of syntax include:

Word order The words in a sentence (or in a line of poetry) may be arranged in an order that puts strong emphasis on a particular word or set of words. This will be especially noticeable if the word order is **unusual**. The term **foregrounding** can be used when particular words are highlighted in this way. If emphasis is placed at the end of a sentence rather than the beginning, this is known as **end-focus**. Another term relevant to word order is **inversion** (or inverted syntax), which occurs when the normal order of words is reversed: for example, saying *Chocolate, I adore* instead of *I adore chocolate*.

Parallelism This occurs when phrases, sentences or lines of poetry have a similar **pattern** or **structure**. Usually one or more words is repeated. In Emily Bronte's poem *Spellbound* the narrator is caught in the middle of a storm, surrounded by hostile forces of nature:

> *Clouds beyond clouds above me,*
> > *Wastes beyond wastes below*

The parallel phrases here are *Clouds beyond clouds* and *Wastes beyond wastes*.

Listing Words or phrases might be arranged into a **list**. If the list includes one or more **conjunctions** ('joining' words such as *and*) this is called **syndetic listing**. If there are no conjunctions the term **asyndetic listing** is used. In Philip Larkin's poem *Mr Bleaney* asyndetic listing is used to describe Mr Bleaney's rented room; note how the starkness of the listing emphasises how bare and bleak the room is:

> *Bed, upright chair, sixty-watt bulb, no hook*
>
> *Behind the door, no room for books or bags –*

Sound

Terms relevant to the use of **sound** in literature include **rhyme**, **onomatopoeia**, **alliteration**, **sibilance**, **assonance** and **dissonance**. These terms are all explained in the Poetry chapter (see pages 20–1), though it is important to realise that techniques such as these can also be found in prose and drama.

Take note

Note how the parallelism, and the words *above* and *below*, reinforce the sense that the narrator is trapped.

Take note

Other aspects of the description contribute to the overall effect. *Sixty-watt bulb* implies there is no lampshade. The *upright* chair does not offer comfort or relaxation.

Exam preparation

When you study a text, look for any distinctive features of language that apply to the text as a whole, and make a note of these (e.g. there might be extensive use of irony).

Revision checklist
Getting started

1 Identify the main differences between GCSE and AS/A2 English Literature.	Confident	Not confident. **Revise** pages 4–5
2 Explain the term 'contexts'.	Confident	Not confident. **Revise** page 5
3 Understand the requirement that you consider alternative 'interpretations' when studying certain texts.	Confident	Not confident. **Revise** page 5
4 Explain the official assessment objectives for your AS or A2 course.	Confident	Not confident. **Revise** pages 6–7
5 Define the term 'genre' and identify the main literary genres.	Confident	Not confident. **Revise** page 8
6 Explain the terms 'form' and 'structure'.	Confident	Not confident. **Revise** page 8
7 List the five types of imagery, linking them to the five human senses.	Confident	Not confident. **Revise** page 9
8 Explain the terms 'metaphor', 'simile', 'personification' and 'symbol'.	Confident	Not confident. **Revise** page 9
9 Define the term 'connotation'.	Confident	Not confident. **Revise** page 9
10 Explain the difference between 'concrete' and 'abstract' vocabulary.	Confident	Not confident. **Revise** page 9
11 Explain the main characteristics of formal and informal language.	Confident	Not confident. **Revise** page 10
12 Define the term 'ambiguity'.	Confident	Not confident. **Revise** page 10
13 Understand the different uses of the term 'irony'.	Confident	Not confident. **Revise** page 10
14 List and explain the main elements of grammar and syntax that are relevant to literary analysis.	Confident	Not confident. **Revise** pages 10–11
15 List and explain terms related to the use of sound in literature.	Confident	Not confident. **Revise** page 11

The three main literary genres are poetry, drama and prose fiction. You'll be studying set poetry texts at both AS and A2, and at A2 you might have to analyse 'unseen' poems (i.e. ones you've never read before) in one of your final exams. The poetry texts you study vary from one exam board to another, but within this chapter you should find material relevant to whichever poet you're studying.

After some introductory tips on studying poetry, the next few sections look at aspects of poetic style, such as language and form. There is some useful terminology here and you should try to make use of these terms when writing essays. A common weakness in many students' answers is that while they write well about the *meaning* of poems they say next to nothing about *how* the poems are written. In fact, sometimes there's no indication that they're writing about poetry at all – the essay could easily be about a play or a novel. Try to show in your answers that you're aware of the distinctive stylistic features of poetry – how poets use rhythm and rhyme, for instance, or how a poem's division into stanzas contributes to its overall effect.

The next sections offer an historical overview of poetry, beginning with Chaucer, who wrote in the 14th century. You can find out from these sections the key features of English poetry during the period in which your set text was written. There is also more detailed discussion of some of the most important individual poets. Finally, there's advice on how to tackle the analysis of a poem.

Exam themes

→ Knowledge and understanding of set poetry texts

→ Use of relevant terminology

→ Awareness of literary contexts (e.g. 'movements' within poetry, such as the Romantics and the Metaphysicals)

Topic checklist

AS ○ A2 ●	AQA/A	AQA/B	EDEXCEL	OCR	WJEC	CCEA
Poetry: study tips	○●	○●	○●	○●	○●	○●
Poetic form and structure	○●	○●	○●	○●	○●	○●
Poetic language 1	○●	○●	○●	○●	○●	○●
Poetic language 2	○●	○●	○●	○●	○●	○●
Rhythm and metre	○●	○●	○●	○●	○●	○●
Chaucer 1	○	○●	●	○●	●	●
Chaucer 2	○	○●	●	○●	●	●
The Metaphysicals		○	●	●	●	●
The Romantics 1	●	○●	○●	○●	●	
The Romantics 2	●	○●	○●	○●	●	
Victorian poetry	○	○●	○●	○●	●	○
First World War poetry	●			○		
Other 20th century poetry	○●		○●	●	○●	○
Analysing poems	○●	○●	○●	○●	○●	○●
Practice poems	○●	○●	○●	○●	○●	○●

Poetry: study tips

This section gives you some tips on how to approach the study of a set poetry text.

Links

Advice on reading and analysing individual poems can be found on pages 40–1.

Checkpoint 1

What general term is used for the background influences on a work of literature?

Take note

Think also about the **sequence** of poems in the book. Who put them in this order? If it was the poet, the sequence might be important.

Checkpoint 2

What is an **assessment objective**?

First reading

→ You can prepare for your first reading of the poems you've been set to study by doing some very basic **background research**. If you're studying a collection of poems by a single author, find out some key facts about the author's life. When did they live? Did they have a profession other than writing? Is much known about their personal life? If you're studying an anthology of some kind – for example, you might be studying a collection of Romantic or Metaphysical poetry – you could again find out when the poems were written, and also what the main characteristics of this type of poetry are. However, don't spend too long on this kind of research. It helps to have some sense of the poet behind the poems, but more detailed background research can be carried out later. Often the text you are studying will have an introduction of some kind, and this should provide you with enough background information to get started.

→ Find out the poems you are required to study (it may not be the whole book), and read them. If the poems are quite short, read each one two or three times. At this stage, your aim is just to get **a general sense of what the poems are about**, so don't worry if the meaning of particular lines or verses isn't clear to you. There may even be whole poems that leave you puzzled. If you're feeling completely stuck, and the poems don't make any sense to you at all, a study guide or other reference book might help (see 'Carrying out research and getting extra help' below).

→ As you read the poems, look for **links** between them. What areas of life is the poet interested in? Do certain **subjects** recur? Are similar **attitudes** expressed in several of the poems?

Studying the text

→ Your first reading will give you a **general overview** of the text. You're now ready to study it in more depth.

→ Identify the aspects of the text you need to concentrate on by finding out the particular **assessment objectives** for this unit or module. For example, it might be important for you to know about how the poems reflect aspects of their **context**, or about different possible **interpretations** of the poems.

→ As you study the poems, keep an organised set of **notes**. Your teacher at school or college will probably give you more guidance on this, but here is some general advice. You'll need detailed notes on **each poem** you study. You also need to identify **links** between the poems, showing which **themes** are relevant to each poem. One simple way of doing this is to have a separate sheet on which the themes are set out as headings, with the relevant poems listed underneath. If you are studying Romantic poetry, for example, headings might include 'childhood', 'nature' and 'the imagination'. You should also think about **form** and **style**. Again you could have a sheet identifying key features (e.g. 'sonnets', 'extended metaphors'), with a list of relevant poems under each heading.

→ If you're allowed to, **annotate** the book itself, underlining or highlighting key passages, writing brief comments or explanations in the margins, and noting cross-references to other poems. Note though that if you'll be taking the book into the examination there will be a limit on how much annotation you're allowed to have.

→ With many poetry texts, it can be useful to identify perhaps seven or eight **key poems**. These will be poems that, taken together, cover all of the key themes in the text and that are the poet's best work or are especially representative of the poet's main strengths and characteristics. Get to know these poems well and, if the opportunity arises in the exam, write about one or more of them. Remember though that you'll still need a good overall knowledge of the text, as the question might involve you having to write about other poems as well.

Carrying out research and getting extra help ●●●

→ As mentioned above, the assessment objectives for the relevant AS or A2 unit might require you to know about the **context** of the poems, or about different **interpretations** of them. Even if this is not a requirement, you might well find that researching these aspects of the text helps your understanding of the poems anyway. For more advice see pages 148–59 and 160–5.

→ Listening to an **audio recording** of the poems can be helpful. For some modern texts there are recordings of the poets themselves reading their own work. **Sound** is an especially important feature of poetry, and listening to readings can help you to appreciate the effects of such features as stress, rhyme and rhythm.

→ You should make full use of any **additional information included in the book** you are using. For example, many editions of poetry texts have helpful introductions, notes, glossaries and so on.

→ Your teacher might point you in the direction of other helpful books and sources of information. There might also be **study guides** you can buy and **online revision materials**. Be careful here though as the quality can vary greatly and they are not all specifically aimed at AS/A2 students. It is also impossible for them to cover everything you need to know, though they can be a useful aid to study.

Checkpoint 3

When was the **Romantic** period in English literature?

Take note

As with all literary texts, it's important to develop your own readings of the poems that you study. Think about the ideas and emotions expressed in the poems, and how you respond to them.

Take note

You might also find there are interesting and helpful **interviews** with the poet – in print, online or on tape/CD.

Exam preparation

As soon as you find out the poetry text you will be studying, carry out some **background research** (see 'First reading' above).

Poetic form and structure

All of the AS/A2 specifications require you to look closely at the **language, form and structure** of the texts you are studying. Pages 18–21 are about aspects of poetic language. This section looks at form and structure.

What are form and structure?

Analysing form and structure involves thinking about a text's overall shape and organisation. In the case of poetry, **form** means types of poem (sonnets, odes and so on) and also the kinds of organisational technique poets use to present their ideas (such as couplets or stanzas). **Structure** is a broader term for the overall arrangement of a poem. Form is part of this, but structure also includes the sequence of ideas (e.g. how a poem begins or ends).

Lyric poetry

Most poems can be described as **lyric poetry**. A lyric poem expresses an individual's thoughts and feelings. Lyrics are usually quite short, and the most common subject is love. Within lyric poetry, the most important forms or genres include **sonnets**, **odes** and **elegies** (see below).

Sonnets

A **sonnet** is a poem of 14 lines, with a rhythm usually based on the **iambic pentameter** and often conforming to a specific **rhyme scheme**. The two most common kinds of sonnet are the **Petrarchan** and the **Shakespearean**:

→ The **Petrarchan** sonnet has a rhyme scheme that divides the poem into two sections, an **octave** (the first eight lines) and a **sestet** (the last six lines). The rhyme scheme is usually *abbaabba* (octave), *cdecde* or *cdcdcd* (sestet).
→ The **Shakespearean** sonnet has three **quatrains** (units of four lines each) and ends with a **couplet** (a pair of rhyming lines). The usual rhyme scheme is *abab*, *cdcd*, *efef*, *gg*.

The sonnet was originally an Italian form and entered English poetry in the 16th century. The earliest English sonnets were love poems, and love has continued to be the topic most strongly associated with sonnets. Poets have however also used the form for a great variety of other subjects: **religious** sonnets are common, and the **Romantic** poets in particular wrote many sonnets about **nature**.

In thinking about how the form of a particular sonnet contributes to its overall effect, look closely at **the relationship between the different sections of the poem**. The divisions often correspond to shifts in meaning or attitude. In Petrarchan sonnets, for example, the octave sometimes outlines a situation or problem, while the sestet offers a response to it. In Shakespearean sonnets, the final couplet may expess a concluding thought or introduce a new idea.

Take note

Form and **structure** are not quite the same thing, but the words are closely linked and in practice are often used interchangeably.

Links

For more on the **iambic pentameter**, see page 22.

Links

Metre and **rhyme** are important aspects of poetic form. See pages 22 and 23.

Odes

An **ode** is an elaborate lyric poem, often extending over several stanzas, addressed to a person, object or abstract idea (the subject is normally indicated by the title). Usually they are serious poems that praise the person or thing addressed, and meditate upon its qualities. Well-known examples include Keats's *Ode To A Nightingale* and Shelley's *Ode To The West Wind*.

Elegies

An **elegy** is a poem that mourns someone's death, such as Milton's *Lycidas*, written in memory of Edward King, a friend who died at sea. The term is also sometimes applied more generally to solemn, contemplative poems. Thomas Gray's famous *Elegy Written In A Country Churchyard* is a reflective poem about death.

Narrative poetry

Apart from the lyric, the most common type of poetry is **narrative poetry**. This is poetry that tells a story. Before novels became popular in the 18th century, stories were traditionally told in verse, and even after the arrival of the novel many poets continued to write narrative poetry. The two main types of narrative poem are the **epic** and the **ballad**:

→ **Epics** are long poems, often about mythical heroes, and often with grand, impressive settings and elements of the supernatural. An example is Milton's *Paradise Lost*, a long religious poem about the fall of man.
→ **Ballads** tell stories in simple, everyday language. The emphasis is on action and dialogue, with description usually kept to a minimum. Many ballads use the traditional **ballad metre**: rhyming **quatrains** (four-line stanzas) of alternate four-stress and three-stress lines. Another common feature is the use of a **refrain** – the regular repetition of words or lines, usually at the end of a stanza.

Stanzas

Within poems, the most commonly used organisational technique is the **stanza**. This is a separate section of a poem consisting of several lines of verse. Many poems are divided into stanzas of equal length (e.g. three or four lines). Four-line stanzas, known as **quatrains**, are especially common, and are often combined with a regular **metre** and **rhyme scheme**. When poems are organised into stanzas, think about why this is and about the relationship between the stanzas. How does the poem change and develop as it moves from stanza to stanza? Are there important contrasts between individual stanzas?

Exam preparation

On page 43 there is a **sonnet** by the Romantic poet Percy Bysshe Shelley. See page 33 for an analysis question on this poem.

Checkpoint 1

Keats, Shelley and other poets of their time are often grouped together. What name is given to this group of poets?

Checkpoint 2

Can you think of other art forms where the term **epic** is commonly used?

Checkpoint 3

In which century did Milton live?

Take note

Stanzas are also sometimes known as **verses**, especially if they are short and of a regular length.

Poetic language 1

Checkpoint 1

The effect of these lines is reinforced by the use of **enjambement**. What does this statement mean?

The next two sections look closely at poetic **style** – how poets use language. The terms covered in this first section all relate to **vocabulary** – the poet's choice of words.

Connotations

The <u>connotations</u> of a word are its **associations** – the emotions, <u>sensations and attitudes that it evokes.</u> Very broadly, words can have **positive** or **negative** connotations, but you should also try to be more precise about the particular connotations of specific words. In this quotation from Elizabeth Barrett Browning's sonnet *How Do I Love Thee?* several of the words have similar connotations:

> *I love thee to the depth and breadth and height*
> *My soul can reach, when feeling out of sight*
> *For the ends of Being and ideal Grace.*

Note how many of the words and phrases here have connotations of space and distance, emphasising the extent of Browning's love: *depth, breadth, height, reach, out of sight, ends.*

Formality

Formal vocabulary tends to be associated with more serious subjects and also with older texts. <u>**Informal** language is sometimes used to suggest a speaking voice</u>, to add a <u>sense of realism</u> or to create humour. It is more common in modern poetry, but can occur in older poems, as the opening of *The Good Morrow* by the 17th century poet John Donne illustrates:

> *I wonder by my troth, what thou and I*
> *Did till we lov'd?*

Here the direct, largely **monosyllabic** vocabulary, the **colloquial** expression *by my troth*, and the **rhythmic stress** on *Did* combine to create the impression of natural speech.

Simplicity and complexity

If vocabulary is noticeably **simple** or **complex**, consider *why* this kind of vocabulary has been used, and think about the *effects* that it has. In Christopher Marlowe's *The Passionate Shepherd To His Love* simple, unsophisticated vocabulary helps to create an idealised picture of unpretentious rural life:

> *Come live with me and be my Love,*
> *And we will all the pleasures prove,*
> *That hills and valleys, dales and fields*
> *Or woods or steepy mountain yields.*

As this quotation illustrates, simple words are often **monosyllabic** (i.e. they only have one syllable), whereas more complex vocabulary tends to be **polysyllabic**.

Ambiguity ●●●

Ambiguous language has more than one possible meaning. Poets use language in an especially concentrated way, and words and phrases often have more than one level of meaning. The Philip Larkin poem *Here* describes a journey northwards to Hull, a journey which ends at the coast. The poem's last words are *out of reach*, suggesting that here is where the poet can find peace and solitude (it is a place beyond the reach of others), but also that what he desires is in fact unattainable (he wants it but it is out of reach).

Imagery ●●●

In its broadest sense, **imagery** refers to any aspect of a piece of writing that appeals to the reader's senses – a description of what something looks like, for example, or of a sound or a taste. There are technical terms for imagery that appeals to each of our senses: **visual imagery** (sight); **auditory imagery** (hearing); **tactile imagery** (touch); **olfactory imagery** (smell); **gustatory imagery** (taste).

The term **imagery** also refers to the use of **comparisons**, specifically **similes**, **metaphors** and **personification**. A **simile** is a comparison that uses the words *like* or *as*. A **metaphor** goes one stage further and describes something as if it actually were something else – what is said is not literally true. The Ted Hughes poem *The Jaguar* begins with a description of animals in a zoo, emphasising how captivity has made them passive and lifeless: tigers and lions *Lie still as the sun* (simile); a coiled snake *Is a fossil* (metaphor).

If a poet continues with a metaphor, developing it over several lines (or sometimes over a complete poem), this is known as an **extended metaphor**. William Blake's *A Poison Tree* uses the extended metaphor of a tree to represent anger towards another person. The growth of the tree, described over the course of the poem, corresponds to the growth of the narrator's anger.

Personification occurs when something that is not human or alive is described as if it were. This example is from Wordsworth's description of London in *Composed Upon Westminster Bridge*:

Dear God! the very houses seem asleep,
And all that mighty heart is lying still!

Watch out!

Note that simple language does not necessarily mean simple ideas – the Romantic poet William Blake is an example of a writer who often uses direct, uncomplicated vocabulary to express complex thoughts and attitudes.

Checkpoint 2

What term is used for a word or phrase with a double meaning which is **humorous**?

Take note

When you come across a comparison in a poem, ask yourself these questions:
→ What are the two things that are being compared? Be as precise as you can.
→ How are they similar? (Often there is more than one similarity.)
→ What is conveyed or achieved by the comparison? For example, the comparison may highlight a particular characteristic of the thing that is being described.
→ What is the significance of the comparison in relation to the poem as a whole? There may be links with other poems in the text, or the comparison may relate in some way to an important theme.

Checkpoint 3

Why is it appropriate to refer to London as a *mighty heart*?

Exam preparation

See pages 29, 31, 33 and 35 for poetry analysis questions relevant to the terms covered in this and the next two sections.

Poetic language 2

This section looks at some other aspects of poetic style.

Grammar and syntax

Here are some aspects of grammar and syntax that might be considered when looking at the poet's use of language in a poem.

Types of sentence Does the poem have any **questions**, **commands** or **exclamations**? If so, what effect do they have? At the beginning of Jonathan Swift's *A Satirical Elegy On The Death Of A Late Famous General*, a series of exclamations suggests a natural speaking voice, and also helps to create the tone of mock concern:

> *His Grace! impossible! what, dead!*
> *Of old age too, and in his bed!*

Word order Look for how word order might cause particular words to be **foregrounded** (brought to the reader's attention). In Tennyson's line *And rarely smells the new-mown hay* the arrangement of words stresses the word *rarely*. Placing a word at the beginning of a line can be another way of emphasising it.

Parallelism This is the repetition of similar grammatical structures: phrases, lines or sentences have a similar **pattern**. In William Blake's *London*, parallelism strengthens the impression that Blake is surrounded by misery and oppression:

> *In every cry of every Man,*
> *In every Infant's cry of fear,*
> *In every voice, in every ban,*
> *The mind-forg'd manacles I hear.*

In this example, parallelism is created by the series of **phrases** beginning with the word *every*.

First person If a poem is written in the **first person** (using words such as *I* and *me*), be careful not to assume the poet is necessarily the narrator. What kinds of feelings, attitudes and tone does the narrator have, and how does the language of the poem reflect this? What view of the narrator does the poet have, and what view is the reader intended to have? Does the poem take the form of a **dramatic monologue** – an extended piece of speech by an imaginary character or **persona**?

Sound

Rhyme Rhymes are easy to spot, and you won't get much credit for simply saying they're there. Instead, you should think about any **effects** that the rhymes have. For example, rhymes can help to give a poem a lively, jaunty rhythm, a sense of narrative pace or an impression of order and harmony.

Terminology

Grammar is a broad term for the rules that govern how we form and use words. **Syntax** is an aspect of grammar that refers more specifically to the arrangement of words into sentences.

Checkpoint 1

What famous novel was written by **Jonathan Swift**?

Checkpoint 2

What does *rarely* mean here?

Checkpoint 3

Explain the difference between **first**, **second** and **third person**.

Rhyming usually involves the **ends** of lines, and pairs of lines that rhyme in this way are called **couplets**. **Internal rhyme** is when words rhyme *within* the line:

> *The ship was cheered, the harbour cleared*

Half-rhymes (or **pararhymes**) occur when the rhyme is not quite complete; usually the consonants in the rhyming words match but the vowels do not, as in *burn* and *born*. The First World War poet Wilfred Owen often used this technique (see page 37).

Onomatopoeia This occurs when words imitate the sounds they describe: when we say the words out loud, we can actually hear the sound. This line is from *Wind*, a poem by Ted Hughes describing a violent storm:

> *The woods crashing through darkness, the booming hills*

Here the onomatopoeic words are *crashing* and *booming*.

Alliteration This is when two or more words begin with the same sound. You should only refer to alliteration if you can also explain the effect that you think it has. In Gerard Manley Hopkins's *Spring* alliteration is used to help create an impression of vigorous natural energy and growth:

> *When weeds, in wheels, shoot long and lovely and lush*

Sibilance This is the repetition of *s*, soft *c*, *sh* and *z* sounds. The opening line of Keats's *To Autumn* uses sibilance to evoke a soft, pleasant atmosphere:

> *Season of mists and mellow fruitfulness!*

Assonance is the rhyming of vowel sounds within two or more words, as in another line from Keats's poem:

> *Then in a wailful choir the small gnats mourn*

Here the rhyming vowel sounds are in *small* and *mourn* (note also the use of **onomatopoeia** in *wailful*).

Take note

The **words** that are rhymed may be significant – rhyming brings them together, and you should consider whether linking them in this way has any effect (the words might, for instance, have contrasting meanings or connotations).

Terminology

The arrangement of rhymes within a poem as a whole is called the **rhyme scheme**. Certain types of poem, such as the **sonnet** (see page 16) have standard rhyme schemes.

Take note

The opposite of **assonance** is **dissonance**, which occurs when sounds are so different they clash with each other, creating a discordant effect.

Exam preparation

See pages 29, 31, 33 and 35 for poetry analysis questions relevant to the terms covered in this section and the sections on pages 18–19 and 22–23.

Rhythm and metre

Rhythm is a broad term for the pace or 'movement' of a poem. **Metre** is a more precise term, referring to the pattern of stressed and unstressed syllables in a line of poetry.

Metre

There are five main patterns of stressed and unstressed syllables, listed below. Any poem is unlikely to conform rigidly to a particular metre; there will usually be occasional variations, with extra stressed or unstressed syllables. However, earlier poems in particular usually have a regular underlying metre. Depending on the metre, the pattern of stresses will be made up of groups of two or three syllables. Each of these groups is called a **foot**.

Iambic

Here an unstressed syllable is followed by a stressed one:

> When _I_ have _fears_ that _I_ may _cease_ to _be_

This line by Keats has five pairs of syllables, or five feet. This particular form of the iambic metre is known as the **iambic pentameter**, the most common metre in English poetry. Unrhymed poetry based on the iambic pentameter is known as **blank verse**.

Trochaic

This is the second most common metre, and is the reverse of the iambic metre. Again there are pairs of syllables, but here the pattern is stressed–unstressed:

> _Simple Simon met_ a _pieman_

Dactylic

Each foot has three syllables, one stressed followed by two unstressed:

> _Half_ a league, _half_ a league,
>   _Half_ a league _onward_

Take note

This is a good example of metre reinforcing **meaning**. Always look for this.

In this example (from Tennyson's _The Charge of the Light Brigade_) the last foot is trochaic: _onward_. Note how the dactylic metre helps to create the sense of cavalry charging into battle.

Take note

The **anapaestic** metre is often found in **narrative poems** (poems which tell stories).

Anapaestic

Again the feet have three syllables, this time two unstressed followed by a stressed:

> Through _all_ the wide _border_ his _steed_ was the _best_

The first foot here – _Through all_ – is iambic.

Spondaic

The foot here has two successive stressed syllables. This metre is usually only found in part of a line:

Rocks, <u>caves</u>, <u>lakes</u>, <u>fens</u>, <u>bogs</u>, <u>dens</u> and <u>shades</u> of <u>death</u>

Other aspects of rhythm

Enjambement

This is when the sense of one line continues into the next, without a pause or punctuation mark at the end of the first line.

End-stopped line

This occurs when the end of a line coincides with a grammatical pause, which is usually indicated by a punctuation mark.

Caesura

This is a pause, usually in the middle of a line, and usually shown by a punctuation mark:

As of some one gently rapping, rapping at my chamber door

Analysing rhythm

Metre can be difficult, and in an exam it is not worth spending time trying to work out the metre of a poem if it is not clear to you quite quickly. You should still be able to make some comment on the rhythm of the poem. Try to imagine how the poem would sound when read aloud, and think about the effects of heavily stressed words, of enjambement and of the pauses suggested by the punctuation. Does the rhythm seem to be **fast** or **slow**? Look for **changes** in the rhythm and, above all, try to identify places in the poem where the rhythm corresponds in some way to the **meaning**. In Coleridge's *The Ancient Mariner*, for example, the rhythm quickens when it is describing a ship travelling at high speed:

The fair breeze blew, the white foam flew

Later, when the ship is becalmed, the rhythm slows:

Day after day, day after day,
We stuck, nor breath nor motion

> **Checkpoint 1**
>
> This line has three spondaic feet, then the poem returns to its usual iambic metre for the last two feet. What is the effect of having so many heavily stressed syllables in this line? (The line is from Milton's *Paradise Lost* and describes a perilous journey.)

> **Take note**
>
> In this example from *The Evacuee* by R.S. Thomas, **enjambement** helps to convey the speed of someone rushing downstairs: *And now the noise and not the silence drew her / Down the bare stairs at great speed.*

> **Checkpoint 2**
>
> What effect is achieved by the repetition of *rapping* here?

> **Checkpoint 3**
>
> In what other ways does the language here convey a sense of the ship being *stuck*?

> **Exam preparation**
>
> See pages 29, 31, 33 and 35 for poetry analysis questions relevant to the terms covered in this section and the sections on pages 18–21.

Chaucer 1

The next two sections are about Geoffrey Chaucer, whose works are often on AS/A2 English Literature specifications.

The Canterbury Tales

The Canterbury Tales is a collection of stories told by a group of imaginary pilgrims who are travelling from London to the shrine of St Thomas a Becket at Canterbury. The opening poem, *The General Prologue*, introduces the pilgrims and outlines their plan for a story-telling competition. Each pilgrim is meant to tell four stories, two on the outward journey and two as they return. There are over 30 pilgrims, so if Chaucer had completed his ambitious project there would have been over 120 Tales. In fact there are only 24 Tales, scattered over an assortment of manuscripts. While some of these manuscripts only contain one Tale, others contain sequences of several Tales, so that the intended order of these particular poems is clear. Although incomplete, *The Canterbury Tales* is still a massive achievement and indisputably a landmark in the history of English Literature.

Chaucer's use of a pilgrimage as a **framing device** for the Tales had two main advantages. Firstly, it enabled him to present a comprehensive portrait of medieval English life. His pilgrims, brought together by a shared desire to travel to Canterbury, are drawn from a range of social classes and have a variety of occupations. They are partly **representative** figures, with characteristics typical of their respective professions, but vivid physical descriptions and the creation of strong, distinctive personalities ensure that many of the pilgrims are also strikingly individual. Secondly, in the Tales themselves, Chaucer was able to explore an equally varied mix of subjects and genres. He often matches Tale to teller, so that the Tale functions not just as a story in its own right but also as an expression of the character of the pilgrim narrating it (see 'Tales and their tellers' and 'Types of Tale' on pages 26–7).

Chaucer's language

The language of Chaucer's time is known as **Middle English**. It is a combination of **Old English** (also known as **Anglo-Saxon**) and words of **French** derivation, which steadily entered the language after the Norman Conquest in 1066 (an estimated 10,000 words of French origin were absorbed into English over the following 300 years). There are interesting contrasts in the two types of vocabulary: Anglo-Saxon words tend to be short and blunt, while French words are often longer and sound more refined and sophisticated. Chaucer's poetry exploits these differences. The **Miller**, for example, an aggressive and foul-mouthed Canterbury pilgrim, is associated with predominantly Anglo-Saxon vocabulary:

> 'By goddes soul,' quod he, 'that wol nat I;
> For I wol speke, or elles go my wey.'

Checkpoint 1

Who was Thomas a Becket?

Checkpoint 2

What does the word *prologue* mean?

Take note

Make sure you know if the Tale you are studying is part of a sequence. There may be important contrasts or similarities between your Tale and the Tales which precede or follow it.

Background

Geoffrey Chaucer was born around 1340 and died in 1400. He was born into the affluent middle class, but became a high-ranking courtier and diplomat, so also moved in royal circles and among the aristocracy. At the same time, as a Londoner who grew up in a busy part of the city, Chaucer would have been very familiar with the ordinary life of the streets. One of the most notable features of *The Canterbury Tales* is Chaucer's insight into the kinds of lives led by people from a range of backgrounds, and what we know of Chaucer's own life helps us to understand where this insight came from.

Checkpoint 1

Anglo-Saxon itself was a language which evolved due to the influence of foreign invaders. Where did they come from?

In contrast, French vocabulary is employed when Chaucer describes the **Prioress**, a nun who despite her calling is keen to appear elegant and fashionable: *curteisie, plesaunt, amiable*.

Tips on reading Middle English ●●●

When you answer exam questions on a Chaucer poem you need to support your points with quotations from the original Middle English text. Getting used to working with Chaucer's language inevitably takes time but here are a few tips:

→ When you first encounter a page of Middle English it is bound to look strange to you. Don't be put off by this – everyone has the same experience. If you try reading through it, you should find that you can form a general idea of what much of it is about. Many Middle English words are still in use today, though the spelling has sometimes changed. Often it's the vowels that are now different: *Whan*, the first word of the *General Prologue*, is our 'When'. Doubling of consonants is another common feature, as in *Aprill* for 'April'. **Syntax** (the sequence of words in a sentence) is also sometimes different, so playing around with the word order can help as well.

→ Some words and phrases will still make no sense at all, but can be understood with the help of notes and a glossary. Most modern editions of Chaucer texts have these. Make full use of them, and if you're able to annotate your book write in the meanings of difficult words – it saves you having to look them up twice!

→ Complete modern English versions of Chaucer texts can be helpful, but be careful not to become too dependent on them. Your answers need to be based on analysis of the original text.

→ Try to get hold of an audio recording of the poem, read in Middle English. This can help you get a sense of the meaning, and is also important because Chaucer was working within an **oral** literary tradition. Works such as *The Canterbury Tales* were intended to be read aloud to groups of listeners, and often the **sound** of words is used to achieve particular effects.

→ Once you have got over the hurdle of understanding what Chaucer's words mean, try to **appreciate** his use of language. Look for ambiguity (double meanings), irony, imagery and so on.

Watch out!

The meaning of some words has changed over time. For example, *sentence* when used by Chaucer means 'opinion' or 'meaning'. The notes or glossary in your edition will usually point out when this occurs.

Take note

David Wright's *Chaucer: The Canterbury Tales* (Grafton) is a good modern English version.

Take note

If you can't obtain an audio recording, try reading parts of the text aloud yourself. Editions of Chaucer texts often include guidance on pronunciation.

Exam preparation

Find out if the Tale you are studying is part of a **sequence** (see 'The Canterbury Tales' above). If it is, read the other Tales in the sequence. (To save time, you might want to read them in translation.)

Chaucer 2

This second section on Chaucer focuses more closely on *The Canterbury Tales*.

The General Prologue ●●●

The General Prologue is the poem that introduces *The Canterbury Tales*. It establishes the situation of a pilgrimage to Canterbury and explains that the pilgrims will tell each other stories on their outward and return journeys. Most importantly, it provides detailed descriptions (or *portraits*) of many of the pilgrims. If you are studying one of the Tales it is likely that a portrait of the character narrating it appears in *The General Prologue*, and it is worth analysing this carefully, as the opinions and values of the narrator are usually an important aspect of the Tale (see 'Tales and their tellers' below).

The General Prologue itself has a **narrator**, who commentators sometimes refer to as 'Chaucer the pilgrim'. This is to distinguish him from the real Chaucer ('Chaucer the poet'), because the two are not the same. Instead Chaucer has created a gullible, impressionable figure who is generally in awe of his fellow pilgrims, endorsing their own high opinions of themselves and blind to their moral shortcomings.

The device of a **naïve narrator** enables Chaucer to make extensive use of **irony**. For example, when the Merchant – a self-important, rather shady businessman – is twice described as *worthy*, Chaucer's apparent praise is not to be taken at face value. This irony often creates humour and is also a means of drawing the reader into the poem: because we cannot trust the narrator's judgements, we must judge the pilgrims for ourselves. Sometimes it is hard to be sure what Chaucer really wanted us to think. The portrait of the Knight has usually been seen as genuinely positive and respectful, but some recent critics have suggested that the campaigns in which he has fought in fact make it more likely that we should view him as an unprincipled mercenary.

Take note

This alternative view of the **Knight** is argued in detail in *Chaucer's Knight* by Terry Jones (published by Methuen).

Tales and their tellers ●●●

A typical Canterbury Tale can be read on two levels:

→ as a self-contained story, with its own setting, characters, themes and so on;
→ as an exploration of the character of the poem's narrator, whose attitudes and personality are expressed through the Tale he or she tells.

These two dimensions are not rigidly separate, and a discussion of one aspect will often inevitably involve reference to the other. Nevertheless, coming at a Tale from these two directions will usually help to clarify your understanding of the text.

In building up a picture of the narrator of a Tale, ideas and information can be gleaned from a variety of sources:

→ The **portrait** of the relevant pilgrim in *The General Prologue* (as discussed above).

→ The **beginning** and **end** of the Tale, when the narrator may engage in conversation with the Host or other pilgrims. Sometimes these sections of the Tale are known as **prologues** and **epilogues**.

→ The **main body** of the Tale. There may be moments where the narrator intervenes to comment on characters or events, or longer passages (known as **digressions**) where the narrator interrupts the Tale to hold forth on a relevant topic. Other evidence within the Tale can be more subtle. For example, characters may possess some of the narrator's own characteristics, or the moral that can be drawn from the Tale may reflect the narrator's attitudes. More broadly, the general setting and content of the Tale may be appropriate to the pilgrim narrating it. For example, the bawdy Tale told by the Miller clearly matches his character, while the aristocratic milieu of *The Franklin's Tale* suggests the Franklin's social aspirations.

→ The **context** of the Tale, in terms of its significance in relation to other Canterbury Tales. For example, *The Miller's Tale* follows *The Knight's Tale* and in some respects parodies it. *The Merchant's Tale* and *The Franklin's Tale* both belong to a group of Tales which present contrasting views of marriage.

Types of tale ●●●

When you are studying one of the Tales, it is also helpful to have some understanding of the literary traditions and genres Chaucer was working within. The concept of *The Canterbury Tales*, with pilgrims from very different backgrounds taking turns to narrate stories, enabled Chaucer to present many different types of Tale. Sometimes he ridicules tired or cliched traditions by creating Tales which undermine or parody them, while at other times he is more conventional.

These are a few of the **forms**, **genres** and **traditions** he drew upon:

→ **Courtly love** This is a set of conventions related to the presentation in literature of romantic love. Several of Chaucer's Tales replicate the feelings, settings and situations associated with courtly love, though they do this in varying ways.

→ **The fabliau** This was a type of story that originated in early French poetry. It was characterised by coarse, bawdy humour. *The Miller's Tale* is a poem rooted in this tradition.

→ **Fables** These are stories with a definite moral or message, usually with animals as characters. *The Nun's Priest's Tale* uses this genre.

→ **Sermons** In telling their stories the narrators sometimes use techniques associated with medieval preachers. *The Pardoner's Tale*, for example, has many of the characteristics of a medieval sermon.

Take note

The Host is an innkeeper. The pilgrimage begins at his inn in London. He offers to accompany the pilgrims on their journey, and takes charge of the story-telling competition.

Checkpoint 1

What is a **milieu**?

Checkpoint 2

What is a **parody**?

Take note

The Knight's Tale appears respectful towards **courtly love** conventions and presents them relatively straightforwardly, but in *The Merchant's Tale* they are grotesquely parodied.

Checkpoint 2

A famous collection of animal **fables** is attributed to an Ancient Greek writer. What is this collection of fables known as?

Exam preparation   answers: page 44

Text A on page 42 is the portrait of the Miller from *The General Prologue*. With close reference to the use of language in the portrait, write about Chaucer's presentation of the character.

The Metaphysicals

The term **Metaphysical poetry** is applied to the work of a group of 17th century poets, including John Donne, George Herbert, Henry Vaughan, Richard Crashaw and Andrew Marvell.

Features of Metaphysical poetry ●●●

Here are some of the main characteristics of the Metaphysical poets:

→ They adopt an **intellectual** approach to emotional and spiritual issues. Their poems often take the form of elaborate, detailed **arguments**, and demonstrate their **knowledge** of contemporary discoveries in science, medicine, exploration and so on.

→ The complexity of their ideas is often reflected in dense, tortuous **syntax** (sentence construction), developing lines of thought that can be difficult to disentangle.

→ They are noted for their **wit** – meaning cleverness rather than humour, though their poems are often witty in that sense as well. Sometimes they display their intelligence in a rather self-conscious way, as if they are 'showing off'.

→ Their poems include unusual and surprising **images**. They use **conceits** – elaborate, extended metaphors based on unexpected comparisons between dissimilar objects.

→ Many of their poems involve **conflict** of some kind. For example, the poetry of **Donne** and **Herbert** often expresses religious doubts and uncertainties. Donne's love poetry frequently presents relationships in which there is disharmony. In both these poets there is a tension between religious faith and sensual pleasure. The early 17th century was a time of political, social and religious turbulence, and the restless quality of much Metaphysical poetry might be said to reflect this.

→ They are fond of **paradoxes** and **puns**. The deliberate contradictions and double meanings in their poems reinforce the impression of conflict and also demonstrate again their ingenuity and wit.

→ Their poems frequently recreate the rhythms and vocabulary of **everyday speech**. Colloquial language is used, and poems often have a **dramatic** quality, with a strong sense of the narrator's speaking voice (as in the Donne poem that begins, *For God's sake hold your tongue, and let me love*).

John Donne ●●●

The life of **John Donne** (1572–1631) helps to account for the emotional turmoil evident in much of his poetry, and his preoccupation with conflict, deceit, faithfulness and betrayal. He was raised as a Catholic but converted to Protestantism, eventually becoming an Anglican priest and Dean of St Paul's Cathedral. His brother was arrested for his faith (accused of harbouring a Catholic priest) and died in prison. Several years before he entered the priesthood Donne secretly married the young daughter of a nobleman, who reacted furiously, arranging for

---

Links

Several of the Metaphysical poets lived at the same time as **Shakespeare**. For more on late 16th and early 17th century society, see pages 116–17 and 152–5.

Take note

In the 18th century, when poetic style was more restrained and controlled, Samuel Johnson criticised the Metaphysicals for their *'combination of dissimilar images . . . The most heterogeneous ideas are yoked by violence together.'* (*Heterogeneous* means made up of very different elements.)

Checkpoint 1

What is a **paradox**?

Donne to be imprisoned. After his release Donne endured a long period of financial hardship and struggled to restore his social position.

The two main strands in Donne's poetry are **love** and **religion**. Donne's approach to both topics is intensely passionate, and one of the main characteristics of his work is its drive, energy and confidence. The Holy Sonnet *Batter my heart* is a representative poem. It begins dramatically, with an audacious command to God: *Batter my heart, three-person'd God*. Much of the poem is built around two extended metaphors or **conceits**. In one Donne compares himself to a besieged town, captured by the devil but longing for God to seize him back. In the other he is the woman in a love triangle, wanting a relationship with God but *betroth'd* to the devil. The final line is a **paradox**, a startling image that fuses eroticism and religion: if he is ever to be *chaste* (pure), God must *ravish* (rape) him.

George Herbert ●●●

George Herbert (1593–1633) was born into a wealthy, aristocratic family, but after a prolonged period of indecision abandoned the prospect of worldly advancement and became a humble country parson. All of his poems are about religion and they record his struggle between faith and doubt. Many of his poems begin in anger or despair but move towards resolution and acceptance. *The Collar*, one of Herbert's finest poems, is an example of this. The title itself is **ambiguous** and **metaphorical**, suggesting both a priest's collar and the restrictions that Herbert feels serving God places upon him. The poem opens in a mood of defiance, with Herbert determined to abandon the priesthood, but closes on a note of submission, as he hears a voice calling *Child* and responds obediently with *My Lord*. The poem is also typical in its convincing evocation of a **speaking voice**, a quality Herbert shares with Donne. Several of his poems are in effect conversations with God, employing colloquial vocabulary and peppered with questions and exclamations. Another similarity with Donne is that Herbert often constructs complex **intellectual arguments**, though his **imagery** is generally simpler and makes less use of scholarship and learning. He had a strong interest in the **technical** aspects of poetry, and experimented with a variety of **forms** and **metres**. *Easter Wings* is an **emblem** poem, in which the pattern of the words on the page creates a visual image. The verses are structured so that they resemble the outstretched wings of angels.

Take note

Donne's **prose** writings are also of note. The well-known phrases *No man is an island* and *For whom the bell tolls* are both from one of his *Meditations*.

Checkpoint 2

Why in this line is God described as *three-person'd*?

Checkpoint 3

Explain what **ambiguous** means.

Exam preparation answers: pages 44–5

Text B on page 42 is *The Good Morrow* by John Donne. Write a close analysis of this poem, focusing in particular on features that are characteristic of Metaphysical poetry.

The Romantics 1

The next two sections are about the Romantic poets. After a general overview of Romantic poetry, this section focuses on Wordsworth.

Features of Romantic poetry

The poets of the late 18th and early 19th centuries did not think of themselves as members of a recognizable literary group, and only became known as 'Romantics' retrospectively (in the 1860s). There are many differences between individual poets of this period, but they also tend to have certain ideas, attitudes and approaches to poetry in common. Some of these are listed below:

→ There was a **reaction against the ideas of the 18th century**, in particular rejecting the emphasis on the importance of order, control and rationality. (The 18th century is sometimes known as 'the Age of Reason'.)

→ **Emotion** is valued, and explored in poetry. **Wordsworth** argued that 'all good poetry is the spontaneous overflow of powerful feelings'. **Blake** attacked the idea that 'Men are admitted into Heaven . . . because they have curbed and govern'd their Passions'.

→ There was an interest in the workings of the **individual** consciousness, and in **personal experience**. Again this was a contrast to the 18th century, when poetry tended to have more public themes and to be preoccupied with society, manners and morals.

→ There was a strong belief in the power of the **imagination**. This is reflected in poems which evoke ancient, exotic worlds and in an interest in the supernatural. **Wordsworth** was interested in the relationship between imagination and perception, in how the mind interacts with the external world, transforming the impressions it receives.

→ There was an enthusiasm for **nature**, with the countryside seen as superior to towns and cities (the opposite view was more common in the 18th century). Aspects of nature that had not been shaped and ordered by human intervention were especially admired; mountains are a recurring symbol of beauty and mystery in Romantic verse.

→ Appreciation of nature and uneasiness about the effects of industrialisation led to a nostalgia for **simple rural life**, for an environment in which people lived and worked in harmony with the natural world. There was a new interest in the attitudes and experiences of ordinary country people, because their way of life had not been corrupted by the artificialities of city living.

→ This regard for unspoilt, natural man can be linked with the Romantics' interest in **childhood**, as a period in life when perception of the world has not been distorted by the conventions of adult society.

→ In terms of **poetic style**, many Romantic poets continued to use traditional forms (such as the sonnet), but there was also an attempt to use language which was **simpler** and closer to **everyday speech**.

Take note

If you are studying a text by an individual Romantic poet, knowledge of the Romantic movement as a whole will help your understanding of the text's **context**.

Take note

The first half of the 18th century is known as the **Augustan** period in English literature. The most important poet from this time was **Alexander Pope**.

Take note

Shelley's poem *Ozymandias*, which is about the statue of a pharaoh in the Egyptian desert, is an example of this interest in the ancient world. The poem is on page 43.

18th century poets tended to use more formal vocabulary and their belief in regularity and order was reflected in the widespread use of the heroic couplet, which was much less popular in the Romantic period.

Wordsworth ●●●

All of the features listed above are associated with **William Wordsworth** (1770–1850). Several of them come together in *The Prelude*, a long autobiographical poem divided into 13 sections or 'Books'. The poem is subtitled 'Growth of a Poet's Mind', and is very much an account of **moral and spiritual development** rather than a simple narration of important events. The early Books vividly recreate Wordsworth's childhood years in the Lake District, exploring how nature shaped the growth of his consciousness. The simple physical enjoyment of nature experienced during his earliest years is gradually replaced by a response to the natural world that is more spiritual and more conscious. He begins to be aware of hidden forces at work within nature, and of the complex ways in which humanity is related to the non-human universe. His experiences of nature, whether joyful or unsettling, slowly mould his character:

> *Fair seed-time had my soul, and I grew up*
> *Foster'd alike by beauty and by fear*

Later Books in *The Prelude* include passages on his unhappy time at university and his visits to France in the early 1790s. The French Revolution was then in its infancy, and Wordsworth became seriously committed to the republican cause. Subsequent events, notably the increasing violence of the revolution and war between Britain and France, led to disillusionment and by 1795 his support for France was at an end.

Most of Wordsworth's other major works are found in the two volumes of *Lyrical Ballads*. The first of these was a joint venture with **Samuel Taylor Coleridge**, though Wordsworth wrote most of the poems. He explained in his *Preface* that his aim was to write about *'low and rustic life'*, using *'the real language of men'*. Not all of the poems are consistent with these principles, but there are many rural ballads and narratives, with characters drawn from the poorest classes of society. *Tintern Abbey*, in the first volume, is a very different kind of poem – a reflective, autobiographical work with an elevated, meditative tone. The second volume includes the Lucy poems, a set of beautiful poems about a dead girl.

Checkpoint 1

What is an **heroic couplet**?

Checkpoint 2

What does the word *prelude* mean? Do you know why Wordsworth gave the poem this title?

Links

For more on **Coleridge**, see page 32.

Checkpoint 3

What does *rustic* mean?

Exam preparation   answers: page 45

Text C on page 43 is *A slumber did my spirit seal*, one of Wordsworth's Lucy poems (see above). Write a close analysis of the poem, examining both its meaning and the poet's use of language, form and structure.

The Romantics 2

Along with Wordsworth, Blake and Coleridge constitute the 'first generation' of Romantic poets. The leading poets of the second generation were Keats, Shelley and Byron.

Blake ●●●

William Blake (1757–1827) was a Romantic poet with a particularly strong interest in **society**, and the effects that its rules and institutions had on the individual. Blake believed strongly in individual freedom, and was opposed to established institutions (such as the church and the state) which he thought stifled this freedom. In *Songs Of Innocence And Experience*, poems which celebrate the innocent, uncorrupted joy of childhood are set against poems which show how this joy was destroyed by oppression and exploitation.

An important stylistic feature of Blake's poetry is his use of **symbolism**: clear, concrete images are used to represent more abstract ideas. Another characteristic of his poetry is the use of **simple**, **direct vocabulary**, though the apparent straightforwardness of his diction can be deceptive, as the underlying meaning is often more complex.

Although he was the earliest of the Romantic poets (his first works pre-date those of Wordsworth and Coleridge), Blake's ideas and the clarity of his language make him seem the most modern.

Coleridge ●●●

As explained on page 31, **Samuel Taylor Coleridge** (1772–1835) collaborated with Wordsworth on the *Lyrical Ballads*. Coleridge later explained that when they planned the book it was agreed that Wordsworth's poems would *'give the charm of novelty to the things of every day'*, while Coleridge's endeavours *'should be directed to persons and characters supernatural'*. Coleridge only contributed four poems, but one was *The Rime Of The Ancient Mariner*, his most famous work. It tells the haunting story of a sailor who shoots an albatross. His ship is becalmed, all his shipmates die and he learns that he must suffer for what he has done. The poem is rich in **symbolism** and succeeds both as a surreal adventure story and as a **moral allegory** about sin and redemption. Coleridge's interest in the exotic and as the mysterious was also reflected in *Kubla Khan*, a dreamlike vision of a landscape which is part-paradise, part-nightmare.

Keats ●●●

John Keats (1795–1821) is especially associated with two particular kinds of poem: long **narrative** poems (such as *The Eve Of Saint Agnes*) and shorter **odes** (such as *To Autumn* and *Ode On A Grecian Urn*). The narrative poems evoke mythic, medieval worlds and are richly descriptive. The subject-matter of the odes is less exotic but running through all of Keats's poetry is a preoccupation with art, beauty and transience. These three themes most clearly come together in *Ode On A Grecian Urn*, where Keats celebrates the capacity of art to preserve

---

Take note

In *A Poison Tree,* Blake uses the image of a tree to represent anger. See page 19.

Take note

An **allegory** is a story with at least two levels of meaning: the surface meaning and one or more hidden meanings. Often in allegories human characters represent (or personify) abstract ideas.

Checkpoint 1

What is an **ode**?

human experience and withstand the passing of time, while also recognising that the figures carved on the urn, though perfect and unchanging, are cold and lifeless. In *To Autumn* Keats's characteristic **sensuous imagery** is used to portray the natural world, with its continuous cycle of change, decay and rebirth. Keats suffered a tragically early death, and in much of his poetry there is a pervasive sense of his own mortality.

Shelley

Like Blake, **Percy Bysshe Shelley** (1792–1822) used his poetry to explore **social and political issues**. He was a radical thinker who rebelled against conventional morality and attacked organised religion and the political establishment. He believed that repressive forces within society stifled the imagination and restricted human freedom. He also celebrated **nature** in poems such as *Ode To A Skylark* and *Ode To The West Wind*, where the unrestrained energy of natural forces mirrors the spiritual and emotional freedom he craves:

> *A heavy weight of hours has chained and bowed*
> *One too like thee: tameless, and swift, and proud.*

Shelley was an idealist who thought that the poet's belief in the power of the imagination, and search for beauty and perfection, could be instruments for change within society.

Byron

The reputation of **George**, **Lord Byron** (1788–1824) stems partly from his poetry but also from his anarchic, eventful life. As with some modern celebrities, his riotous behaviour and turbulent love life both scandalised and fascinated the society of his day. The adjective 'Byronic' – still used to describe someone who is charismatic, mysterious and passionate – is similarly based partly on the man himself and partly on the heroes of his **narrative** poems, notably *Don Juan*. As a poet Byron is admired for his story-telling skills, and also for the irreverent **humour** evident in his verse **satires**. His literary reputation has declined since the 19th century, but in his own lifetime he was a popular and influential writer.

Checkpoint 2

What does the term **sensuous imagery** mean?

Take note

Like Keats, **Shelley** died young. He drowned in a boating accident in Italy.

Checkpoint 3

What is a **satire**?

Exam preparation   answers: page 45

Text D on page 43 is the sonnet *Ozymandias* by Shelley. Write a close analysis of the poem, focusing in particular on those features which are characteristic of Romantic poetry.

Victorian poetry

'**Victorian poetry**' is a broad term applied to poets who wrote during the reign of Queen Victoria (1837–1901), although it covers a large number of writers whose works sometimes have only a limited amount in common.

Overview

Unlike the **Romantic** poets, Victorian poets do not as a group represent a clear break from the past, although they share with the Romantics a belief in poetry as a vehicle for **emotional expression**. Their continued use of **traditional verse forms** distinguishes them from the **Modernist** poets who succeeded them, though the pessimism of later Victorian poetry anticipates the alienation and despair of much 20th century poetry.

Alfred, Lord Tennyson (1809–92) was very popular in his own lifetime, though his critical standing has declined since. In particular, he has been accused of sentimentality, and of having technical skills as a poet but ideas which are shallow and conventional. Several of his best works (such as *The Lady Of Shallott*) are narrative poems based on classical myth and medieval legend. His best-known poem is *In Memoriam*, an **elegy** which expresses Tennyson's grief over the sudden death of a friend, Arthur Hallam. Tennyson became Poet Laureate, and as Britain's 'national poet' wrote poems in response to historic events, such as *The Charge Of The Light Brigade*.

Robert Browning (1812–89) is especially noted for his **dramatic monologues**, poems which bring vividly to life the personalities of a variety of imaginary characters. He creates through the skilful use of language a range of different voices, refraining from direct comment on the morality of his characters and instead allowing them to reveal themselves through their attitudes and manner of speaking. Browning's language, which is often close to everyday speech, contrasts with that of Tennyson, which is more formal and more traditionally 'poetic'.

Browning's wife was **Elizabeth Barrett Browning** (1806–61), one of several important 19th century women poets. She was an early feminist, and much of her poetry reflects her radical political views, as well as expressing freely and openly her passion for her husband. *How Do I Love Thee?* is a celebratory poem, filled with the sense that her relationship with Browning had liberated her from a life of restraint and confinement.

The major literary achievement of **Emily Bronte** (1818–48) was the novel *Wuthering Heights*, but she also wrote several powerful poems. Threatening images of wild, untamed nature run through her poetry, as in *Spellbound*, where a violent storm is used to suggest psychological and emotional disturbance.

Christina Rossetti (1830–94) wrote several conventional love poems, though more unusual is the veiled sexuality of *Goblin Market*, ostensibly a children's poem.

The key poets of the later Victorian period were **Hopkins** and **Hardy**.

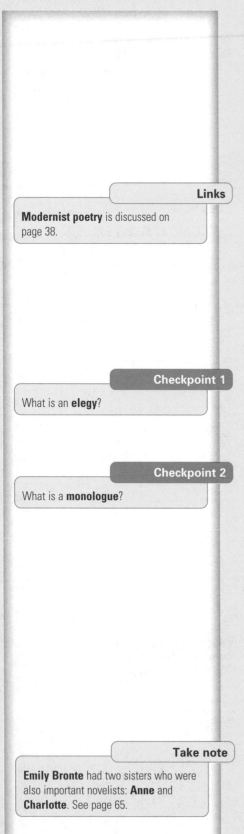

Links

Modernist poetry is discussed on page 38.

Checkpoint 1

What is an **elegy**?

Checkpoint 2

What is a **monologue**?

Take note

Emily Bronte had two sisters who were also important novelists: **Anne** and **Charlotte**. See page 65.

Hopkins

Gerard Manley Hopkins (1844–89) was a Jesuit priest whose poetry was not published until 1918, many years after his death. His work was original and experimental, and became an important influence on 20th century poetry. (He is considered the most 'modern' of the Victorian poets.) His main themes are **religion** and **nature**. He believed that the glory of God was expressed in the beauty of nature, but also despaired at humankind's increasing alienation from God. His poetry has several distinctive stylistic features:

→ Hopkins coined the word **inscape** to refer to the unique inner identity that any object or experience has. The aim of his poetry was to capture the hidden essence of whatever he was describing. In his view, language used in a conventional way failed to do this.

→ One result of this objective is that Hopkins's **vocabulary** is **unusual** and **inventive**. He creates new words, uses obscure dialect and Old English vocabulary, and joins words together in surprising combinations.

→ His use of **grammar** is equally **unconventional**. Syntax is compressed, with subjects and verbs missing, or words are placed in an unusual order.

→ The effects of **sound** and **rhythm** are extremely important in Hopkins's poetry. One of the reasons for Hopkins's unorthodox vocabulary is that words are often chosen as much for their sound as for their meaning. Similarly, traditional grammatical rules are broken in order to achieve a rhythmic effect. Hopkins makes extensive use of such devices as onomatopoeia, alliteration, assonance and rhyme. He also employs what he called **sprung rhythm**, a freer approach to traditional metre which enabled him to capture the soaring movement of a bird in flight (in *The Windhover*) or the dynamic exuberance of natural growth (in *Spring*).

Take note

A newly invented word or phrase is known as a **neologism**.

Hardy

Thomas Hardy (1840–1928) wrote many well-known novels, but he was also an important poet, whose work influenced later British poets such as Philip Larkin. Like his novels, his poems often present human beings as the helpless victims of forces beyond their control – *Convergence Of The Twain*, about the sinking of the Titanic, is an example of this. He was a prolific writer who also wrote many **narrative** poems, as well as poems about **nature**, **rural life**, **war** and the passing of **time**. Many critics consider his finest work to be the *1912–13 poems*, a group of poems written after the death of his wife.

Checkpoint 3

Can you name any novels written by **Thomas Hardy**?

Exam preparation   answers: page 45

Text E on page 43 is *The Self – Unseeing* by Thomas Hardy. Write a close analysis of this poem, examining both its meaning and the poet's use of language, form and structure.

First World War poetry

The poetry of the **First World War** (1914–18) is often set for AS/A2 study.

Background

Unlike previous wars, the First World War was fought by armies comprising literally millions of men, drawn mostly from the civilian populations of the countries involved. These armies inevitably included many writers experiencing military conflict for the first time. There were also reasons why they felt compelled to write about what they saw: the horrific nature of the war, the heartlessness and incompetence of many of their generals, and widespread ignorance in Britain about the reality of the conflict.

Take note

A poem which describes the mood in Britain when war broke out is *MCMXIV* by Philip Larkin (written not at the time, but about 45 years later).

Early verse

Response to the declaration of war in August 1914 was almost universally positive. One reason for this was that the war was expected to be short; it was generally assumed that Britain would secure an easy victory. Another was that the vast majority of people had no first-hand experience of war. The country's most recent wars had been fought by professional soldiers and far from Britain. When the army asked for recruits in 1914 there was an enthusiastic response, and within two months 750,000 had volunteered to fight. Poetry written at the start of the war reflects this sense of optimism and excitement. It tends to glorify the conflict, with romantic images of heroism, patriotism and noble sacrifice. The poet most strongly associated with this phase of the war is **Rupert Brooke** (1887–1915), whose sonnet *Peace* welcomes the outbreak of fighting in its opening line:

Now, God be thanked Who has matched us with His hour.

Another typical poem is **Herbert Asquith's** *The Volunteer*, which uses images of medieval chivalry to celebrate the life of a clerk, whose empty peacetime existence (*Toiling at ledgers in a city grey*) is contrasted with his noble death in battle: *His lance is broken; but he lies content.*

Checkpoint 1

What are *ledgers*?

Later responses

By 1915 it was apparent that the war would be much longer, and the number of casualties much greater, than people had first thought, though many in Britain remained ignorant of the horrors being experienced by those fighting in France. Poetry about the war, however, began to change, partly because several soldier-poets wanted civilians at home to know the truth. Writers such as **Wilfred Owen** (see below), **Isaac Rosenberg** and **Robert Graves** brought a new kind of **realism** to English poetry, with deliberately disturbing images of violence and death. The romantic, idealised language of earlier war poetry was replaced by vocabulary which was stark and direct, often incorporating soldiers' slang. Another approach was **satire**, with poems which mocked with bitter humour a variety of targets: incompetent generals, smug, insensitive civilians, lying propagandists. **Siegfried Sassoon**

(1886–1967) is especially associated with this satirical approach. In *Base Details* he imagines life as a major, stationed far from the front line and able when the war is over to *toddle safely home and die – in bed*.

Wilfred Owen ●●●

Wilfred Owen (1893–1918) is usually regarded as the major poet of the First World War. In his poems are found many of the recurring **themes** and attitudes of the war poets: the horrors of trench warfare; the common humanity of soldiers on both sides; anger at the futility and senselessness of the conflict, and of war in general; bitter questioning of the decisions taken by politicians and military leaders.

His poems also adopt a number of different styles and approaches to the subject of war. There are brutally **realistic** descriptions of life and death on the front line, but also gentler, more elegiac passages. In some poems there is **irony** and **satire**. One of Owen's best-known poems, *Dulce Et Decorum Est*, has an ironic title: the words are the beginning of a Latin quotation (it appears in full at the end of the poem) which means, 'It is sweet and proper to die for the fatherland'. In the poem Owen shows his contempt for the unthinking patriotism of this sentiment by describing in unsparing detail the reality of a gas attack.

A distinctive stylistic feature of Owen's poetry is his use of **half-rhyme** (also known as **pararhyme**). This occurs when consonants are similar but vowel sounds are different, as in this example from *Miners* (Owen is comparing soldiers digging trenches in France to miners digging for coal):

> I thought of some who worked dark pits
>> Of war, and died
> Digging the rock where Death reputes
>> Peace lies indeed.

Here the half-rhymes are *pits/reputes* and *died/indeed*. Half-rhymes give Owen's poetry a feeling of dislocation and disharmony, more appropriate to his presentation of war than the sense of order and stability that full rhymes might create.

Checkpoint 2

Explain how the title *Base Details* is ambiguous.

Take note

Siegfried Sassoon wrote prose as well as poetry. His *Memoirs Of An Infantry Officer* is a semi-autobiographical book about the First World War.

Take note

Like several other First World War poets, Wilfred Owen was killed in the war. He died a week before the war ended.

Checkpoint 3

Are any other techniques associated with the use of sound evident in this extract?

Take note

Owen also uses **sound** in other ways, as in *Anthem For Doomed Youth*, where techniques such as **onomatopoeia** and **alliteration** are used to evoke the sounds of battle: *wailing shells, the stuttering rifle's rapid rattle*.

Exam preparation

If you are studying the poetry of the First World War, choose **two** poems that you have studied which have contrasting attitudes to the conflict. Write an essay comparing the two poems.

Other 20th century poetry

This summary of 20th century poetry excludes the First World War poets discussed in the previous section (pages 36–37). It identifies some general movements and trends, and also looks in more detail at the work of some poets who are often set for AS/A2 study.

Overview

Poetry since 1900 has been extremely varied, but listed below are some broad movements and groupings:

→ **Modernist poetry**, which is associated with the first half of the 20th century, is often seen as a response to the feelings of alienation and insecurity created by two World Wars and continued technological change. Modernist poets such as **T.S. Eliot**, **W.B. Yeats** and **Ezra Pound** wrote complex, experimental poetry which deliberately rejected traditional forms and conventions, reflecting a sense of disintegration and confusion. They developed **free verse**, which broke with the patterns of regularly stressed syllables and standard line lengths found in traditional metre. The modernist approach remained influential in the second half of the century and much recent poetry is in this tradition.

→ In contrast to the Modernist poets, there have also been more **traditional**, anti-experimental poets – notably **Thomas Hardy** (see page 35), who began writing in the 19th century but lived until 1928, and **Philip Larkin** (see below).

→ The later decades of the 20th century saw the emergence of a number of important women poets, coinciding with the growth of **feminism**. Examples include **Carol Ann Duffy** (see below), **Sylvia Plath** and **Fleur Adcock**.

→ English language poetry has become increasingly **multicultural**. The poetry of **Grace Nichols**, for example, reflects on her experiences as a black woman living in Britain, and on the slavery of her West Indian ancestors. Another important Afro-Caribbean poet is **Benjamin Zephaniah**, who has lived in both Britain and Jamaica.

Ted Hughes

Much of the poetry of **Ted Hughes** (1930–98) is about **nature**, emphasising its raw violence and power. The forces of nature in Hughes's poetry (often represented by animals) are ungovernable, and oblivious to human beings. In *Wind* the inhabitants of a house are cowed by the ferocity of the storm raging outside. *The Jaguar* is about an animal in a zoo, but the big cat disregards its captivity, striding about its cage as if traversing *wildernesses of freedom*.

Checkpoint 1

Can you name any poems written by **T.S. Eliot**?

Checkpoint 2

Ted Hughes became the Poet Laureate (the national poet, who writes poems to mark important national occasions) in 1984. Who is the Poet Laureate today?

Checkpoint 3

Ted Hughes was married to a famous American-born poet, who committed suicide. He wrote about their relationship in a collection of poems called *Birthday Letters*. Who was she?

Seamus Heaney ●●●

Seamus Heaney (born 1939) is from Northern Ireland, and several of his most thought-provoking poems are about **Irish history and politics**. Like Hughes (an early influence) he also writes about the **natural world**. Often his poetry delves into the past, exploring his own **childhood**, **Irish history** and **ancient legend and myth**. He has a strong interest in the history of language, and *Beowulf* is a powerful modern version of an epic Old English poem.

Philip Larkin ●●●

Philip Larkin (1922–85) was (and remains) a very popular poet, who is admired for his ability to evoke **ordinary**, **everyday life**, while also moving beyond the surface of familiar social reality to uncover more profound truths about the nature of human experience. The development from a particular situation to a general reflection about life is found in many of his poems. In *Dockery And Son*, for example, a return visit to his old Oxford college prompts the narrator to consider the direction his life has taken, culminating in the observation that *Life is first boredom, then fear*, and *Whether or not we use it, it goes*. Larkin's poems often have **first-person narrators**, and most of these poems are clearly autobiographical. The **passing of time** and the **inevitability of death** are recurring themes. His poems, including those that deal with love relationships, are often about failure, but negativity is balanced by Larkin's humanity and the sense that he is continually reaching towards hope and fulfilment.

> **Take note**
>
> At the beginning of his writing career, Philip Larkin wrote two novels: *Jill* (1946) and *A Girl In Winter* (1947).

> **Take note**
>
> During his lifetime, Philip Larkin published four volumes of poetry: *The North Ship* (1945), *The Less Deceived* (1955), *The Whitsun Weddings* (1964) and *High Windows* (1974).

Carol Ann Duffy ●●●

The poetry of **Carol Ann Duffy** (born 1955) encompasses a rich variety of themes. These include: **childhood**; **family relationships**; **memory and the past**; **the passing of time**; **heterosexual and lesbian love**; **politics**. Often these themes overlap, as when poems about childhood draw on Duffy's own memories and reflect on the passing of time. *In Mrs Tilscher's Class* is a poem about the innocence of children in a primary school (which *glowed like a sweet shop*) and their approaching adolescence, prefigured in the transmutation of tadpoles into frogs. The children's dash through the schoolgates symbolises the rapid transition from one phase of life to another. Duffy also uses a variety of **poetic forms**, most notably the **sonnet** and the **dramatic monologue**.

> **Take note**
>
> An example of a **dramatic monologue** by Carol Ann Duffy is *The Captain Of The 1964 'Top Of The Form' Team*, in which an embittered middle-aged man longs for the confidence and success of his schooldays.

> **Exam preparation**
>
> If you are studying a 20th century poet, choose **two** of their poems: one which you think is very typical, and another which you think is untypical. Write an essay justifying your choice.

Analysing poems

Here are some tips on analysing individual poems, including previously 'unseen' poems, which you might be asked to write about in an exam.

Getting started

Read the poem carefully. Don't jump to conclusions concerning what it is about. If the meaning is unclear, look again at the beginning and end, as this often helps. If there are particular lines or phrases you can't understand, don't worry too much. You don't need to comment on every word in the poem, and you won't be penalised for admitting that you find part of a poem obscure – provided you don't keep saying this!

Begin by asking yourself these questions about the poem:

→ What is it about?
→ What is it *really* about?

In answering the first question, you only need to address the simple, surface meaning of the poem. Who is narrating the poem? What are they describing? If the poem tells some kind of story, what happens? If the poem is expressing a feeling of some kind, what is it? In answering the second question, you need to think more deeply about the poet's intention. What attitude do they have towards the subject matter of the poem? How is the reader intended to react? How would you describe the theme (or themes) of the poem? Does the poem have some kind of moral or 'message'?

Developing your response

Develop your response by looking in more detail at what different parts of the poem **mean**, and by looking at the poem's **style**. Identify important stylistic features, and consider how these contribute to the overall effect and to the poem's meaning. Key aspects to consider include:

Form and structure

How has the poem been organised? Does it conform to an identifiable poetic form (e.g. the sonnet)? How does it begin, develop and end? Do particular sections of the poem contrast with each other?

Poetic voice

What **tone** does the poem have – bitter, playful, ironic, regretful? If the poem is in the first person, has the poet created a **persona** (a narrator who is clearly distinct from the author)? If so, what view does the poet have of this character, and what view is the reader intended to have (sympathetic? disapproving?).

Vocabulary

What general points can be made about the vocabulary of the poem? Is it formal or informal? Simple or complex? What kind of mood or atmosphere does the vocabulary create? Are there any other **patterns** in the vocabulary, such as groups of words with similar connotations?

Links

See pages 16–17 for more on poetic **form** and **structure**.

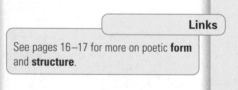

Checkpoint 1

If a poem does not use the first person, what 'person' is it most likely to be written in?

Links

There is more on poets' use of **vocabulary** on pages 18–19.

Are there individual words and phrases that are especially powerful or significant? Is any of the vocabulary ambiguous? Are there words that contrast with each other?

Imagery

Does the poem make use of metaphors, similes or personification? How do the comparisons work and what effects do they have? Are there any links between the images used?

Grammar and syntax

Are there parts of the poem where word order is especially unusual or significant? What types of sentences are used – for example, are there exclamations, or questions? How about sentence length – are any sentences unusually long or short? What tenses are used in the poem (past, present, future)? Are there changes of tense that are significant?

Sound and rhythm

Does the poem have a regular rhythm or metre? Are there places where the rhythm changes? If so, how and with what effect? Is there any use of devices such as alliteration, assonance and onomatopoeia?

Links to other poems ●●●

If the poem is part of a set text you are studying, you need to consider how it links to other poems in the book. Are there **themes** that are also found in other poems? Are the **attitudes** expressed similar to those in other poems? Are there **stylistic features** that are also found elsewhere? Do any of these aspects **contrast** with other poems in the book?

Final thoughts ●●●

Finally, how successful do you consider the poem to be? Which aspects of the style are especially effective? Does the poem 'work' for you? If the poem is part of a set text, in what ways is it typical, or unusual?

Checkpoint 2

What are **connotations**?

Links

See page 19 for more on poetic **imagery**.

Links

Grammar and **syntax** are discussed in more detail on page 20.

Links

See pages 21–3 for a fuller discussion of **sound**, **rhythm** and **metre**.

Checkpoint 3

What is **assonance**?

Take note

Other aspects of the poem's **context** might also be important, including for example the **period** when it was written.

Examiner's secrets

Examiners definitely like, and will reward, a genuine, well-argued personal response to a poem.

Exam preparation

There are practice poetry analysis questions on pages 27, 29, 31, 33 and 35.

Practice poems

The poems below are for use with the practice exam questions for this chapter.

Take note

The question for this poem is on page 27.

Examiner's secrets

Consider the impressions of the Miller's character created by his physical appearance and the references to his behaviour.

Text A

The MILLERE was a stout carl for the nones;
Ful big he was of brawn, and eek of bones.
That proved wel, for over al ther he cam,
At wrastlinge he wolde have alwey the ram.
He was short-sholdred, brood, a thikke knarre;
Ther was no dore that he nolde heve of harre,
Or breke it at a renning with his heed.
His berd as any sowe or fox was reed,
And therto brood, as though it were a spade.
Upon the cop right of his nose he hade
A werte, and theron stood a toft of heris,
Reed as the brustles of a sowes eris;
His nosethirles blake were and wide.
A swerd and bokeler bar he by his side.
His mouth as greet was as a greet forneys.
He was a janglere and a goliardeys,
And that was moost of sinne and harlotries.
Wel koude he stelen corn and tollen thries;
And yet he hadde a thombe of gold, pardee.
A whit cote and a blew hood wered he.
A baggepipe wel koude he blowe and sowne,
And therwithal he broghte us out of towne.

Take note

The question for this poem is on page 29.

Examiner's secrets

The imagery in the second and third stanzas is especially characteristic of Metaphysical poetry.

Text B

I wonder by my troth, what thou, and I
Did, till we lov'd? were we not wean'd till then?
But suck'd on countrey pleasures, childishly?
Or snorted we in the seaven sleepers den?
T'was so; But this, all pleasures fancies bee.
If ever any beauty I did see,
Which I desir'd, and got, t'was but a dreame of thee.

And now good morrow to our waking soules,
Which watch not one another out of feare;
For love, all love of other sights controules,
And makes one little roome, an every where.
Let sea-discoverers to new worlds have gone,
Let maps to other, worlds on worlds have showne,
Let us possesse one world, each hath one, and is one.

My face in thine eye, thine in mine appears,
And true plaine hearts doe in the faces rest,
Where can we finde two better hemispheares
Without sharpe North, without declining West?
What ever dyes, was not mixt equally;
If our two loves be one, or thou and I
Love so alike, that none doe slacken, none can die.

Text C

A slumber did my spirit seal;
    I had no human fears:
She seemed a thing that could not feel
    The touch of earthly years.

No motion has she now, no force;
    She neither hears nor sees;
Rolled round in earth's diurnal course,
    With rocks, and stones, and trees.

Take note

The question for this poem is on page 31.

Examiner's secrets

Think about the change in tense between the first and second stanzas.

Text D

I met a traveller from an antique land
Who said: Two vast and trunkless legs of stone
Stand in the desert . . . Near them, on the sand,
Half sunk, a shattered visage lies, whose frown,
And wrinkled lip, and sneer of cold command,
Tell that its sculptor well those passions read
Which yet survive, stamped on these lifeless things,
The hand that mocked them, and the heart that fed:
And on the pedestal these words appear:
'My name is Ozymandias, king of kings:
Look on my works, ye Mighty, and despair!'
Nothing beside remains. Round the decay
Of that colossal wreck, boundless and bare
The lone and level sands stretch far away.

Take note

The question for this poem is on page 33.

Take note

Ozymandias is the Greek name for the Egyptian pharaoh Rameses II (1304–1237 BC).

Text E

Here is the ancient floor,
Footworn and hollowed and thin,
Here was the former door
Where the dead feet walked in.

She sat here in her chair,
Smiling into the fire;
He who played stood there,
Bowing it higher and higher.

Childlike, I danced in a dream;
Blessings emblazoned that day;
Everything glowed with a gleam;
Yet we were looking away!

Take note

The question for this poem is on page 35.

Answers
Poetry

Poetry: study tips

Checkpoints

1 Context.
2 In all of the components of your AS or A2 course, marks are allocated according to how far you have succeeded in achieving certain assessment objectives. For example, one of the objectives is that you should demonstrate 'knowledge and understanding' of the texts that you have studied. See pages 6–7.
3 The Romantic period was in the late 18th and early 19th centuries. For more on the Romantic period in English poetry, see pages 30–3.

Poetic form and structure

Checkpoints

1 Romantic poets.
2 The term 'epic' implies a story on a grand scale, and can be used (for example) in relation to novels and films as well as poems.
3 The 17th century. Milton lived from 1608–74.

Poetic language 1

Checkpoints

1 Enjambement occurs in poetry when the sense of one line continues into the next, and the end of the first line has no punctuation mark. In this example, enjambement emphasises the extent of the poet's love, because the description of it is not contained within single lines, but reaches out from one line into the next.
2 Pun (or play on words).
3 The image is appropriate because London is the capital city of England, just as the heart is the central organ in the body.

Poetic language 2

Checkpoints

1 *Gulliver's Travels*.
2 *Rarely* here means 'unusually well' – the hay has a special, unusually fine smell.
3 First person involves the use of pronouns such as *I*, *me* or *we*. Second person uses words such as *you* and *your*, while third person refers to *he*, *she*, *it*, *they* etc.

Rhythm and metre

Checkpoints

1 The effect is to emphasise the many obstacles that have to be overcome during the journey that is being described. The line does not flow smoothly or quickly, because the heavy stresses slow it down.
2 The repetition of sound helps to suggest the repeated knocking on the door. *Rapping* is also an example of onomatopoeia (see page 21), which adds to the effect.
3 The use of repetition (*day*, *nor*) also plays a part.

Chaucer 1

Checkpoints

1 Thomas a Becket was an Archbishop of Canterbury who was murdered in Canterbury Cathedral in 1170. After his death he was declared a saint (in 1172), and the cathedral became a shrine, visited by Christian pilgrims.
2 An introductory section in a literary or musical work.
3 Anglo-Saxon was influenced by the language of the Angles and the Saxons, Germanic tribes who invaded England from northern Germany and southern Denmark in the fifth century. The Vikings, who began invading England from Scandinavia towards the end of the eighth century, were another influence on the development of English before the Norman Conquest of 1066.

Chaucer 2

Checkpoints

1 Social world/environment.
2 A humorous imitation of another work.
3 *Aesop's Fables*.

Exam preparation

The vividly detailed description of the Miller invests the character with primitive energy and strength. His physical appearance is part of this – he is *short-sholdred* and *brood*, with a coarse, overpowering ugliness: the hairy wart on his nose, the wide, black nostrils, the *greet* mouth. The imagery associates him with animals: his beard is red like a *sowe or fox*, and the hairs on his wart are also red, like *the brustles of a sowes eris*. Powerful verbs convey his energy and suggest a potential for violence: *heve*, *breke*. The discordant sound of the bagpipes he plays matches his noisy, raucous personality.

The Metaphysicals

Checkpoints

1 A statement or situation that is apparently contradictory but which is nevertheless true.
2 *Three-person'd* is a reference to the Holy Trinity: the Father, Son and Holy Spirit (or Holy Ghost).
3 Having more than one possible meaning.

Exam preparation

The confident, conversational opening of this poem is typical of Donne, and the sense of a strong personal voice is characteristic of Metaphysical poetry in general. The rhythmic stress on *Did*, the use of a colloquialism (*by my troth*) and the series of questions all suggest natural speech. The range of imagery, and the display of knowledge and intellect, are also characteristically Metaphysical, with references to global exploration and the two *hemispheares*. Complexity and ambiguity are other features of the language of Metaphysical poetry. The poem is ostensibly a declaration of the strength and intensity of a love relationship, but there are underlying doubts. Some lines could imply the relationship is claustrophobic: *each hath one, and is one; My face in thine eye, thine in mine appears*. When the poem states *If ever any beauty I did see . . . t'was but a dreame of thee*, does this only refer to past relationships? Or does it imply the woman he is addressing remains elusive and does not live up to his 'dreame' of her?

The Romantics 1

Checkpoints

1 A pair of rhyming lines based on the iambic pentameter (i.e. each line has five pairs of alternately stressed syllables).
2 A prelude is an introductory section, serving as an opening to a longer work. *The Prelude* by Wordsworth was originally intended to be the introduction to a work called *The Recluse*, which was never completed.
3 Rural, connected to the countryside. The word has connotations of simplicity, lack of urban sophistication.

Exam preparation

This poem contrasts the poet's state of mind before and after a loved one's death. The first stanza tells of the deluded belief he once had that she was immortal. *Slumber* implies a dream-like state from which he would eventually awake; *seal* similarly suggests that he was enveloped in a false security from which reality was excluded. As he now recognises, he was foolish to have no *human fears* because the woman **was** a human being and therefore subject to mortality. The second stanza then registers the shock of her death, which has destroyed the poet's delusion and forced him to acknowledge reality. Buried in the earth, she is as dead as rocks or stones. The poet's cruel loss has given him a new awareness of the impersonal forces which govern the universe; the unfeeling inexorability of these forces is reflected in the use of the coldly scientific word *diurnal*.

The Romantics 2

Checkpoints

1 A long poem addressed to a person, object or idea.
2 Writing (especially description) that appeals to the senses.
3 Humorous writing that has a serious purpose (often political or moral). Usually something is ridiculed in order to make serious criticisms of it.

Exam preparation

Like several other Romantic poets, Shelley was interested in myths and the ancient world. This sonnet is about a ruined statue of an Egyptian pharaoh. The destruction of the statue shows the power of time and how pride comes to nothing – it is overtaken by inevitable death and decay. As the inscription on the statue shows, Ozymandias saw himself as *king of kings* and thought other *mighty* rulers would look on his statue and *despair*, because they could not hope to match his achievements. But his works now lie in ruins, the vast, empty desert surrounding the statue emphasising that his power has been reduced to nothingness.

Victorian poetry

Checkpoints

1 A poem that mourns someone's death, though the term is also sometimes applied more generally to solemn, contemplative poems.
2 A lengthy speech delivered by one person.
3 Hardy's novels include *Tess Of The D'Urbevilles, The Mayor Of Casterbridge, The Return Of The Native, Jude The Obscure, Far From The Madding Crowd*.

Exam preparation

Like many of Hardy's poems, *The Self – Unseeing* considers the passing of time and views the past from the perspective of the present. Hardy recalls a joyful experience from his childhood, and recognises his inability to appreciate the value of the experience at the time. The poem is based on a return visit to Hardy's birthplace and childhood home at Higher Bockhampton. Every line in the opening stanza stresses the passage of time: the *ancient* floor is *Footworn and hollowed and thin*, the door is described as *former* because it is no longer there, and the feet that once passed through it belonged to his parents, who are now dead. The second stanza evokes a typical childhood scene: Hardy's mother *smiling into the fire*, while his father exuberantly played the violin. In the third stanza Hardy's response to the experience as a child is described: he *danced in a dream*, suggesting both happiness and the lack of awareness that is confirmed in the poem's last line.

First World War poetry

Checkpoints

1 Books that are written in, usually containing financial accounts.
2 *Base* has a double meaning. It refers to a military base, but also implies the major's life and attitudes are shameful.
3 Alliteration is also present, with the hard 'd' sounds creating an aural impression of digging into rock.

Other 20th century poetry

Checkpoints

1 T.S. Eliot's most famous poem is *The Waste Land*. Other poems include *Four Quartets, The Hollow Men, Ash Wednesday* and *Old Possum's Book Of Practical Cats*.
2 Andrew Motion.
3 Sylvia Plath.

Analysing poems

Checkpoints

1 Third person.
2 The associations that a word or phrase has – what is suggested by it.
3 Assonance occurs when the vowel sounds within words rhyme.

Revision Checklist
Poetry

By the end of this chapter you should be able to:

1	Explain the terms 'lyric poetry', 'sonnet', 'ode', 'elegy', 'narrative poetry' and 'stanza'.	Confident	Not confident. **Revise** pages 16–17
2	Understand the significance when analysing poetic vocabulary of connotations, levels of formality, simplicity or complexity of language, ambiguity and imagery.	Confident	Not confident. **Revise** pages 18–19
3	Understand the key features of grammar relevant to the analysis of poetry.	Confident	Not confident. **Revise** page 20
4	Understand the key features of sound relevant to the analysis of poetry.	Confident	Not confident. **Revise** pages 20–21
5	Recognise the five main metres of English poetry.	Confident	Not confident. **Revise** pages 22–23
6	Explain the term 'blank verse'.	Confident	Not confident. **Revise** page 22
7	Define the terms 'enjambement', 'end-stopped line' and 'caesura'.	Confident	Not confident. **Revise** page 23
8	Explain the concept of *The Canterbury Tales*.	Confident	Not confident. **Revise** page 24
9	Explain the role of *The General Prologue* within *The Canterbury Tales*.	Confident	Not confident. **Revise** page 26
10	Identify the key features of Metaphysical poetry.	Confident	Not confident. **Revise** page 28
11	Identify the key features of Romantic poetry.	Confident	Not confident. **Revise** page 30
12	Identify some of the key features of Victorian poetry.	Confident	Not confident. **Revise** page 34
13	Explain the context and some of the main characteristics of First World War poetry.	Confident	Not confident. **Revise** page 36
14	Offer an overview of some of the key movements and poets within other 20th century poetry.	Confident	Not confident. **Revise** pages 38–39
15	Approach the analysis of a poem with confidence.	Confident	Not confident. **Revise** pages 40–41

As with poetry, you'll definitely be studying one or more prose texts during your AS or A2 course. This will usually be a novel, but it might be a collection of short stories. A difference from GCSE is that whereas at GCSE you may have focused on some key extracts, at AS/A2 it's important that you know the *whole* text. This means you'll need to read it independently, ideally a few times. Another difference is that you'll need in your written work to demonstrate a more sophisticated understanding of some of the techniques that novelists use. This includes, for example, characterisation, narrative perspectives and the use of settings. Several of the sections in this chapter look at these features.

There is also an historical overview, covering the major periods and the important authors in the development of the novel. In the 20th century, American and post-colonial novelists became increasingly important, and there's a section on these. Finally, there's advice on analysing prose fiction extracts. In your exams, you might have to analyse an extract from your set text, or possibly (at A2) an unseen extract (i.e. one taken from a text you've not actually studied before).

Exam themes

→ Knowledge and understanding of set prose texts

→ Use of relevant terminology

→ Awareness of literary contexts (e.g. important phases or periods in the development of the novel)

Topic checklist

AS ○ A2 ●	AQA/A	AQA/B	EDEXCEL	OCR	WJEC	CCEA
Novels: study tips	○●	○●	○●	○●	○●	○●
Form and structure in novels	○●	○●	○●	○●	○●	○●
Settings in novels	○●	○●	○●	○●	○●	○●
Narrative technique in novels	○●	○●	○●	○●	○●	○●
Characters in novels	○●	○●	○●	○●	○●	○●
Use of language in novels 1	○●	○●	○●	○●	○●	○●
Use of language in novels 2	○●	○●	○●	○●	○●	○●
18th and 19th century novels	●	○	○	○	○	○
Austen and the Brontes		○	○	○	○	○
Dickens and Hardy	●	○	○		○	○
20th century novels	○	○		○●	○●	●
American and post-colonial novels	○	○	●	○●	●	●
Analysing prose extracts	○●	○●	○●	○●	○●	○●
Practice extracts	○●	○●	○●	○●	○●	○●

Novels: study tips

Here is some initial advice on how to go about studying a novel at AS or A2.

Reading the book ●●●

→ If you can, **read the book before you begin studying it** at school or college. Often you'll be able to find out in advance the texts you are studying, and if it is an A2 book you might well be asked to read it over the summer holiday.

→ The purpose of this first reading is to get a **general idea** of the storyline, characters and so on. You may want to give some thought to 'deeper' aspects such as themes and the writer's use of language, but there is nothing wrong with leaving these until later.

→ If reading the book proves to be hard going, set yourself **targets** for getting through it (such as 50 pages a week). Students sometimes struggle with the first few chapters of novels, but once you settle into the story you should find reading the book becomes less difficult, and an enjoyable experience. But if you only read it when you feel like it, and only read a few pages at a time, there is a danger you'll never actually finish it at all.

→ **If understanding what is 'going on' in the novel is difficult**, you could get help from a relevant study guide (see 'Extra help' below). These often contain detailed plot summaries, which you can refer to as you're going along.

→ You might find it helpful to listen to an **audio version** of the book. Try to make sure you get an unabridged (complete) reading if one is available – local libraries often stock these.

Studying the book ●●●

→ Ideally, an examination text should be read **three** or more times:
  → an initial reading to get a **general grasp** of the book (see above);
  → a second, more careful **analytical** reading;
  → a final re-reading for **revision** purposes.
The second of these is the most important – this is when you examine the book in detail.

→ You need to know **what to look for, and what to concentrate on**. Finding out the relevant **assessment objectives** for the course component is crucial – for example, it might be especially important to know about how the novel reflects its social and historical context. Do you need to *compare* the book to another text? If the book is a coursework text, do you know what the coursework task will be?

→ In analysing a novel, you usually need to focus on these areas: the overall **structure**, including how the plot develops; the **setting**; the author's **narrative technique**; the presentation of **characters** and their relationships; **themes**; use of **language**.

Checkpoint 1

What term is used for the storyline of a novel or play?

Watch out!

When planning your revision schedule, make sure you allow time for re-reading the novel. You may need to start this early!

Checkpoint 2

What are **assessment objectives**?

Links

Later in this chapter you'll find guidance on all these topics.

→ Your teacher will probably give you advice on organising your **notes**, but usually it is a good idea to have notes related to all the topic areas above. In addition, it is helpful to have:

  → **chapter summaries** (key points, 'what happens' in terms of the plot etc.);

  → **key quotations** (lists of quotations, organised under headings – specific themes, characters etc.).

→ If you're allowed to, **annotate** the book, highlighting key passages, writing brief comments in the margins and so on. Note though that if you're taking the book into an examination, there are regulations limiting the amount of annotation you can have.

Carrying out research and getting extra help ●●●

→ When you first begin reading the novel, you might want to carry out some **preliminary research** to find out a bit more about the author, the period when the novel is set etc. The **Internet** and public or school/college **libraries** are obvious places to start.

→ When you are studying the book, you can carry out **more detailed research**. Depending on the assessment objectives for the course component, it might for example be important to find out about the novel's historical context, or how it has been interpreted by critics.

→ Make use of any **notes**, **introductory material** etc. in the book itself. Editions of older novels in particular often have helpful additional sections, and it is a mistake to ignore these.

→ For many set texts, there are inexpensive **study guides** you can buy and free **online revision materials**. Note though that some study guides are for GCSE rather than AS/A2 courses, and some online sites are for American students so don't directly address AS/A2 requirements.

→ You might be able to watch a **film or television adaptation** of the novel you are studying. Be careful here, as adaptations sometimes make significant changes to the storyline. It is usually best to watch the adaptation *after* you have read the book. Watch for changes to the original novel, and think about why these were made. Do they make the storyline simpler, or place greater emphasis on particular characters? Think also about how the director and the actors have **interpreted** the novel. Has the director successfully conveyed the novel's main ideas and themes? Do you agree with the way the characters are played and presented?

Links

For more on selecting and using quotations, see page 175.

Checkpoint 3

Why is it best to watch a film or television adaptation **after** reading the book rather than before?

Exam preparation

After carrying out the relevant research, make a list of key facts about the life of the author of the novel you are studying. Highlight any facts which seem to be linked to the novel, explaining the connections.

Form and structure in novels

Form and **structure** are broad terms which are sometimes used interchangeably, though form can refer more specifically to the **genre** of a novel, while structure includes organisational aspects such as the **plot** and the division of a novel into chapters.

Checkpoint 1

Explain the term **conventions**.

Types of novel ●●●

The **genre** of a novel can be a useful starting-point when considering the overall shape or pattern of the book. You might find that the author follows the **conventions** of the genre quite closely, or seeks to achieve particular effects by going against convention in some way. You might also find that the novel is in fact a **mix of genres**. These are some of the most common genres:

→ The **social novel** – addresses social issues such as poverty and inequality. Several of Charles Dickens's novels fall into this category.

→ The **historical novel** – set in the past. The author attempts to recreate a different historical period.

→ The **futuristic novel** – set in the future. George Orwell's *Nineteen Eighty-Four* and Margaret Atwood's *The Handmaid's Tale* are examples. A related genre is **science fiction**.

→ The **fantasy novel** – creates a make-believe world, often with a hint of the **supernatural**. This genre can be contrasted with **realism** or **naturalism** (where characters and events are true to life).

→ The **Gothic novel** – a type of horror story, especially associated with 18th and 19th century English literature. Mary Shelley's *Frankenstein* is an example. This genre is discussed more fully on page 62.

→ **Magic realism** – a blend of realism and fantasy. Strange, fantastic events occur in a realistic setting. Angela Carter is a modern writer associated with this genre.

→ The **epistolary novel** – takes the form of letters written by the main characters. It was popular in the 18th century, but some more recent fiction also uses this form (e.g. Alice Walker's *The Color Purple*).

→ The *Bildungsroman* – a German term for a novel that charts the growth of a character from early years to maturity. Dickens's *Great Expectations* and *David Copperfield* are examples.

Checkpoint 2

Explain the terms **satire** and **parody**.

→ The **comic novel** – has several variations, including **satire** or **parody**.

→ The **mystery novel** – about strange or mysterious events. Usually we read on because we want to unravel the mystery. A related genre is the **detective novel** or **thriller**.

→ The **romantic novel** – a term used in a variety of ways. 'Romance' can mean taking the reader away from the ordinary and mundane, into a world which is extraordinary or ideal. The term is also more narrowly associated with stories about love. Emily Bronte's *Wuthering Heights* is a romantic novel in both senses.

→ The **adventure novel** – has an emphasis on exciting action, and often involves challenges, journeys and exotic locations.

Plot

The term **plot** refers to the events of a novel (the storyline) and how these are *organised* by the novelist. The pattern or plan that the author imposes on the action of the novel reflects the author's underlying purposes – for example, a sequence of events involving a series of mishaps may be devised in order to encourage us to be sympathetic towards a character.

When you are considering plot, think about how the overall organisation of the novel, and particular events or sequences of events, illustrate important themes in the novel, or help to convey aspects of the novel's characters. Think also about the kinds of effects the development of the plot has on the reader – for example, parts of the plot may generate a feeling of **suspense**, or the story may have an exciting **climax**.

Look at the **order** of events. Usually narratives are **linear**, which means events are presented in a chronological sequence, but this is not always the case.

Other aspects of structure

Structure is a broad term that includes plot but also covers all other aspects of a novel's organisation.

Chapter divisions are important **structural devices**: chapters might be **juxtaposed** in order to highlight some kind of contrast, or there might be **'cliffhanger endings'** to chapters. Many 19th century novels were originally **serialised**, and it is helpful to know where these divisions originally occurred. As with television soap operas, the intention at the end of an instalment was usually to leave the reader anxious to know how the plot would develop.

As well as conventional chapters, there are other ways of ordering and presenting material, and you should always try to identify the purpose and effect of these. Ian McEwan's *Enduring Love*, for example, ends with two appendices. *The Handmaid's Tale* has a set of 'Historical Notes'.

Other structural techniques include **symbols** or **motifs** that might be repeated during the course of a novel. Alternatively, **imagery** with positive connotations in one part of the book might contrast with imagery that has negative associations in another part.

Take note

Atwood's *The Handmaid's Tale* has frequent **flashbacks**, and we are given alternative versions of certain events. Martin Amis's *Time's Arrow* is an experimental novel which tells the story of a man's life backwards in time, beginning with his death and ending with his childhood.

Take note

Beginnings and **endings** of novels are important structurally. The beginning might introduce important themes or characters. The close of a novel might provide some kind of resolution, or be open-ended and ambiguous.

Take note

Narrators can be important structural devices. You should think about how the narrator guides us through the story. What does the narrator tell us about, and what is omitted? Does the narrator comment on the development of the story, for example by referring to future events?

Checkpoint 3

What is a **motif**?

Exam preparation

What **genre** does the novel you are studying belong to? Make a list of elements in the novel which are characteristic of this genre.

Settings in novels

This section looks at some of the ways in which **settings** and **locations** might be important in a novel.

Setting and historical context

Setting can play an important part in creating the **historical period** when the action of the novel takes place. William Golding's *The Spire* is set in the Middle Ages and is about the construction of a cathedral spire. Almost all of the events in the novel take place within the grounds of the cathedral, reflecting not only the inward-looking obsessiveness of the novel's central character (Jocelin, the cathedral dean), but also the role of a medieval cathedral as a focal point for the local community.

Oscar Wilde set *The Picture Of Dorian Gray* in his own time, and most of the novel's action occurs in Victorian London. Wilde's use of location highlights the divisions in Victorian society, the gulf between rich and poor: we move from a glittering aristocratic world of luxurious apartments and leisurely dinner parties to the squalor of shabby lodging houses and dingy opium dens. Dorian Gray's own journeys between these locations symbolise his divided self and parallel his steady descent into moral corruption.

Setting and themes

As the above examples illustrate, settings are often used to help convey a novel's main ideas or **themes**. A setting may have a **symbolic** significance, which means it is used to **represent** something – usually, a set of ideas, attitudes or values. In Jane Austen's *Mansfield Park* the country estate that gives the novel its title is associated with order and morality, civilised values which are threatened by the influence of the Crawfords, a brother and sister who visit the house. *Return Of The Native* by Thomas Hardy is dominated by its setting: the tragic events of the novel unfold against the formidable backdrop of Egdon Heath, used to symbolise the unchanging elements of life. Egdon is described as being what *it always had been*, and as having *an ancient permanence which the sea cannot claim*.

Contrasts between settings can be important to the development of themes. Mansfield Park is contrasted with the disorder of Portsmouth (the heroine Fanny Price's family home) and the lax morality of London (where the Crawfords spend most of their time). In Emily Bronte's *Wuthering Heights*, the two main settings are Wuthering Heights itself (a farmhouse on the Yorkshire moors) and another house nearby, Thrushcross Grange. The houses symbolise contrasting values and approaches to life. Wuthering Heights, a working farm, is associated with the forces of nature and with intense, unrestrained emotion. Thrushcross Grange, a luxurious family residence, is associated with social refinement and control of the emotions. The locations of the houses reinforce this contrast: Wuthering Heights is set in wild and unprotected moorland (*wuthering* means exposed to violent winds), whereas Thrushcross Grange is set in a sheltered park.

Checkpoint 1

Jocelin, the central character of *The Spire*, might be described as **solipsistic**. What does this mean?

Links

For more on **Jane Austen**, see page 64.

Links

See page 67 for more on **Thomas Hardy**.

Links

Emily Bronte is also discussed on page 65.

Setting and character

Settings can also reflect aspects of the novel's **characters**. In the case of *Wuthering Heights*, the characters who live at Wuthering Heights tend to be strong and passionate, while those at Thrushcross Grange are delicate and sensitive. In Charles Dickens's *Great Expectations*, Wemmick (a lawyer's clerk who becomes a friend to the hero Pip) keeps his personal and professional life rigidly separate, and the drawbridge which cuts his house off from the outside world symbolises this. When he is engaged in his professional duties he has a hard, self-contained manner, but at home he is more human and less robotic. The quirky eccentricity of his house (which he calls 'the Castle') symbolises this emotional freedom. It is surrounded by a small moat, and has a cannon which is fired at nine o'clock each night and a flagpole from which a flag flies every Sunday. Wemmick explains, *'The office is one thing and private life is another. When I go into the office, I leave the Castle behind me, and when I come into the Castle I leave the office behind me.'*

Links

For more on **Charles Dickens**, see page 66.

Setting and atmosphere

Settings are also important in evoking an appropriate **mood** or **atmosphere** for particular episodes in a novel. In *Great Expectations*, when Pip first arrives in London the descriptions of the city give it a depressing, unwholesome atmosphere, prefiguring Pip's disillusionment and the disappointment of his expectations:

> *So, I came into Smithfield; and the shameful place, being all asmear with filth and fat and blood and foam, seemed to stick to me. So I rubbed it off with all possible speed by turning into a street where I saw the great black dome of St Paul's bulging at me from behind a grim stone building which a bystander said was Newgate Prison. Following the wall of the jail, I found the roadway covered with straw to deaden the noise of passing vehicles; and from this, and from the quantity of people standing about, smelling strongly of spirits and beer, I inferred that the trials were on.*

Links

In **Gothic novels**, settings play an important part in creating a supernatural atmosphere (see page 62).

Checkpoint 2

What does **prefiguring** mean?

Checkpoint 3

Comment closely on the use of language in this extract.

Exam preparation   answers: page 76

Text A on page 74 is from *A Passage To India* by E.M. Forster. It is a description of Chandrapore, the novel's setting. The events of the novel take place in India in the early part of the 20th century, when the country was ruled by the British. Comment on the impressions of Chandrapore created by this description, including what it suggests about the relationship between the British and Indian communities.

Narrative technique
in novels

The narrator of a novel might be one of the characters, or an invisible, **third-person** narrator. In both cases, the way a story is told almost inevitably implies a view of the characters and events described. In analysing a novel you need to decide what this view is, and how far it appears to be shared by the author.

Third-person narrators

A **third-person narrator** is not involved in the world of the story and refers to characters using third-person pronouns such as *he*, *she* and *they*. This is the most common form of narration. The narrator is usually **omniscient**, which means 'all-knowing'. In other words, everything in the novel's fictional world is known to them, and they can switch freely from character to character, and from location to location.

An omniscient narrator can be **intrusive** or **unintrusive**. Intrusive narrators intervene in the novel to comment directly on characters and events, often making explicit moral judgements. Some 19th century authors such as George Eliot and Jane Austen are associated with this approach. Unintrusive narrators are **invisible**. They describe the events of the story but do not comment on them, although a view may well be **implicit** in the language that is used.

A novel can have a third-person narrator, but still be narrated mainly or exclusively from the **perspective** of one of the characters. An example is William Golding's *The Spire* (see page 52), which is told mainly from the perspective of Jocelin, the dean of the cathedral. The effect is to distance us from the character, so that we view him critically even as we share his private thoughts.

First-person narrators

A **first-person narrator** refers to *I* and *me*. The narrator is usually the novel's central character, but can also be a secondary character who is a witness to the events described (Nelly Dean, one of the main narrators in *Wuthering Heights*, is an example of this). An advantage of first-person narration is that it enables the author to present a character's thoughts and emotions very directly. Often the narrator is viewing events **retrospectively**, recognising with the wisdom of hindsight their own foolishness or naivety. In *Great Expectations* the narrator, Pip, is a mature adult, recalling the illusions and misjudgements of his childhood and youth.

Because we view events from the narrator's perspective, and because their private thoughts are shared with us, there is a tendency for the reader to **identify** with the narrator. In some cases, this may be what the author intended, but remember the narrator is a **character** the author has created, and may well have been given flaws and weaknesses. Try to identify these, and consider how far the narrator's view of events can be relied upon (see 'Unreliable narrators' below).

Take note

Relevant technical terms that can be used here are **intradiegetic** (= in the world of the story) and **extradiegetic** (= outside the world of the story).

Take note

F. Scott Fitzgerald's *The Great Gatsby* is an example of a novel where, although the narrator is a character within the story (Nick Carraway), the distinction between author and narrator has been deliberately blurred. Carraway refers to *this book* and makes remarks such as *Reading over what I have written so far*. Nevertheless the distinction still exists, and it is important to remember that Carraway is a character created by Fitzgerald, and not just a thinly disguised version of Fitzgerald himself.

Multiple narrators

A novel has **multiple narrators** if more than one character tells the story (the novel will often alternate between them). This device is often used to give the reader **different perspectives** on the same events. A **framed narrative** occurs when the main narrative is contained within another narrative. *Wuthering Heights* is again an example of this. The novel begins with Lockwood describing to the reader his experiences during a visit to Yorkshire. The narrator then becomes Nelly Dean, who tells Lockwood the history of the people who live at Wuthering Heights. This second narrative takes up most of the book, though Lockwood occasionally reminds us of his presence (as Nelly Dean's audience), and he takes over the role of narrator again for the close of the novel. Another example is Joseph Conrad's *Heart Of Darkness*, where Marlow is the main narrator, while the 'outer narrator' is an unnamed character who is among a group of people listening to Marlow's account of his journey to the African Congo.

Narrative voice

The character of a narrator is created partly through the opinions and attitudes they express, and partly through the **language** the narrator uses. The **narrative voice** might, for example, reflect the narrator's personality, age or regional background. Mark Twain's *The Adventures Of Huckleberry Finn* is a late 19th century novel in which the narrator is a young, uneducated American boy. The opening of the novel uses **informal vocabulary** and **non-standard grammar** to create an immediate sense of the narrator's natural speaking voice:

> *You don't know about me without you have read a book by the name of The Adventures Of Tom Sawyer; but that ain't no matter. That book was made by Mr Mark Twain, and he told the truth, mainly. There was things which he stretched, but mainly he told the truth.*

Unreliable narrators

An **unreliable narrator** is a narrator whose judgement is flawed. In the opening chapters of *Wuthering Heights* Lockwood comically makes several mistaken assumptions about the people he meets. The device of an unreliable narrator is a way of drawing the reader into the novel, as it forces us to question the narrator's views and form our own judgements.

Checkpoint 1

What is a **perspective**?

Checkpoint 2

What other term can be used for an individual's distinctive use of language (or 'voice')?

Checkpoint 3

Identify examples of **non-standard grammar** in this extract.

Take note

As with *The Great Gatsby* (see above), note how Mark Twain plays with the separation between author and narrator in this extract.

Take note

Some narrators (whether first- or third-person) **speak directly to the reader**. The earlier quotation from *The Adventures Of Huckleberry Finn* is an example of this (*You don't know me . . .*). One effect is usually to encourage a **closer relationship** between narrator and reader. As with the device of an unreliable narrator, we sometimes need to be on our guard here: how far should we identify with the narrator, and share their view of events?

Exam preparation   answers: page 76

Text B on page 74 is from *The Adventures Of Huckleberry Finn* by Mark Twain (see 'Narrative voice' above), a sequel to *The Adventures Of Tom Sawyer*. Examine Twain's presentation of the narrator (Huck), commenting closely on the author's use of language.

Characters in novels

As at GCSE, many AS/A2 examination questions involve writing about the **characters** of the novel you have studied. The main difference is that at AS/A2 you need to show more awareness that the characters have been **created** by the author to serve particular purposes within the text.

Characters as fictional constructs

Students sometimes make the mistake of writing about characters in novels as if they were real people. Imagining the characters created by an author is of course part of the enjoyment of reading novels, but you should only refer to what is disclosed about them in the pages of the book. Don't speculate about additional biographical details, such as relationships you imagine they might have had before the story started. Instead, demonstrate your awareness that they are **fictional constructs** – that is, imaginary people created by the author to serve specific purposes and functions within the novel. You can do this by writing things like *Austen uses X to illustrate the theme of . . .* , or *X is important to the development of the plot.*

Presentation of character

Examination questions often ask you to comment on how a character is **presented**. This means looking at the methods used in creating the characters and influencing the reader's response to them. Some of the most important methods are listed below.

Appearance

Physical **appearance** (including clothing) is often used to express important aspects of a character. This is the initial description of Joe Gargery in *Great Expectations*:

> *Joe was a fair man, with curls of flaxen hair on each side of his smooth face, and with eyes of such a very undecided blue that they seemed to have somehow got mixed with their own whites. He was a mild, good-natured, sweet-tempered, easy-going, foolish, dear fellow – a sort of Hercules in strength, and also in weakness.*

Here the characteristics mentioned in the second sentence are initially indicated by the description of Joe's physical appearance in the first sentence. Joe's gentleness and good nature are suggested by *the curls of flaxen hair on each side of his smooth face*, while his weakness of character is apparent in his *eyes of such a very undecided blue*.

Direct comment

Explicit comments might be made about the character by the author, narrator or other characters (as in the *Great Expectations* extract above). Jane Austen is associated with frequent **authorial comment** on her characters, as when Lady Bertram in *Mansfield Park* is described as *a woman of very tranquil feelings, and a temper remarkably easy and indolent.*

Take note

This does not mean that characters are not sometimes **based** on real people. The term **projection character** is used for a character who resembles in some ways the book's author. In *The Picture Of Dorian Gray* Lord Henry Wotton, who dazzles London society with his outrageous wit, has strong similarities to Oscar Wilde himself. However, the resemblance is rarely complete. In *Dorian Gray* it is likely that Basil Hallward (who is very different to Lord Henry) reflects other, contrasting aspects of Wilde's character.

Checkpoint 1

The second sentence here contains **asyndetic listing**. What does this mean?

Watch out!

Comments about characters are not always to be taken at face value. Lockwood in *Wuthering Heights* is an example of an **unreliable narrator**, whose judgements are often mistaken.

Imagery and symbolism

A character may be strongly associated with particular **images** or **symbols**. In *Wuthering Heights* Heathcliff is associated with natural imagery, reflecting his primitive strength and savagery. Two characters compare him to *whinstone* (hard rock). Nelly Dean says that the contrast between Heathcliff and Edgar Linton *resembled what you see in exchanging a bleak, hilly, coal country for a beautiful fertile valley*. Even the name *Heathcliff* has connotations of wild, rugged nature.

Speech and thought

Characters are also revealed through what they say and think. As well as *what* characters say, you should consider *how* they say it: a character's **idiolect**, or use of language, is often significant.

Action

How a character **acts** is important. This includes both broad patterns of behaviour (Heathcliff's carefully plotted revenge against the Linton family shows his ruthlessness), and smaller, individual actions which are still revealing. In E.M. Forster's *A Room With A View*, Lucy Honeychurch's openness to new experience is contrasted with the repressed nature of her older cousin, Miss Bartlett. At the end of the first chapter, this is reflected in the characters' contrasting behaviour when they return to their hotel rooms (they are staying in Florence): Lucy *opened the window and breathed the clean night air*, whereas Miss Bartlett *fastened the window-shutters and locked the door*.

Role of a character ●●●

Another aspect of the presentation of a character is the **role** that the character plays in relation to the rest of the book – the **importance** of the character to the novel as a whole. Think about:

→ **The plot** How important is it to the storyline? How do plots influence the events that occur in the novel?
→ **The themes** Does the character represent or illustrate any of the main ideas in the novel? What are their attitudes and values?
→ **Relationships with other characters** Do they have important relationships with any of the other characters? Are these relationships used to reveal anything about the other characters?

> **Checkpoint 2**
>
> Jane Austen's novels employ **omniscient narrators**. What does this mean?

> **Take note**
>
> As the example of Heathcliff illustrates, characters' **names** can be revealing. In *Great Expectations*, Pip's name is appropriate because over the course of the novel we see him *grow* – the book begins with his earliest childhood memory and traces his development into a mature adult.

> **Checkpoint 3**
>
> If one character in a novel is described as the **antithesis** of another character, what does this mean?

Exam preparation   answers: page 76

Text C on page 75 is a description of Mrs Joe Gargery, a character in Charles Dickens's *Great Expectations* (see 'Appearance' above). Write a close analysis of the extract, examining how Dickens presents the character to us.

Use of language in novels 1

It is important that when you write about a novel you make close reference to the author's **use of language**. The next two sections identify some aspects of language that are often worth comment.

Vocabulary ●●●

Connotations

The **connotations** (or associations) of the vocabulary used are important. Look for **positive** or **negative** connotations, and also for the more specific associations that particular words can have. Try to find **patterns** in the writer's use of vocabulary, such as the repeated use of words with similar or contrasting associations. 'Counterparts' in James Joyce's *Dubliners* is a short story about an embittered, frustrated clerk in a solicitor's office. Words with connotations of anger and aggression run through the story: *furious, rage, savage, revengeful, annoyed, enraged*.

Checkpoint 1

What term can be used for vocabulary that evokes a strong emotional response?

Formality and informality

Formal vocabulary is especially associated with older texts – Jane Austen's novels, for example, generally have a formal tone or **register**. However, it can also be found in more recent texts, where it is often used to reflect **character**. In Kazuo Ishiguro's *The Remains Of The Day*, for example, the narrator is Stevens, the butler to an English aristocrat. His language reflects his stiff, reserved manner:

> *I can say I am in agreement with those who say that the ability to draw up a good staff plan is the cornerstone of any decent butler's skills. I have myself devised many staff plans over the years, and I do not believe I am being unduly boastful if I say that very few ever needed amendment.*

Checkpoint 2

Explain, with close reference to the language used, how this extract creates a sense of Stevens's character.

This quotation also illustrates how vocabulary, along with other aspects of language, is important in creating a **narrative voice**. A contrasting text is Graham Swift's *Last Orders*, whose narrators include a working-class Londoner:

Take note

Levels of formality can vary within a single novel – for example, one character may speak more formally than another.

> *Bernie pulls me a pint and puts it in front of me. He looks at me puzzled, with his loose, doggy face, but he can tell I don't want no chit-chat. That's why I'm here, five minutes after opening, for a little silent pow-wow with a pint glass. He can see the black tie, though it's four days since the funeral. I hand him a fiver and he takes it to the till and brings back my change.*

Take note

Another aspect of this extract's informality is the presence of **non-standard grammar** – for example, the double negative *I don't want no chit-chat*.

The vocabulary here is notably **informal**, with the use of **colloquialisms** such as *chit-chat*, *pow-wow* and *fiver*.

Imagery

The term **imagery** is sometimes applied to any aspect of a text that appeals to the reader's senses. For example, novels often include passages of **visual description**, perhaps describing a novel's setting or a character's appearance. More specifically, imagery means the use of **comparison**. Look for examples of **metaphor**, **simile** and **personification**, and for the effects that they have. In the passage below from *Wuthering Heights*, imagery is used when Catherine compares her feelings for Edgar Linton with those that she has for Heathcliff:

> *My love for Linton is like the foliage in the woods. Time will change it, I'm well aware, as winter changes the trees. My love for Heathcliff resembles the eternal rocks beneath – a source of little visible delight, but necessary.*

The imagery here conveys the contrast between the enduring nature of her love for Heathcliff and the relative superficiality of her feelings for Edgar.

Related terms are **symbol** and **motif**. A **symbol** is something used to represent something else, such as an abstract idea or concept. In William Golding's *The Spire*, the pit which is dug to explore the foundations of a medieval cathedral is a symbol of evil and corruption: it is *the roof of hell*, and when the foundations begin to shift they are like *Some form of life; that which ought not to be seen or touched, the darkness under the earth, turning, seething, coming to the boil*. When Jocelin (the cathedral dean and the novel's central character) seeks to escape from his own corruption and the corruption around him he climbs into the cathedral tower, symbolically distancing himself from all that is represented by the pit, which viewed from the tower was *no more than a black dot*. In the same novel the spire itself is a complex symbol, used to represent a variety of ideas, including religious faith (it is described as *a diagram of prayer*) and sexual desire.

A **motif** is an element such as an image, phrase or action which occurs repeatedly in a work of literature. In Oscar Wilde's *The Picture Of Dorian Gray* there are frequent references to knives and daggers, anticipating the climax of the novel, when Dorian plunges a knife into his own portrait.

Checkpoint 3

Explain the terms **metaphor**, **simile** and **personification**.

Take note

This extract includes **natural imagery**, which writers often use.

Exam preparation

See page 61 for a question relevant to this and the next section.

Use of language in novels 2

This second section on language looks at some aspects of **grammar** and **syntax**, and briefly considers the role of **dialogue** in novels.

Grammar and syntax

Grammar is a broad term for the rules that give structure to our use of language. **Syntax** refers more specifically to the way words are arranged to form sentences. Some aspects of grammar and syntax that are often worth comment are listed below.

Types of sentence

Look for **questions**, **exclamations** and **commands**, and consider the effects of using these kinds of sentence. The extract below from *The Picture Of Dorian Gray* occurs soon after Dorian has noticed that the portrait has strangely begun to change; the series of questions reflects his anxiety:

> *Was it all true? Had the portrait really changed? Or had it been simply his own imagination that had made him see a look of evil where there had been a look of joy? Surely a painted canvas could not alter?*

Sentence length

Sentences that are noticeably **long** or **short** can have a variety of effects. Think about the meaning of the passage, and consider why it is appropriate to have short or long sentences. In this example from Charles Dickens's *Hard Times*, the lengthy sentence combines with the use of **repetition** to create an impression of tedium and monotony (Dickens is describing Coketown, the industrial town where the novel is set):

> *It contained several large streets all very like one another, and many small streets still more like one another, inhabited by people equally like one another, who all went in and out at the same hours, with the same sound upon the same pavements, to do the same work, and to whom every day was the same as yesterday and tomorrow, and every year the counterpart of the last and the next.*

Sentence structure and patterning

Word order in sentences can be used to achieve particular effects. Sometimes the intention is to **foreground**, or highlight, a particular part of the sentence. In this example from E.M. Forster's *A Passage To India* the word *Dead* is foregrounded by placing it at the beginning of the sentence:

> *Dead she was – committed to the deep while still on the southward track . . .*

Checkpoint 1

What effect do the **short sentences** have here?

Take note

This extract also uses **parallelism** (see 'Sentence structure and patterning' below).

Checkpoint 2

Another useful term that relates to the order of words in a sentence is **end-focus**. What does it mean?

If parts of a sentence have a similar pattern or structure, this is known as **parallelism**. In this example from *Great Expectations*, the series of similar (or parallel) phrases encourages sympathy for Magwitch (an escaped convict) by emphasising how much he has suffered:

A man who had been soaked in water, and smothered in mud, and lamed by stones, and cut by flints, and stung by nettles, and torn by briars.

Non-standard grammar

Non-standard grammar occurs when the use of language breaks the rules and conventions of Standard English. This might, for example, be done to make the language appear realistic, or to suggest a character's regional background or social class. In *Great Expectations*, non-standard grammar helps to create the regional dialect spoken by the convict Magwitch:

You fail, or you go from my words in any partickler, no matter how small it is, and your heart and your liver shall be tore out, roasted and ate. Now, I ain't alone, as you may think I am. There's a young man hid with me, in comparison with which young man I am a Angel.

Examples of non-standard grammar here include *a Angel* (for 'an Angel'), and *tore*, *ate* and *hid* (for 'torn', 'eaten' and 'hidden'). Note how **non-standard spelling** is also used, to suggest Magwitch's **accent**: *partickler*.

Dialogue ●●●

Dialogue is often used in novels to **reveal character** or **develop relationships** between characters. An author will often give a character a distinctive **idiolect**, an individual way of speaking that reflects the character's personality and attitudes. In *The Picture Of Dorian Gray* Lord Henry Wotton often speaks in **epigrams**, clever sayings which reflect his cynicism and wit: *Men marry because they are tired; women, because they are curious: both are disappointed.*

The **interaction** between characters in dialogue can be important. It might indicate characters' attitudes towards each other, or who has the dominant role in a relationship.

Checkpoint 3

This quotation from *Great Expectations* includes several **passive verbs**. Identify them, and explain what passive verbs are.

Take note

As the quotation from *Great Expectations* shows, parallelism can give a sentence a repetitive rhythm. The **rhythm** of a sentence is also affected by the use of **punctuation**. In this quotation from *Odour of Chrysanthemums*, a short story by D.H. Lawrence, the slow, clumsy movement of a train is reflected in the broken, stilted rhythm of the sentence: *The small locomotive engine, number 4, came clanking, stumbling down from Selston with seven full wagons.*

Take note

Other purposes that might be served by dialogue include:
→ to illustrate and develop a **theme**;
→ to move the **plot** forward;
→ to gain a specific response from the reader (e.g. it might be intended to entertain).

Exam preparation answers: page 77

Text D on page 75 is the opening of *Wuthering Heights* by Emily Bronte. Examine closely how Bronte uses language to present the characters of Lockwood (the narrator) and Heathcliff.

18th and 19th century novels

The next few sections provide a historical overview of the novel, beginning with the 18th and 19th centuries.

Links

The following writers are discussed separately: **Jane Austen** (page 64); **the Bronte sisters** (65); **Charles Dickens** (66–7); **Thomas Hardy** (67).

The rise of the novel

Although there are earlier forms of writing that can be seen as forerunners of the novel, the first true English novels appeared in the early 18th century, notably *Robinson Crusoe* and *Moll Flanders* by **Daniel Defoe** (1660–1731). A contemporary of Defoe was **Jonathan Swift** (1667–1745), author of *Gulliver's Travels*, a powerful satire which viciously mocks the ways of mankind, as well as political parties and other established institutions of his time.

The other major 18th century novelists were **Samuel Richardson** (1689–1761), **Henry Fielding** (1707–54) and **Laurence Sterne** (1713–68). Richardson wrote **epistolary novels**, where the story is told through letters written by the major characters. Fielding's works (such as *Joseph Andrews* and *Tom Jones*) are comic, and closer in form to the modern novel. In particular, he made use of an **intrusive omniscient narrator**, a technique discussed on page 54. Sterne was an experimental novelist, who in *Tristram Shandy* discarded the notion of a conventional (linear) plot, narrating events in an apparently random order and frequently departing from the main storyline to digress on other topics and relate subsidiary episodes. His approach was very influential on later novelists, and he is seen as the pioneer of **'stream of consciousness' writing**, which is strongly associated with 20th century writers such as James Joyce and Virginia Woolf. This is writing which aims to represent the natural, disordered flow of a character's thoughts and emotions.

The Gothic novel

The 18th century also saw the emergence of what became known as the **Gothic novel**, a literary genre that retained its popularity into the 19th century. Novels within this tradition are stories of the macabre and the supernatural, set in haunted castles, eerie graveyards and wild, desolate landscapes.

The word *Gothic* originally had medieval associations, and the first Gothic novel, Horace Walpole's *The Castle Of Otranto* (published in 1764) is set in southern Italy in the Middle Ages. Other Gothic novels of the 18th century include *The Monk* by Matthew Lewis (1796) and William Beckford's *Vathek* (1786). The most famous examples of the genre in the 19th century are *Frankenstein* by **Mary Shelley** (1797–1851) and Bram Stoker's *Dracula* (1897). *Frankenstein* has more subtlety and depth than most examples of the genre, with a sympathetic portrayal of the cruelty and rejection experienced by the monster.

The Gothic novel was an influence on several of the most important novelists of the 19th century. **Jane Austen** satirised it in *Northanger Abbey*, and there are Gothic elements in the novels of **Dickens** and **the Bronte sisters**. Today the genre survives in popular horror fiction and films, and there are also connections with **magic realism** (see page 50) and the work of writers such as **Angela Carter**.

The popularity of the Gothic novel in the late 18th and early 19th centuries can be linked to the **Romantic** movement in the poetry of the period (see pages 30–33). Both developments reflected a growing interest in the power of the imagination, and a willingness to rebel against the 18th century belief in rationality and order.

19th century novels ●●●

The 19th century, especially the middle decades, is regarded as the great age of the novel. The major novels of the period are generally characterised by a combination of **psychological complexity** and **social realism**. They explore the morality and emotional life of individual characters, while also addressing broader contemporary issues such as the effects of the Industrial Revolution and of social class divisions. The works of **Jane Austen**, **the Brontes**, **Charles Dickens** and **Thomas Hardy** are discussed in the next two sections of this chapter (pages 64–7). Other important 19th century novelists include:

George Eliot (1819–80) Significant features of her novels (such as *Middlemarch* and *The Mill On The Floss*) include the realistic portrayal of provincial life, depth of characterisation and a strong interest in moral values.

Anthony Trollope (1815–82) He established the idea of the **novel-sequence** in English fiction, with series of novels (the 'Barsetshire' series and the 'Palliser' novels) in which characters appear in more than one book.

Elizabeth Gaskell (1810–65) Her novels, such as *Mary Barton* and *North And South*, portrayed sympathetically the plight of working people and reflected her belief in social justice.

Henry James (1843–1916) He was American by birth but lived in England for much of his life. He developed a complex prose style in order to explore in a precise, detailed way the psychological development of his characters. His novels include *Washington Square*, *The Portrait Of A Lady* and a ghost story, *The Turn Of The Screw*.

Oscar Wilde (1854–1900) A writer more celebrated for his plays (see page 99), but *The Picture Of Dorian Gray* is an important work, a horror story which also satirises Victorian society and scrutinises fashionable ideas of the time (such as aestheticism and hedonism). The book's veiled references to homosexuality have led to it being described as the first gay novel.

Checkpoint 1

Can you name any **Romantic** poets?

Checkpoint 2

Do you know the titles of any of Anthony Trollope's novels?

Take note

Another significant 19th century novelist was **William Makepeace Thackeray** (1811–63). His most important work was *Vanity Fair*, a satirical examination of the materialism and corruption of fashionable society.

Checkpoint 3

Can you name any of Oscar Wilde's plays?

Exam preparation

If you are studying an 18th or 19th century novel, write an essay outlining some of the ways in which the book reflects the period when it was set. Consider social, historical and literary contexts.

Links

See pages 148–9 for advice on writing about contexts.

Austen and the Brontes

This section focuses on the most important women novelists of the 19th century, **Jane Austen** and the **Bronte sisters**.

Jane Austen

The novels of **Jane Austen** (1775–1817) usually focus on the dilemmas of upper-class young women, torn between the expectations of society and the promptings of their own moral conscience. Her novels remain popular today, celebrated for their social comedy and astute, ironic observation.

Important features of Austen's novels include:

→ They portray **a narrow section of society** (the rural gentry) and have **a limited number of characters**. She once said in a letter that *'Three or four families in a country village is the very Thing to work on'*. Unlike the novels of Dickens, her books do not have a broad social canvas, and there is limited reference to the political and social issues of the day.

→ Her novels have however survived the test of time because they address **universal** themes, examining the strengths and weaknesses of **human nature** and the **moral choices** that people face. In particular, she explores the moral issues surrounding **love** and **marriage**.

→ Her novels typically have a **young heroine** who wrestles with the difficulties involved in choosing a suitable marriage partner: Elizabeth Bennet in *Pride And Prejudice*, Fanny Price in *Mansfield Park*, Emma Woodhouse in *Emma*, Anne Elliot in *Persuasion*. In making their choice, Austen's characters acquire **self-knowledge** and an understanding of **the principles that should govern their behaviour** (a combination of a strong sense of morality and trust in their own emotions and intuition).

→ Running through Austen's novels is a belief in **social order** and **emotional restraint**. In this respect she might be seen as **untypical** of her age, when there was a movement towards emotional and imaginative freedom (e.g. in Romantic poetry). Austen's values are closer to those of the earlier 18th century, when reason, decorum and moderation were favoured.

→ Austen's novels use an **omniscient third-person narrator** (see page 54), who presents characters with **ironic detachment**, exposing their failings and misjudgements through the clever use of wit, understatement and subtle sarcasm.

→ Her use of **dialogue** is another important stylistic feature. It is often **comic** and characters' relationships are frequently explored through **verbal duels**.

The Bronte sisters

The **Bronte sisters** were **Emily** (1818–48), **Charlotte** (1816–55) and **Anne** (1820–49). They grew up with their widowed father (a clergyman)

Take note

Jane Austen wrote six novels: *Northanger Abbey, Sense And Sensibility, Pride And Prejudice, Mansfield Park, Emma* and *Persuasion. Northanger Abbey* (her earliest book, though not published until after her death) gently satirises the **Gothic novel** genre (see page 62).

Checkpoint 1

Explain what *universal* means here.

Links

For more on the Romantic movement, and what came before it, see pages 30–33 and 154–5.

Checkpoint 2

What do the terms **omniscient** and **third-person** mean?

Take note

You may see Bronte written as Brontë in some texts.

in an isolated village close to the Yorkshire moors. Their family life was blighted by a series of tragedies, including illness and early deaths. The emotional intensity of their domestic environment and the rugged beauty of the moors clearly inspired much of the **drama**, **passion** and **violence** that characterise their novels. The works of the Brontes are also notable for their portrayal of **strong women characters**, who defy convention and are **fiercely independent**.

Emily Bronte

The most highly regarded of the Bronte sisters' works is *Wuthering Heights*, Emily's only novel. It tells of the doomed, passionate love relationship between Catherine Earnshaw and the mysterious Heathcliff. Catherine decides, disastrously, to marry for social advantage. The novel explores Catherine's motives and the consequences of her action, and powerfully evokes the wild Yorkshire moors that are the story's setting. Other important aspects of the book include Bronte's narrative technique, which involves the use of **multiple narrators** (see page 55), and the construction of the **plot**. The narration of the story involves several flashbacks and **time-shifts**, and also spans two generations, with one set of characters both mirroring and contrasting with the other.

Charlotte Bronte

Charlotte Bronte's most important work is *Jane Eyre*, a ***Bildungsroman*** which traces the narrator's journey towards maturity and fulfilment. The novel begins with Jane's childhood years as an orphan; she then becomes a governess, falls in love with her employer, and after overcoming a variety of difficulties and obstacles is finally able to marry him. The book is in places melodramatic and sensational (the **Gothic** elements include a madwoman hidden away in an attic), but it is also a serious and complex study of a woman's moral development.

Anne Bronte

Anne Bronte wrote *The Tenant Of Wildfell Hall*, which like *Jane Eyre* portrays a strong female character overcoming adversity to find eventual happiness. Helen Huntingdon endures a deeply unhappy marriage before finally rebelling against her husband (and against social convention), firstly by refusing to share a room with him and then by running away with their son to begin a new life. She finds love with another man, and her husband's death means she can marry him.

Checkpoint 3

Can you name the village in Yorkshire where the Bronte family lived?

Take note

A ***Bildungsroman*** is a novel that traces the development of a character, usually from childhood to maturity.

Exam preparation

See page 61 for a question on an extract from Emily Bronte's *Wuthering Heights*.

Dickens and Hardy

The most important male novelists of the 19th century were **Charles Dickens** and **Thomas Hardy**. Hardy lived until 1928, but stopped writing novels after the publication of *Jude The Obscure* in 1895.

Charles Dickens

The childhood years of **Charles Dickens** (1812–70) were spent in Kent and London. Much of his childhood was happy, but when he was 12 his father was imprisoned for debt and Dickens himself was sent by his family to work in a blacking factory, making polish for shoes. These distressing experiences remained with Dickens for the rest of his life, and there are repeated echoes of them in his novels; the Dickens biographer Peter Ackroyd describes them as *'a pressing pain which he needed continually to explain and to assuage'*. As an adult, he began his writing career in journalism, but achieved rapid success as a novelist with *The Pickwick Papers*, published in instalments in 1836–7. Many more novels followed, and long before his death Dickens was firmly established as the most popular novelist of his time.

Some important aspects of Dickens's work are listed below.

→ He was one of the first writers to use the novel to address social issues and concerns; there is a strong element of **social criticism** in his books. He has a strong **sympathy for the marginalised in society** (the poor, convicts), and draws attention to social injustice.

→ In some novels (notably *Hard Times*) he **criticises the effects of the Industrial Revolution**. In *Hard Times* the grinding monotony of factory life is complemented by an equally soulless education system, where the emphasis is on teaching children nothing but 'facts'. Dickens uses the novel to attack the philosophy of **utilitarianism** (the belief that everything should be judged by its usefulness).

→ Another frequent target is the **legal system**, which punishes the innocent, lets the guilty escape and is populated by lawyers who act out of self-interest rather than any desire for justice.

→ **Attitudes to wealth** are a recurrent theme in his novels. He shows how people can be motivated by greed and how our perception of others can be influenced by their wealth and social status.

→ **Childhood** is another important theme. Children in Dickens's novels often experience fear and humiliation, and are the victims of neglect or cruelty. The adult characters we are encouraged to admire are frequently ones who treat children with generosity and kindness.

→ Dickens's **characterisation** has been both praised and criticised. He created a huge number of memorable characters, and the central characters in his novels are usually carefully portrayed, but many of his lesser characters have been described as thin and one-dimensional.

→ **Humour** is an important element in Dickens's novels. His later works tend to be darker and more pessimistic, but even here there is

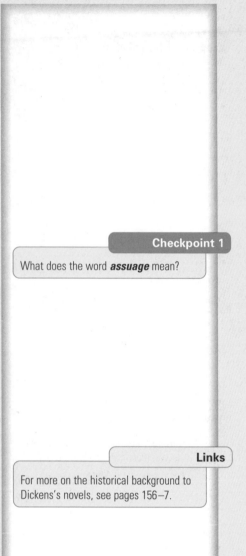

Checkpoint 1

What does the word *assuage* mean?

Links

For more on the historical background to Dickens's novels, see pages 156–7.

Checkpoint 2

Can you name any Dickens novels in which a **child** is the central character for a major part of the novel?

E.M. Forster

The works of **E.M. Forster** (1879–1970) often concern the barriers people have to overcome in forming relationships. *A Passage To India* depicts India under British rule, exploring relationships between people of different races. In *A Room With A View* the central characters have to overcome social convention and prejudice to find love. Characters often also have to be liberated from their own emotional repression. Another notable feature of Forster's novels is his use of comedy, both in his portrayal of his characters' awkward attempts to 'connect' with each other, and as a tool to expose the absurdity of narrow-minded attitudes.

James Joyce

James Joyce (1882–1941) was an experimental writer who is especially associated with the **stream of consciousness** technique, which aims to capture as accurately as possible an individual's flow of thoughts. In seeking to achieve this effect conventional punctuation and sentence construction are sometimes abandoned. *Ulysses*, a novel about a day in the life of its central character, is in this tradition. Joyce also wrote the autobiographical novel *A Portrait Of The Artist As A Young Man*, and *Dubliners*, a collection of short stories notable for their realistic portrayal of Dublin life, and for their use of **epiphanies** – moments in the lives of individuals which reveal fundamental truths.

Checkpoint 3

Who is the hero of the novel *Ulysses*?

William Golding

William Golding (1911–93) achieved immediate success with his first novel, *Lord Of The Flies*, about a group of middle-class schoolboys stranded on a desert island. After initially attempting to maintain the rules and restraints of civilised society, they steadily descend into barbarism. A trilogy of sea novels, beginning with *Rites Of Passage*, again explored the behaviour of a small, isolated social group, in this case the crew and passengers of a ship on a long sea voyage. Another important Golding novel is *The Spire*, about the building of a medieval cathedral spire. In this novel the cathedral, and the spire itself, take on a range of symbolic and metaphorical meanings. The central character, Jocelin, is a man blinded by pride and delusion, but in the course of the novel he slowly acquires self-awareness.

Take note

The central idea of *Lord Of The Flies* was inspired by an earlier, more idealistic adventure story about a group of boys shipwrecked on an island: *The Coral Island* by R.M. Ballantyne.

Ian McEwan

The early works of **Ian McEwan** (born 1948) often centre on violent, macabre events. His later novels retain dark, disturbing elements but also tackle broader social and political themes. *Saturday*, for example, is set on the day of a terrorist attack on London.

Exam preparation

See page 53 for a question on E.M. Forster's *A Passage to India*.

American and post-colonial novels

During the 20th century, many of the finest novels written in English were by **American** novelists. In recent decades **post-colonial** literature has also been increasingly important.

American novels

Mark Twain

The Adventures Of Huckleberry Finn by **Mark Twain** (1835–1910) is regarded by many as the first great American novel. Huck Finn, the narrator, is a young boy who escapes from his brutal father and travels down the Mississippi on a raft, accompanied by Jim, a runaway slave. The river journey is a narrative device that enables Twain to incorporate a variety of episodes and characters. The novel works on one level as a humorous and exciting adventure story, but it is also a denunciation of slavery and an attack on the values of adult, supposedly 'civilised' society. Natural, **colloquial** language is used to narrate the story, creating a realistic impression of Huck's southern dialect (see page 55). Twain's use of language and the novel's central idea of a journey of discovery were both enormously influential on later American fiction.

F. Scott Fitzgerald

The most important novels by **F. Scott Fitzgerald** (1896–1940) are *The Great Gatsby* and *Tender Is The Night*. Both novels examine critically the values of wealthy, pleasure-seeking Americans, drawing on Fitzgerald's own experience of the 'high life' following his marriage to the glamorous Zelda Sayre. *Tender Is The Night* charts the disintegration of Dick and Nicole Diver's marriage, and Dick Diver's increasing disillusionment with the moral emptiness of his life after he abandons a career as a doctor. Looking back, he wished *he had always been as good as he had intended to be*.

J.D. Salinger

The Catcher In The Rye by **J.D. Salinger** (born 1919) is a novel very much in the tradition of *Huckleberry Finn* (see above). The teenage narrator, Holden Caulfield, has a series of escapades in New York after running away from an exclusive boarding school. He is an acerbic commentator on the materialism and pretentiousness of the adult characters he encounters, but is also an idealist who gradually comes to terms with an imperfect world. As with *Huckleberry Finn*, a strength of the novel is the language used to narrate the story: Holden speaks to the reader with the authentic voice of an American teenager. In the decade that followed the novel's publication in 1951, youthful rebellion became a familiar element in American and British culture – in drama, fiction, films and popular music – and J.D. Salinger played a major part in initiating this tradition: *The Catcher In The Rye* expressed the restlessness and dissatisfaction of the young in a language they could recognise and understand.

Checkpoint 1

Huckleberry Finn was the sequel to another novel. Do you know its name?

Checkpoint 2

Huckleberry Finn has a **first-person narrator**. What does this mean?

Take note

F. Scott Fitzgerald was also an accomplished writer of short stories.

Take note

Since the 1960s **J.D. Salinger** has apparently continued to write, but he chooses not to publish his work. He is very protective of his privacy and his photograph never appears on the dust-jackets of his books.

Alice Walker

Alice Walker was born in 1944 in the American South, the daughter of black sharecroppers. As a young woman in the 1960s she was active in the civil rights movement in Georgia and Mississippi. Her most famous novel, *The Color Purple*, is about the struggle of black women living in Georgia in the first half of the 20th century. Racism is one of the book's major themes, but it is also a feminist work which celebrates the central character's triumph over sexism. It is an **epistolatory novel** (see page 62), constructing the narrative from a series of letters.

Charles Frazier

One of the most highly regarded American novels of recent years is *Cold Mountain* by **Charles Frazier** (born 1950). It is an epic historical novel in which the two central characters, Inman and Ada, strive for romantic fulfilment against the violent backdrop of the American Civil War (the book is set in 1864). Frazier's evocation of the vast landscape of the American South is another key element in the novel.

Post-colonial novels ●●●

The term **post-colonial literature** is used for writing from, or about, countries that gained independence from colonial rule in the 20th century. Often these countries once formed part of the British Empire, including for example India, parts of Africa and several Caribbean islands. Many post-colonial writers have chosen to write in English though some, such as the novelist **V.S. Naipaul** and the poets **Grace Nichols** and **Derek Walcott**, make use of local Creole languages as well as Standard English. Many post-colonial novelists look back to a time when the identity of their peoples was suppressed by colonial rule, and forward to the difficulties involved in creating a new post-colonial identity. **Diaspora** is another important theme. This refers to the experience of migration and of living in another country (in the case of many post-colonial writers, this is England).

Major post-colonial novelists include **Chinua Achebe** (born 1930), a Nigerian who has been described as the founding father of modern African literature. His novel *Things Fall Apart* is set in the 1890s and tells how Okonwo, the leader of an Igbo community, resists the attempts of missionaries and local government to impose their authority on Igbo society and culture. **Timothy Mo** (born 1950) is an example of a **diasporic** writer. His novel *Sour Sweet* is a revealing portrayal of London's Chinese community.

Checkpoint 3

The Red Badge Of Courage is another novel set during the American Civil War. Do you know who wrote it?

Take note

Creole languages are found in former colonies and have evolved through the interaction of local, native languages and the language of the colonisers.

Exam preparation

See page 55 for a question on Mark Twain's *The Adventures of Huckleberry Finn*.

Analysing prose extracts

Links

Much of the advice in the 'Writing essays' sections (pages 172–5) is also relevant to these kinds of exam questions.

Different types of questions are set on extracts from prose texts. For example, the extract might be unseen or from a text you have previously studied. With set texts, the question usually specifies an extract, but you might be asked to select your own extracts for comment and analysis.

Getting started

Whether the extract is unseen or from a set text, a good way to start is to read the extract once or twice and develop an **overview** of it. (With set texts, the extract might be a complete chapter of the book, in which case you will only have time to remind yourself of the chapter by looking quickly over it.) What are the **purposes** of the extract? For example, is the writer portraying **characters**, or describing a **place** or a piece of **action**? What is the **narrative viewpoint** (see below)? What kinds of **feelings** and **attitudes** does the writer seem to be encouraging in the reader? Are characters portrayed sympathetically or unsympathetically? If a setting is described, are the impressions you form of it generally positive or negative? Concentrate in particular on those aspects of the extract that will help you to answer the specific **question** that has been set.

If the extract is from a set text, your knowledge of the novel as a whole should make it easier for you to answer the above questions. You will also need to think about the **context** of the extract. **Where** in the set text does it occur? How is what happens here important? What aspects of the **characters** are illustrated? Are any of the novel's **themes** evident? Do any elements in the extract **echo**, or **contrast** with, other parts of the book? Be careful though not to spend too much of the answer writing about the rest of the novel. Usually, a substantial part of the answer needs to be devoted to a close analysis of the extract (you should make sure before the exam that you know the requirements of your AS or A2 specification with regard to this).

It's important to consider both **content** and **style**. In other words, you need to discuss the **meaning** of the extract (answering the kinds of questions mentioned above) and also look at the author's use of **language, form and structure**. More advice on analysing these stylistic features is given below.

Narrative viewpoint

Checkpoint 1

Explain the difference between **first-person** and **third-person** narration.

→ Is the narration **first-person** or **third-person**?
→ What kind of **narrative voice** is created (especially important with first-person narration)?
→ What kind of relationship exists between **narrator and reader**? Is the reader addressed directly?

Language

Vocabulary
→ How **formal** or **informal** is the vocabulary used? Is there any regional **dialect**, or **colloquial** vocabulary?
→ What are the **connotations** of individual words? Are there groups of words with similar connotations?
→ Is any use made of **imagery**, including **similes**, **metaphors** or **personification**?
→ Is the **sound** of any of the words significant? Are devices such as **onomatopoeia** and **alliteration** used?
→ How does the vocabulary contribute to the impressions conveyed of **characters**, **setting** or **atmosphere**?
→ Are any aspects of the vocabulary **characteristic of the novel as a whole**?

Grammar and syntax
→ Are any sentences unusually **long** or **short**?
→ Is **word order** important in any of the sentences?
→ Are techniques such as **parallelism** and **repetition** used in structuring any of the sentences?
→ Does the structure of any of the sentences have a **rhythmic** effect?
→ Are there any **questions**, **commands** or **exclamations**? What effect do they have?
→ Is **tense** significant?
→ Is any of the grammar **non-standard**?

Form and structure

→ Are there any particular comments you can make about how the extract **begins** and how it **ends**?
→ What about what happens in between – how does the extract **develop**?
→ Is **paragraphing** significant? Do changes in paragraphs correspond to changes in perspective (point of view) or tone?
→ Do any aspects of the extract reflect the **genre** of the novel?
→ In terms of the development and organisation of the **whole novel**, how is this extract significant? Is it a turning-point? Does it parallel, or contrast with, other episodes in the book?

Examiner's secrets

In examination answers, students would often have gained higher marks if they had commented more fully on **language**.

Checkpoint 2

What are **connotations**?

Take note

If the extract includes **dialogue**, there are other questions you can ask:
→ How does the speech of **individual characters** differ? Do their ways of speaking reflect aspects of their characters?
→ How do characters **interact**? What does the dialogue reveal about **relationships** between characters?
→ How does the author's (or narrator's) **accompanying commentary** influence the way we interpret the dialogue?
→ How close is the dialogue to **natural speech**?

Checkpoint 3

Explain the term **non-standard grammar**.

Exam preparation

See pages 53, 55, 57 and 61 for some prose fiction analysis questions.

Practice extracts

The extracts below are for use with the practice exam questions for this chapter.

Take note

The question for this extract is on page 53.

Examiner's secrets

A key sentence in this extract is the first sentence in the second paragraph.

Text A

Chandrapore was never large or beautiful, but two hundred years ago it lay on the road between Upper India, then imperial, and the sea, and the fine houses date from that period. The zest for decoration stopped in the eighteenth century, nor was it ever democratic. In the bazaars there is no painting and scarcely any carving. The very wood seems made of mud, the inhabitants of mud moving. So abased, so monotonous is everything that meets the eye, that when the Ganges comes down it might be expected to wash the excrescence back into the soil. Houses do fall, people are drowned and left rotting, but the general outline of the town persists, swelling here, shrinking there, like some low but indestructible form of life.

Inland, the prospect alters. There is an oval maidan, and a long sallow hospital. Houses belonging to Eurasians stand on the high ground by the railway station. Beyond the railway – which runs parallel to the river – the land sinks, then rises again rather steeply. On this second rise is laid out the little Civil Station, and viewed hence Chandrapore appears to be a totally different place. It is a city of gardens. It is no city, but a forest sparsely scattered with huts. It is a tropical pleasance, washed by a noble river. The toddy palms and neem trees and mangoes and peepul that were hidden behind the bazaars now become visible and in their turn hide the bazaars . . . Especially after the rains do they screen what passes below, but at all times, even when scorched or leafless, they glorify the city to the English people who inhabit the rise, so that newcomers cannot believe it to be as meagre as it is described, and have to be driven down to acquire disillusionment. As for the Civil Station itself, it provokes no emotion. It charms not, neither does it repel. It is sensibly planned, with a redbrick Club on its brow, and further back a grocer's and a cemetery, and the bungalows are disposed along roads that intersect at right angles. It has nothing hideous in it, and only the view is beautiful; it shares nothing with the city except the overarching sky.

Take note

The question for this extract is on page 55.

Examiner's secrets

In considering the language of this extract you should especially look at vocabulary and grammar.

Take note

The *sugar-hogshead* referred to here is a large barrel in which Huck sometimes sleeps.

Text B

Now the way that the book winds up, is this: Tom and me found the money that the robbers hid in the cave, and it made us rich. We got six thousand dollars apiece – all gold. It was an awful sight of money when it was piled up. Well, Judge Thatcher, he took it and put it out at interest, and it fetched us a dollar a day apiece, all the year round – more than a body could tell what to do with. The Widow Douglas, she took me for her son, and allowed she would sivilize me; but it was rough living in the house all the time, considering how dismal regular and decent the widow was in all her ways; and so when I couldn't stand it no longer, I lit out. I got into my old rags, and my sugar-hogshead again, and was free and satisfied. But Tom Sawyer, he hunted me up

and said he was going to start a band of robbers, and I might join if
I would go back to the widow and be respectable. So I went back.

Text C ●●●

Take note

The question for this extract is on page 57.

My sister, Mrs Joe Gargery, was more than twenty years older than I,
and had established a great reputation with herself and the neighbours
because she had brought me up 'by hand'. Having at that time to find
out for myself what the expression meant, and knowing her to have a
hard and heavy hand, and to be much in the habit of laying it upon her
husband as well as upon me, I supposed that Joe Gargery and I were
both brought up by hand . . .

My sister, Mrs Joe, with black hair and eyes, had such a prevailing
redness of skin, that I sometimes used to wonder whether it was
possible she washed herself with a nutmeg-grater instead of soap.
She was tall and bony, and almost always wore a coarse apron, fastened
over her figure behind with two loops, and having a square impregnable
bib in front, that was stuck full of pins and needles. She made it a
powerful merit in herself, and a strong reproach against Joe, that she
wore this apron so much. Though I really see no reason why she should
have worn it at all: or why, if she did wear it at all, she should not have
taken it off every day of her life.

Text D ●●●

Take note

The question for this extract is on page 61.

I have just returned from a visit to my landlord – the solitary neighbour
that I shall be troubled with. This is certainly a beautiful country! In
all England, I do not believe that I could have fixed on a situation so
completely removed from the stir of society. A perfect misanthropist's
heaven: and Mr Heathcliff and I are such a suitable pair to divide the
desolation between us. A capital fellow! He little imagined how my
heart warmed towards him when I beheld his black eyes withdraw
so suspiciously under their brows, as I rode up, and when his fingers
sheltered themselves, with a jealous resolution, still further in his
waistcoat, as I announced my name.

"Mr Heathcliff!" I said.

A nod was the answer.

"Mr Lockwood, your new tenant, sir. I do myself the honour of
calling as soon as possible after my arrival, to express the hope that
I have not inconvenienced you by my perseverance in soliciting the
occupation of Thrushcross Grange: I heard yesterday you had had
some thoughts –"

"Thrushcross Grange is my own, sir," he interrupted, wincing.
"I should not allow anyone to inconvenience me, if I could hinder
it – walk in!"

Examiner's secrets

Note the contrasts in the way
Lockwood and Heathcliff speak.

Answers
Novels

Novels: study tips

Checkpoints

1 Plot.
2 Your AS or A2 marks will depend on how far you have succeeded in achieving certain specified assessment objectives. See pages 6–7.
3 Film or television adaptations of a book often make changes to it – this can cause confusion. Always remember you are studying the book, not someone else's interpretation of it.

Form and structure in novels

Checkpoints

1 These are the usual features, techniques etc. associated with a genre. For example a convention of most types of novel is that the narrative is usually divided into chapters.
2 A 'satire' is a piece of humorous writing that has a serious purpose. Usually something is ridiculed in order to make serious criticisms of it (e.g. many satires have a political purpose). A 'parody' is a humorous imitation of another work. Usually the other work is ridiculed by comically exaggerating or distorting certain of its features.
3 An idea, image, type of character etc. that occurs repeatedly within a single work or a particular body of work (e.g. works that belong to a specific genre or that were written by the same author).

Settings in novels

Checkpoints

1 This is an extreme form of self-centredness. Solipsism as a philosophy or view of life is the belief that the self is all that can be known to exist.
2 To prefigure is to anticipate or look forward to – an early indication of something that is to happen later, or an event that is similar in some way to a later event.
3 The imagery is visual and also very tactile, suggesting the squalor of Smithfield. A tactile effect is also achieved through the use of sibilance (repeated 's' sounds) and alliteration (*filth, fat, foam*). Heavily syndetic listing (listing which uses conjunctions) reinforces the sense that Pip is surrounded by various kinds of unpleasantness.

Exam preparation

The description emphasises the division between the British and Indian communities. The British live outside the centre of Chandrapore, on a rise which looks down on the city. Their ignorance of Indian life is suggested by the way trees *hide* and *screen* aspects of the city, making it appear to them *totally different* to the Chandrapore described to the reader in the first paragraph. The Civil Station associates the British with cold, emotionless efficiency: . . . *it provokes no emotion. It charms not, neither does it repel. It is sensibly planned . . . roads that intersect at right angles.*

Narrative technique in novels

Checkpoints

1 A point of view – a way of looking at or regarding something.
2 Idiolect.
3 There are non-standard verb forms, including *ain't* for 'isn't' and *was* for 'were' (*There was things*). There is also a double negative (*that ain't no matter*) and unconventional grammatical constructions (*without you have read, That book was made by Mr Mark Twain*).

Exam preparation

Twain creates the narrative voice of an uneducated American boy. The extract has a conversational tone, as if Huck is speaking naturally to the reader. The vocabulary includes colloquial expressions such as *lit out, a body* and *winds up*. There is also non-standard spelling, to suggest Huck's lack of familiarity with the word 'civilize' (which becomes *sivilize*). Much of the grammar is non-standard, including double negatives (*I couldn't stand it no longer*) and incorrect verb forms (*I never seen*). Huck emerges as a free spirit, who rebels against attempts to control him and make him conform to the conventions of *regular* society.

Characters in novels

Checkpoints

1 A list without conjunctions. Syndetic listing is a list where the items are linked by one or more conjunctions (i.e. words such as 'and').
2 'Omniscient' means all-seeing and all-knowing. In other words, the narrator knows everything about the world of the novel, including the thoughts and feelings of the characters.
3 The direct opposite.

Exam preparation

The first paragraph establishes Mrs Joe's brutality, though in a humorous way. In the second paragraph Dickens uses physical appearance to indicate character. Her *black hair and eyes* make her sound hard and evil. Note the contrasts with her husband Joe (see page 56): he is *fair*, and whereas he has *smooth* skin, hers is raw – so red that Pip thought she might have washed it with a nutmeg-grater instead of soap (the perspective of a child is used to humorous effect). *Bony* suggests that there is something hard-edged about her appearance. Her apron is a symbol of her aggressive, unyielding nature: it is filled with *pins and needles* and has a *square impregnable bib*. She wears it all day, suggesting she has the air of a martyr and wants everyone to know she is a hardworking housewife.

Use of language in novels 1

Checkpoints

1 Emotive.
2 The main feature here is the formal vocabulary used by Stevens: individual words such as *unduly* and *amendment*, and phrases such as *in agreement with*.
3 A 'metaphor' is a comparison that is not literally true because it refers to something as if it were something else (e.g. 'a blizzard of information'). A 'simile' is a comparison that uses the words 'like' or 'as'. 'Personification' occurs when something that is not human is described as if it were.

Use of language in novels 2

Checkpoints

1 The short sentences help to suggest Dorian's mental turmoil.
2 'End-focus' occurs when the main emphasis falls at the end of a sentence.
3 A 'passive verb' involves using the verb in a way that emphasises the object of an action (the person or thing 'on the receiving end') rather than the person or thing performing the action. The quotation contains a series of passive verbs: *A man who had been soaked* . . . *smothered* . . . *lamed* . . . *cut* . . . *stung* . . . *torn*. The effect is to present Magwitch as a suffering victim.

Exam preparation

It is ironic that Lockwood describes Heathcliff as a *capital fellow* and implies they are similar in temperament, when the extract emphasises their differences. Lockwood appears pompous and rather ridiculous, an impression partly created by the excessive formality of his language when he addresses Heathcliff: *do myself the honour*, *express the hope*, *perseverance*, *soliciting*, *occupation*. In contrast Heathcliff is curt and monosyllabic. He does not speak at all in response to Lockwood's initial greeting (*A nod was the answer*) and interrupts Lockwood's next speech, visibly *wincing* as he does so. He then gives an abrupt command: *walk in!*

18th and 19th century novels

Checkpoints

1 Important Romantic poets include Blake, Wordsworth, Coleridge, Keats, Shelley and Byron.
2 Trollope's novels include *Barchester Towers*, *Can You Forgive Her?*, *The Way We Live Now*, *The Eustace Diamonds* and many others.
3 Wilde's plays include *The Importance Of Being Earnest*, *Lady Windermere's Fan*, *An Ideal Husband* and *A Woman Of No Importance*.

Austen and the Brontes

Checkpoints

1 Themes which are 'universal' are relevant to all times and all societies because they relate to enduring aspects of human nature.
2 An 'omniscient' narrator is all-seeing and all-knowing, in the sense that he or she knows everything about the world of the novel, including the thoughts and feelings of the characters. 'Third person' means the narrator does not directly enter the novel: all characters are referred to using third person pronouns such as 'he', 'she', 'they' etc., and there is no use of the first person pronouns 'I', 'me' etc.
3 Haworth.

Dickens and Hardy

Checkpoints

1 To 'assuage' is to soothe or lessen an unpleasant feeling.
2 Examples include *Great Expectations*, *David Copperfield* and *Oliver Twist*.
3 A 'dialect' is a form of language associated with a specific region or social group.

20th century novels

Checkpoints

1 *Apocalypse Now*.
2 *Sons And Lovers*.
3 Leopold Bloom.

American and post-colonial novels

Checkpoints

1 *The Adventures Of Tom Sawyer*.
2 The narrator uses first person pronouns such as 'I' and 'me'. Usually this means the narrator is a character in the novel, and directly involved in the action.
3 Stephen Crane.

Analysing prose extracts

Checkpoints

1 First person narration involves the use of pronouns such as 'I' and 'me'. With third person narration the narrator is not so directly involved in the world of the novel, referring to all of the characters as 'he', 'she', 'they'.
2 The associations that a word or phrase has.
3 Language which does not conform to the usual grammatical rules and conventions of Standard English. For instance, saying 'I seen him yesterday' instead of 'I saw him yesterday' is non-standard grammar.

Revision Checklist
Novels

1 List and briefly explain ten or more novel genres.	Confident	Not confident. **Revise** page 50
2 Understand the key elements relevant to the discussion of a novel's plot.	Confident	Not confident. **Revise** page 51
3 Explain the different ways that setting might be important in a novel.	Confident	Not confident. **Revise** pages 52–53
4 Explain the difference between first- and third-person narration.	Confident	Not confident. **Revise** page 54
5 Understand what is meant by 'narrative voice'.	Confident	Not confident. **Revise** page 55
6 Outline five or more techniques that might be used to present a character.	Confident	Not confident. **Revise** pages 56–57
7 Understand the significance when analysing a novelist's use of language of connotations, levels of formality and imagery.	Confident	Not confident. **Revise** pages 58–59
8 Understand the key features of grammar relevant to the analysis of language in novels.	Confident	Not confident. **Revise** pages 60–61
9 Recognise the significance of dialogue in novels.	Confident	Not confident. **Revise** page 61
10 Give an outline account of the origins of the English novel.	Confident	Not confident. **Revise** page 62
11 Explain the main features of the Gothic novel.	Confident	Not confident. **Revise** page 62
12 Outline the main characteristics of 19th century novels and list the major novelists of this period.	Confident	Not confident. **Revise** page 63
13 Offer an overview of the main trends in the development of the novel in the 20th century.	Confident	Not confident. **Revise** page 68
14 Identify important American and post-colonial novelists of the 20th century.	Confident	Not confident. **Revise** pages 70–71
15 Approach with confidence the analysis of prose fiction extracts.	Confident	Not confident. **Revise** pages 72–73

As well as Shakespeare (covered in the next chapter), you'll be studying one or more additional plays during your AS/A2 course. This chapter begins with some introductory tips on studying plays, then there are several sections on the techniques that dramatists use, including, for example, aspects of staging and dialogue. It's very important when you write about a play that you show an awareness that it was written to be performed *on stage* rather than read in a book. This might for instance involve considering how an audience might react to a particular scene, or discussing the impact of important actions that occur on stage. To help you with this, you should certainly try to see a live production of the play you are studying, or if this is not possible watch a film or television version.

In other sections in the chapter there is an historical overview, focusing on key periods and major playwrights. This should help you to put the play you are studying into context. The final section is about the analysis of extracts from plays. This is relevant both to questions on extracts from plays that you have studied, and to questions on unseen extracts (from plays you have not encountered before).

Exam themes

→ Knowledge and understanding of set plays

→ Use of relevant terminology

→ Awareness of literary contexts (e.g. important periods in the history of drama)

Topic checklist

AS ○ A2 ●	AQA/A	AQA/B	EDEXCEL	OCR	WJEC	CCEA
Plays: study tips	○●	○●	○●	○●	○●	○●
Dramatic form and structure	○●	○●	○●	○●	○●	○●
Stagecraft 1	○●	○●	○●	○●	○●	○●
Stagecraft 2	○●	○●	○●	○●	○●	○●
Dramatic dialogue 1	○●	○●	○●	○●	○●	○●
Dramatic dialogue 2	○●	○●	○●	○●	○●	○●
Characters in plays	○●	○●	○●	○●	○●	○●
Elizabethan and Jacobean drama	○●	●	●	●	●	●
Restoration drama		●	○●	●		●
18th and 19th century drama	○	●	●	●		●
20th century drama 1	○	○	●	●	○●	○●
20th century drama 2	○	○	○●	●	○●	○●
Analysing drama extracts	○●	○●	○●	○●	○●	○●
Practice extracts	○●	○●	○●	○●	○●	○●

Plays: study tips

Here is some initial guidance on how to tackle the study of a play.

Remember it's a play

When you're studying and writing about a play, it's vital to remember that the text was written to be **performed** rather than read. Think about **visual** aspects such as the set, the positioning of characters on stage, actions and movements and so on. Think also about **aural** aspects including sound effects, music and the pace and rhythm of dialogue. In written answers you'll get particular credit for showing an awareness of **dramatic** elements such as these. Remember also that you should always:

→ refer to how the play affects the **audience** rather than the 'reader';
→ refer to the text as a **play** and never as a 'book'.

It will obviously help if you can **see the play performed on stage**. It's probably best to see a production after you are fairly familiar with the text, so you can note how the directors and actors have **interpreted** the play. Alternatively you might watch a film or television adaptation, though caution is needed here as adaptations sometimes make significant alterations to the original text. A third possibility is listening to an audio recording of a performance. The key thing to remember is that different directors and different actors will offer different **interpretations**, both of the play as a whole and of particular characters. Think about their view of the play, and how it differs from your own. Provided it is relevant to the question, it can be helpful in written answers to refer to productions you have seen, especially if you:

→ refer to a production to show that **different interpretations** of the play or of particular aspects of it are possible;
→ **critically evaluate** a director's or actor's interpretation, explaining how far you agree or disagree with it.

The first reading

When you first get hold of the text, try to read it through fairly quickly. On stage plays are usually no more than two or three hours long, and reading a play shouldn't take much longer than this. Don't skip the list of characters at the front – this often contains useful information, such as characters' rank or status, and who is related to whom. With older plays you might have difficulty understanding some of the language, but try not to let this slow you down too much. The purpose of this first reading is to get a **general idea** of the **plot** (the storyline) and the **characters**. If you find the play especially difficult to follow, you could try making use of any notes included in your edition, or of a relevant study guide (see 'Carrying out research and getting extra help' on the next page). As you are reading, try to keep your **visual imagination** actively engaged – picture the play being performed on stage. Even for this first reading, it is worth looking over the initial **stage directions** carefully, as these often describe the set in considerable detail.

Links

For more on the performance aspects of plays, see pages 84–7.

Take note

Listening to an audio recording of the play as you are reading it can help you to read it more quickly. It may also help you to understand it more easily.

Studying the play

Once you have a general understanding of the play, you need to **study** it in an organised, analytical way. Here are some tips:

→ Find out the relevant **assessment objectives** for this component of the course. This will give you an idea of the areas you need to focus on. Some are fairly standard (see next point), but others can vary. For example, with some texts it is important to know about their **historical context**, but with others this is less important.

→ In analysing the text itself, the key aspects are usually: **plot and structure; characters; themes; use of language; stagecraft** (performance elements). (The rest of this chapter includes guidance on these topics.)

→ Follow your teacher's advice on organising your notes, but having notes on each of the above topics is usually a good idea. In addition, you are likely to need **notes on each scene** (again the topics listed above can be used as headings) and lists of **key quotations** (linked to specific characters and themes).

→ If you're allowed to, **annotate** the text with brief comments, underlinings and so on. (If you're taking the text into the examination with you, there will though be a limit on how much you can write.)

Carrying out research and getting extra help

→ Depending on the assessment objectives for the text, you might need to find out about the **context** of the play and **how critics have interpreted it**. Investigating these areas can in any case help your understanding of the play. For more advice, see pages 148–59 and 160–5.

→ Make use of any **notes** or other **additional information** in your edition of the play.

→ There might be a **study guide** you can buy (or borrow from a library), or **online revision materials**. Use these with care as they are not always aimed at AS/A2 students, and it is very unlikely they will cover everything you need to know.

Links

For more on **assessment objectives**, see pages 6–7.

Checkpoint 1

Explain (with examples if possible) what is meant by **historical context**, and why this might be important to the understanding of a play.

Checkpoint 2

As a general rule, should **quotations** be long or short? Give reasons for your answer.

Checkpoint 3

'A critic is someone who considers a text to have weaknesses or defects.' Is this statement true or false?

Exam preparation

After your first reading of the play you are studying, make a list of the characters who appear in it (there should be a cast list at the beginning of the play). Summarise each character's role in the plot, and your own initial impressions of them.

Dramatic form and structure

When writing about a play that you have studied, you need to show an understanding of dramatic **form** and **structure**. This essentially means you have to know about the **genre** and **organisation** of the play.

Tragedy and comedy ●●●

Traditionally, the two great contrasting genres of drama are **tragedy** and **comedy**.

The word **tragedy** is often used in everyday speech for especially sad or unfortunate events, but in relation to plays it has a more specific meaning. The first definition was provided by the Greek philosopher **Aristotle** in the fourth century BC. Although many other theories and definitions of tragedy have been developed since, attempts to explain what 'tragedy' consists of generally still use Aristotle's ideas as a starting-point. Some of these ideas are summarised below, with the terms that Aristotle used shown in bold.

→ The play has a central character, the **protagonist** or tragic hero. Usually this is someone of high rank or status, with qualities that the audience can admire.
→ The character has a tragic flaw (**hamartia**) which contributes to his downfall.
→ The character experiences a reversal of fortune (**peripeteia**).
→ The audience feel a sense of loss, but also experience a purging of the emotions (**catharsis**), so that at the end of the play feelings of pity and terror have passed, and there is an atmosphere of peace.

If the play you are studying is a tragedy, you should not expect it to conform rigidly to the above principles, but you should find that at least some of these elements are present. You might well want to argue that the supposed 'rules' of tragedy are too simplistic – for example, you might think that the central character has more than one flaw, or that his flaws are not responsible for his downfall.

Like 'tragedy', the term **comedy** doesn't simply have its everyday meaning when applied to drama. Especially in the past, a comedy was a play with a happy ending (the opposite of a tragedy) rather than one that was necessarily funny. **Shakespeare's comedies** are generally love stories in which characters are beset by confusion and misunderstanding but eventually achieve harmony and reconciliation. Later forms of comedy include the **comedy of manners** – a term applied to 17th and 18th century plays which satirised the attitudes and values of high society.

If you are studying a comedy, you are likely to find that it has an underlying **seriousness of purpose**, and you should try to identify this – what 'point' is the playwright making about society, or about certain kinds of people?

Checkpoint 1

Another Greek word used in relation to tragedy is **hubris**. Do you know what this means?

Take note

You might also find that the play deliberately **challenges** conventional ideas of tragedy. For instance, in *Death Of A Salesman* the 20th century American playwright Arthur Miller sought to show the tragedy of an 'average man', rejecting the idea that the tragic hero should be someone of elevated status.

Take note

Some plays are hard to categorise as tragedies or comedies as they have elements of both. These are known as **tragicomedies** (Shakespeare's *The Winter's Tale* is a good example).

Structure

Most plays follow a traditional three-part structure:

→ **Exposition** The first part of the play introduces the characters and 'sets up' a situation, usually by presenting the central characters with some kind of change or challenge.

→ **Complication** The middle part of the play then develops the initial situation; we see the consequences of change and how characters respond to their altered circumstances.

→ **Resolution** The close of the play (also known as the **denouement**) usually involves some kind of restoration of order or equilibrium; characters come to terms with what has taken place.

Pre-20th century plays often conform quite neatly to this pattern. Modern drama is less predictable, with playwrights deliberately going against conventional ideas of structure. For example, a play might end with many unanswered questions, so that there is no real sense of 'resolution'. Nevertheless, many modern plays do broadly have this structure. As with tragedy, you should try to explain *how* (and if) the three-part structure works in the case of your particular text.

Plot and sub-plot

The **plot** of a play is its storyline – 'what happens' in it. A common weakness in examination answers is to describe the plot in too much detail. Nowhere in an answer should you simply 'tell the story' of a play for its own sake. Only refer to details of the plot where they are especially significant, or where they illustrate an argument you are making (e.g. about a character or theme).

A **sub-plot** is a secondary plot which runs alongside the play's main plot. It may involve characters who rarely if ever encounter the characters who feature in the main plot. Often there are **parallels** and **contrasts** between the main plot and the sub-plot, with the sub-plot mirroring the themes of the main plot, but presenting them from a different perspective (in Shakespeare's plays, for instance, the sub-plot is often more comic than the main plot).

Acts and scenes

The division of a play into **acts** and **scenes** is another important structural element. Look for the effects achieved by the **juxtaposition** of scenes, and for contrasts and similarities between particular scenes. In *Death Of A Salesman*, for example, the first Act tends to portray illusions and false hopes, whereas in the second Act the emphasis is on reality and disappointment.

Exam preparation

How far does the play you are studying conform to the **three-part structure** outlined above? Write an essay in which you support your answer with close reference to the play.

Checkpoint 2

The word **exposition** is not only used in relation to drama. What is its usual meaning?

Checkpoint 3

Which Shakespeare play has a **sub-plot** involving the following characters: Bottom the weaver, Quince the carpenter, Snug the joiner, Flute the bellows-mender, Snout the tinker and Starveling the tailor?

Take note

Juxtaposition means positioned next to each other.

Stagecraft 1

You should never lose sight of the fact that plays are written to be performed on stage. The next two sections focus on some important aspects of stagecraft.

The set ●●●

Early plays, including those of Shakespeare, contained little or no information about how they should be staged. When these plays are performed today, the stage **set** will reflect the director's interpretation of the play. Modern playwrights, in contrast, often give very detailed descriptions of what the set should look like. These should be studied closely as they can reveal much about a writer's intentions. Sets can be used to reflect aspects of the characters, to create a particular mood or atmosphere, or to suggest an historical period.

Mike Leigh's *Abigail's Party* is a play set in a suburban London home in 1977. The initial description of the set immediately suggests the values and lifestyle of Beverly and Laurence, the married couple who live there:

> *Laurence and Beverly's house, the ground floor. Room divider shelf unit, including telephone, stereo, ornamental fibre-light, fold-down desk, and prominently placed bar. Leather three-piece suite, onyx coffee-table, sheepskin rug. Open-plan kitchen, dining area with tables and chairs.*

Laurence is a successful estate agent, and Beverly is a woman of expensive tastes. The modern furnishings suggest an ostentatious display of wealth, reflecting both their prosperity and their materialistic outlook on life.

In **Arthur Miller's** *Death Of A Salesman* the set is on a larger scale. The focal point is again the interior of a family home, but we are also aware of the surrounding area:

> *Before us is the Salesman's house. We are aware of towering, angular shapes behind it, surrounding it on all sides. Only the blue light of the sky falls upon the house and forestage; the surrounding area shows an angry glow of orange. As more light appears, we see a solid vault of apartment houses around the small, fragile-seeming home.*

The *towering, angular shapes* and *the solid vault of apartment houses* have a threatening presence, emphasising the *fragile* nature of Willy Loman's home and world. The set for *Death Of A Salesman* is also less **naturalistic** (true to life) than that for *Abigail's Party*. The stage directions make this explicit: *An air of the dream clings to the place, a dream rising out of reality*. This prepares the audience both for Willy Loman's illusions about himself and others, and for the way the play itself departs from naturalism. The action moves back and forth between the past and the present, and when episodes are set in the past the characters step through the invisible 'wall' of the house.

Checkpoint 1

Mike Leigh is also a successful film director. Can you name any of his films?

Links

For more on **Arthur Miller**, see page 103.

Checkpoint 2

Comment on Miller's use of **lighting** here.

Props

Props can also be important; often they have a **symbolic** significance. In **Tennessee Williams's** *A Streetcar Named Desire* a radio symbolises the power struggle between Stanley and Blanche, his wife's sister. When Blanche turns the radio on, Stanley turns it off; later, when she turns it on again, he hurls it out of a window. In *Death Of A Salesman* stockings symbolise Willy's shabby treatment of his wife and contrasting generosity towards his lover. We see Linda mending old stockings, but Willy gives his lover new stockings as a gift.

Stage directions

As well as providing information about the set, playwrights sometimes include descriptions of the **characters** as well. These are obviously not available to an audience watching the play, but authors include them to guide actors and directors, and they are very useful if you are studying the play. In **Brian Friel's** *Translations* the descriptions of Manus and his brother Owen prepare us for the differences in their characters – Manus the serious-minded idealist, Owen a more worldly, extrovert figure:

> *Manus is in his late twenties/early thirties; the master's older son. He is pale-faced, lightly built, intense, and works as an unpaid assistant – a monitor – to his father. His clothes are shabby; and when he moves we see that he is lame.*

> *Owen is the younger son, a handsome, attractive young man in his twenties. He is dressed smartly – a city man. His manner is easy and charming: everything he does is invested with consideration and enthusiasm.*

Some playwrights go beyond external appearance and behaviour in their directions. **Tennessee Williams** is an example of this. In his introductory notes to *The Glass Menagerie*, Amanda is described as *A little woman of great but confused vitality clinging frantically to another time and place . . . she has endurance and a kind of heroism, and though her foolishness makes her unwittingly cruel at times, there is tenderness in her slight person.*

Stage directions can also indicate characters' **actions** and **movements**, and these may be significant. Manus's father Hugh shows his son little affection and is quite dismissive towards him, as we see when *He removes his hat and coat and hands them and his stick to Manus, as if to a footman.*

Checkpoint 3

The term **props** is an abbreviation. What is the full version of the word?

Links

For more on **Brian Friel**, see page 102.

Links

These stage directions are also discussed on page 86.

Exam preparation

See page 87 for an essay question relevant to this and the next section.

Stagecraft 2

In this section we continue to look at the importance of how plays might be presented **on stage**.

Costume

Brian Friel's descriptions of Manus and Owen in *Translations* (see page 85) illustrate how dress can be used to **reflect character**. Manus's *shabby* clothes emphasise his poverty and lack of material ambition. Owen, who left the rural Irish community of Baile Beag in a determined effort to better himself, is in contrast *dressed smartly – a city man*. In the same play the military uniforms of the English soldiers separate them from the rest of the characters, making them visibly outsiders, while also symbolising their authority and power.

In **Harold Pinter's** *The Caretaker* the first character we see is Mick. His behaviour creates an unsettling, rather sinister impression (he says nothing, then exits as soon as voices are heard offstage), and his air of menace is reinforced by his leather jacket. The two other characters, Aston and Davies, then enter. Aston's appearance suggests self-neglect, while Davies's even shabbier dress is the first indication that he is a vagrant:

> Aston wears an old tweed overcoat, and under it a thin shabby dark-blue pinstripe suit, single-breasted, with a pullover and faded shirt and tie. Davies wears a worn brown overcoat, shapeless trousers, a waistcoat, vest, no shirt, and sandals.

Lighting, music and sound effects

A play is an aural and visual experience, and **lighting**, **music** and **sound effects** can make an important contribution to the overall effect. You should consider how they **reflect the mood** at particular points in the play, and how they **reinforce** what is taking place between the characters.

In *A Streetcar Named Desire* Blanche's boyfriend Mitch symbolically turns on a light at the moment he is confronting her with the truth about her past. In contrast, in *Translations* much of the stage is in darkness for the romantic dialogue between Maire and Yolland, enhancing the scene's intimacy. The change in atmosphere for this scene is also signalled by music: the loud fiddle playing of the dance that Maire and Yolland have just left fades, and is replaced by gentler guitar music.

Arthur Miller's *Death Of A Salesman* also makes use of music. At the beginning of the play *A melody is heard, played upon a flute. It is small and fine, telling of grass and trees and the horizon*. The music has associations of happiness and freedom, and soon afterwards when Willy has a happy memory of the past *the flute is heard distantly*.

There is some uncertainty about how much use was made of lighting in **Elizabethan and Jacobean theatre**. It is possible that light was increased or diminished by the use of candles and torches. **John Webster's** *The Duchess Of Malfi* makes particular use of symbolic contrasts between light and darkness, with darkness having clear

Links

For more on **Harold Pinter**, see page 101.

Checkpoint 1

Which monarchs ruled England during the **Elizabethan** and **Jacobean** periods?

connotations of evil, and of moral and spiritual corruption. Scenes where there is intrigue, tension and fear often take place at night. The plays of the time also occasionally used music, as in **Shakespeare's** *Antony And Cleopatra*, when the mysterious sound of *Music i'the air* is taken as a bad omen, signifying that Antony's god Hercules is deserting him.

Apart from music, other sound effects might be significant. In *A Streetcar Named Desire* the occasional roar of a locomotive train is used to reinforce Stanley's role as a character representing the modern industrial age. It also symbolises his menacing strength: in the scene that culminates in Blanche's rape, *The barely audible blue piano begins to drum up louder*, before *The sound of it turns into the roar of an approaching locomotive*.

Performance and interpretation ●●●

However much the playwright uses stage directions and other methods to control how a play is presented, the way it is **interpreted** by producers and actors – from its overall meaning to decisions about how particular lines should be delivered – is still enormously important. If you see a performance of a play you are studying (or watch a film production), you should note how specific roles or episodes in the play are interpreted. When answering an examination question, including brief points about productions you have seen can strengthen your answer, provided they are relevant to the extract or topic you are writing about.

Another crucial element is the presence of a **live audience**. If the play includes **soliloquies** or **asides**, these may be delivered as if the character is speaking directly to the audience, taking them into his or her confidence. Shakespeare's villains – such as Richard III and Iago – often address audiences in this way, so that we are made to feel like fellow conspirators. Some plays have a **narrator**, who guides the audience through the play, perhaps giving them background information or commenting on what they see. Tom Wingfield in **Tennessee Williams's** *The Glass Menagerie* has a dual role, as a narrator who is also one of the play's main characters.

Dramatic irony is a device that exploits the presence of an audience. It hinges on the audience knowing more than the characters: characters say something that has an extra meaning or significance, apparent to the audience but not to the characters themselves.

Checkpoint 2

Which Shakespeare play begins with the line, *If music be the food of love, play on*?

Checkpoint 3

In which American city is *A Streetcar Named Desire* set?

Links

For more on **soliloquies** and **asides**, see page 91.

Take note

Sometimes with **dramatic irony** the significance of what is said only becomes apparent later in the play. Often the effect is of a character's words rebounding on them in some way. For example, Macbeth says *Fail not our feast* to Banquo, hypocritically urging him to attend a banquet even though he then arranges to have Banquo murdered before the banquet takes place. The dramatic irony of Macbeth's words (and of Banquo's reply – *My lord, I will not*) becomes apparent when Banquo does appear at the banquet – as a ghost. See also page 10.

Exam preparation

With reference to the elements of stagecraft discussed in this section and on pages 84–5, write an essay in which you explain how as a director you would stage the opening scene of the play you are studying.

Dramatic dialogue 1

With all the texts you study, it is important to consider the writer's use of **language**. In the case of a play, this essentially means looking closely at the **dialogue**.

Purposes of dramatic dialogue

When you are studying a play, or analysing an extract from the text, you should think about the **effects** and **purposes** that the dialogue has. These can include the following:

→ It may **reveal character**. For example, the dialogue might shed light on a character's attitudes and values, or reveal something interesting about their past. What is said and how it is said are both significant. A character's **idiolect** – the distinctive features of an individual speaker's language – may be used by a writer to reflect important aspects of the character's personality.

→ It may reveal or develop **relationships between characters**.

→ It may contribute to the development of **themes** and **ideas** that are important to the play as a whole.

→ It may give information that is important to the **plot**, or move the storyline forward in some way (e.g. a character might make a significant decision or a key piece of action might occur).

→ It might be used to evoke a particular **mood** or **atmosphere**.

→ It might be intended to generate a specific **reaction from the audience** (such as laughter if the dialogue is humorous).

Note that the above are not mutually exclusive – a piece of dialogue can be doing several of these things at the same time.

Naturalistic dialogue

There are significant differences between dramatic dialogue and the way we speak in real life. To begin with, dialogue in plays is usually much more coherent than in everyday speech, which is often disjointed and littered with pauses, hesitations and unintended repetition. Most importantly, dialogue in plays is not genuinely spontaneous but has been carefully crafted by a writer. This means it has a special kind of intensity because in good dramatic dialogue not a word is wasted – everything goes towards achieving one or more of the dramatic purposes outlined above.

Of course, this does not mean that some playwrights do not try to give the **impression** of natural, everyday speech. Dialogue of this kind is described as **realistic** or **naturalistic**. The dialogue in most of **Mike Leigh's** plays and films is an example of this approach. This is the beginning of *Abigail's Party* (Laurence has just arrived home from work; his wife Beverly greets him):

LAURENCE [*kissing her*]: Hullo.
BEVERLY: Hi.
   [*Laurence puts case on armchair.*]
You're late.

Links

For more on **idiolect**, see page 90.

Checkpoint 1

-lect is a suffix found in several words associated with language. For example, a **sociolect** is a form of language used by a particular social group. What word ending in –*lect* is commonly used for a form of language associated with a particular region of the country?

Checkpoint 2

Not all of the speeches in plays are addressed to other characters (see page 91). In older plays in particular there may be **soliloquies**. What is a soliloquy?

Take note

Another difference between dramatic dialogue and real speech is that in real conversation there are more interruptions, and more simultaneous or overlapping speech.

LAURENCE: Sorry? [*Laurence turns down music.*]

BEVERLY: I said, you're late.

　　[*Laurence pours himself a scotch.*]

LAURENCE: Yes: sorry about that – unavoidable.

BEVERLY: What happened?

LAURENCE: Oh, some clients, they were late.

BEVERLY: Laurence, don't leave your bag on there, please.

LAURENCE: I'll move it in a minute.

BEVERLY: D'you get something to eat?

LAURENCE: No.

BEVERLY: No? I had to throw your pizza away, I'm sorry.

Non-naturalistic dialogue ●●●

Dialogue which has clearly been carefully constructed by a writer, and which is very different from the way people naturally speak, is described as **non-naturalistic** or **stylised**. Many playwrights (especially in previous centuries) did not intend that their dialogue should sound lifelike and realistic, so this does not mean that it is therefore badly written and ineffective. In **Samuel Beckett's** *Waiting For Godot*, there is much **patterning** in the dialogue, with deliberate **circularity** and **repetition** reinforcing a sense of futility and paralysis:

ESTRAGON: Then adieu.

POZZO: Adieu.

VLADIMIR: Adieu.

POZZO: Adieu.

　　[*Silence. No one moves.*]

VLADIMIR: Adieu.

POZZO: Adieu.

ESTRAGON: Adieu.

　　[*Silence.*]

POZZO: And thank you.

VLADIMIR: Thank *you*.

POZZO: Not at all.

ESTRAGON: Yes yes.

POZZO: No no.

VLADIMIR: Yes yes.

ESTRAGON: No no.

Links

See 'Exam preparation' below for an analysis question based on this extract.

Take note

When you are quoting from plays, remember to identify clearly the speakers, and to put speeches from different characters on separate lines.

Checkpoint 3

Waiting For Godot was originally written by Samuel Beckett in another language, then translated by Beckett himself into English. In which language was the play first written and performed?

Exam preparation　　　　　　answers: page 108

Write an analysis of the extract from *Abigail's Party* above. Identify aspects of the language that make the dialogue **naturalistic**, and comment on how this opening to the play presents the characters of Laurence and Beverly, and their relationship.

Dramatic dialogue 2

This second section on dramatic dialogue considers further the different ways that playwrights use language.

Dialogue and character

One of the main purposes of dialogue in plays is to **reveal character**. Obviously the **content** of characters' speeches is important, and needs to be examined for what it tells us (both explicitly and implicitly) about their attitudes, moral values, personalities and so on. The *way* a character speaks is also significant. The term **idiolect** is used for the distinctive features of one individual's use of language. Within a play, a character's idiolect often reveals a great deal. In **Mike Leigh's** *Abigail's Party*, Laurence is a pompous, pretentious character, and this is reflected in his language, which often appears excessively formal:

> BEVERLY: I told you nobody'd like olives, Laurence.
> LAURENCE: Not nobody, Beverly: I like olives. And that's twenty-five per cent of the assembled company.

Dramatic dialogue involves **interaction** between characters, so it is also a way of showing characters' **relationships**. For example, one character might assert **dominance** over another by speaking more, interrupting, controlling the topics of conversation or using commands and questions. In **Harold Pinter's** plays, characters often use language to control and intimidate others, as in this extract from *The Caretaker*:

> MICK: What's your name?
> DAVIES (*shifting, about to rise*): Now look here!
> MICK: What?
> DAVIES: Jenkins!
> DAVIES: Jen . . . kins.
>   *DAVIES makes a sudden move to rise. A violent bellow from MICK sends him back.*
>   (*A shout.*) Sleep here last night?
> DAVIES: Yes . . .
> MICK (*continuing at great pace*): How'd you sleep?
> DAVIES: I slept –
> MICK: Sleep well?
> DAVIES: Now look –
> MICK: What bed?
> DAVIES: That –
> MICK: Not the other?
> DAVIES: No!
> MICK: Choosy.

Checkpoint 1

Explain the difference between *explicitly* and *implicitly*.

Take note

In contrast, Beverly's language is generally very informal: she uses words such as *bloke, cos* (for 'because') and *yeah*.

Links

For an analysis question based on this extract, see 'Exam preparation' on page 91.

Dialogue and atmosphere ●●●

Dialogue can also contribute to the creation of a **mood** or **atmosphere**. The **pace** and **rhythm** of dialogue often have a part to play in this. In **John Webster's** *The Duchess Of Malfi* this exchange between Antonio and Bosola has a **staccato** rhythm, underlining a feeling of tension and unease:

ANTONIO: Bosola?
  [*Aside*] This mole does undermine me – heard you not
  A noise even now?
BOSOLA: From whence?
ANTONIO: From the Duchess' lodging.
BOSOLA: Not I. Did you?
ANTONIO: I did, or else I dreamed.

Checkpoint 2

Explain what you understand by the term **staccato**.

Soliloquies, asides and monologues ●●●

Not all speeches in plays involve interaction with other characters. A **soliloquy** is an extended speech which is heard by the audience but not by the other characters (usually the character speaking is alone on stage). It is a technique especially associated with **Elizabethan** and **Jacobean** plays, including those by **Shakespeare**. In a soliloquy the character reveals his innermost thoughts, sharing these with the audience. An **aside** is a shorter piece of speech, spoken when other characters are present. The character slips in a comment or remark which only the audience hears. A soliloquy is a form of **monologue**, which is a lengthy speech by one character, with or without other characters hearing it or being present. **Alan Bennett's** television plays *Talking Heads* are monologues: each play has one character, who speaks directly to the camera; no one else is seen or heard, other than in one play when a policeman's voice is briefly heard offscreen.

Take note

As with soliloquies, an aside reveals to us what the character is thinking – in the above extract from *The Duchess Of Malfi*, Antonio's distrust of Bosola is shown by the aside *This mole does undermine me.*

Other aspects of language ●●●

With any kind of literary text, including plays, the close analysis of language also involves looking at such things as the **connotations** of words and phrases, the use of **simile** and **metaphor**, the effects of different kinds of **sentence construction** and so on. In particular, you should look for **patterns** in the language that is used. Often there is **imagery** which acquires significance because it is **repeated** through the play. *The Duchess Of Malfi*, for example, presents a generally pessimistic view of human nature, and this is reflected in repeated references to animals (suggesting that much human behaviour is bestial), disease, poison and darkness.

Checkpoint 3

Can you think of another word that has a similar meaning to **connotations**?

Exam preparation   answers: page 108

Write an analysis of the extract from *The Caretaker* on page 90, explaining how the dialogue reflects Mick's domination of Davies.

Characters in plays

This section offers some advice on writing about the **characters** in the plays that you study.

What are 'characters'?

As with novels (see page 56), it is important to remember that characters in plays are **dramatic constructs** (imaginary creations) rather than real people. In written answers you should, for example, avoid speculating about a character's life before and after the play. Instead, you should refer to how the playwright has **presented** the character, and discuss the **dramatic purposes** the character has in relation to the play as a whole (see below).

Characters and their purposes

Every character is in a play for a purpose – be careful not to dismiss minor characters as insignificant. In thinking about the purposes of a character in relation to the play as a whole, it can be helpful to examine how the character is important in terms of:

→ The **plot** – the action of the play. In **Brian Friel's** *Translations*, for example, the character of Yolland (an English soldier) is important in a variety of ways, but he is certainly crucial to the plot: his disappearance (we assume he has been abducted and possibly murdered by Irish rebels) triggers the events that occur in the closing Act of the play.

→ The **themes** – the ideas and issues that run through the play. **Tom Stoppard's** *Professional Foul*, for example, is a television play about the suppression of free speech in communist Czechoslovakia. A character called Pavel Hollar appears only briefly in the play but he is central to the development of this theme. He is used to represent the persecution suffered by intellectual dissidents in Czechoslovakia. He can only obtain work as a cleaner, he asks the central character Anderson (an English professor) to smuggle a thesis out of the country for him because he cannot publish it in Czechoslovakia, and in the course of the play he is arrested and has his flat searched.

→ **How they relate to other characters** For example, Pavel Hollar in *Professional Foul* is important in relation to Anderson and is used to reveal much about him. He is initially a rather distant, self-absorbed character who is reluctant to become involved with Hollar because he does not want to put himself in any danger. However, through Hollar he is made aware of the plight of dissidents and of his own selfishness. His decision to help Hollar shows how he has changed. Characters can also be important because they **contrast** with other characters in the play. In *Translations* the two brothers Owen and Manus are clearly very different, and these differences make each character's strengths and weaknesses more distinct.

The most important character in a play is traditionally known as the **hero** or **protagonist**. The hero is not necessarily 'heroic' in the sense of being noble and courageous: the hero of Shakespeare's *Richard III* is the cunning, malevolent Richard. (The term **anti-hero** is sometimes used for

Take note

This does not mean that characters in plays necessarily lack individuality or complexity, that they are not capable of gaining an emotional response from an audience, or that for the duration of the play we do not 'believe' in them as people. However, when you analyse a play as a work of literature you need to show that you understand the characters have been **created** by the dramatist.

Checkpoint 1

What is a **dissident**?

Checkpoint 2

Sometimes in plays one character is the **antithesis** of another. What does this mean?

a protagonist who, while not necessarily evil or villainous, lacks traditional heroic qualities.) Many plays also have an **antagonist**, the hero's main opponent and often the play's villain. *Othello* conforms to this pattern: Othello is the hero or protagonist, Iago the antagonist and villain.

Ways of presenting characters

If you are writing about how a character is presented in a play, these are some important aspects to consider:

→ How the character is **introduced** by the dramatist. We may be introduced to a character before the character appears, through what others say about him or her. Othello, for instance, is not present in the opening scene of Shakespeare's play, but most of the dialogue is about him. This creates a sense of anticipation in the audience. When a character first appears, there may be **stage directions** that tell us something about the character's personality, attitudes or values. For example, Maire in *Translations* is described as *strong-minded*. The stage directions might also include information about the character's physical appearance, and how they are dressed (as noted on page 86, external appearance is often used to suggest character).

→ What the character **says**, and how they say it. As explained on page 90, a character's **idiolect** (the distinctive way he or she uses language) can be important.

→ How the character **interacts** with other characters, and what is revealed about them by the kinds of relationships they have.

→ **Actions** performed by the character, and their significance. In the opening scene of *A Streetcar Named Desire*, Stanley's raw masculinity is suggested when he enters carrying a parcel of meat, which he tosses to his wife (like a hunter returning home with his kill).

→ How the character **develops** in the course of the play. Do their attitudes and values change? Are their relationships with any of the other characters different in any way? Important characters are more likely to develop than minor ones. Anderson in *Professional Foul* (see above) is a good example of a character who undergoes change.

Checkpoint 3

The words **protagonist** and **antagonist** derive from an ancient civilisation strongly associated with the early development of drama. Which one?

Take note

Shakespeare's plays often begin with information or comment about the central characters before they appear.

Watch out!

A danger of studying a play as a written text is that you overlook the impact of **actions** performed on stage. Be careful not to do this.

Exam preparation   answers: page 108

On page 106 there is an extract from *A Streetcar Named Desire* by Tennessee Williams, in which Blanche and her brother-in-law Stanley meet for the first time. Examine Williams's presentation of the two characters in this extract.

Elizabethan and Jacobean drama

The next few sections consider the main phases in the history of English drama, beginning with the **Elizabethan** and **Jacobean** periods.

Pre-Elizabethan drama

The earliest English plays date from the Middle Ages. They were performed in the open air by bands of travelling players, on wagons as theatre did not yet exist. The **mystery plays** enacted episodes from the Bible. They were a form of religious instruction, but were also intended to entertain, and included comic scenes and dialogue that incorporated the colloquial language of the time. **Morality plays** developed later, in the late 15th and early 16th centuries. The most admired English example is *Everyman*. The plays use **allegory** to deliver moral lessons, with characters who are personifications of abstract concepts such as Knowledge and Strength. Many morality plays feature the **Vice**, a comic character who is nevertheless the personification of evil.

Elizabethan and Jacobean theatre

Plays of this period were written during the reigns of Elizabeth I (1558–1603) and James I (1603–25). England's first theatre was built in 1576, and interest in drama escalated in the years that followed. Many famous dramatists belong to this period, which is regarded as the golden age of English drama. The most notable is of course **Shakespeare**, whose works are discussed in the next chapter (pages 111–46). The best plays of this period offer penetrating insights into society and the human condition, addressing issues of morality, justice, political discord and social corruption, as well as individual human tragedy. Three of the most important Elizabethan and Jacobean playwrights are discussed more fully below.

Christopher Marlowe

The plays of **Christopher Marlowe** (1564–93) illustrate the importance of placing literary works in their historical context. The **Renaissance** (the name given to the resurgence of art and literature that occurred in the 15th and 16th centuries) was a period of new discoveries and ideas, a time when writers, artists and scientists extended the frontiers of knowledge. The heroes of Marlowe's plays are over-reachers, characters who push at the boundaries of human potential. *Dr Faustus* has a hero who wants to possess all knowledge. He sells his soul to the devil, entering into a pact which gives him limitless power and pleasure for 24 years, after which he will go to hell. Marlowe incorporates elements from the earlier morality plays, using Good and Bad Angels to personify good and evil, and showing on stage a parade of the Seven Deadly Sins. However, plays such as *Dr Faustus* also helped to initiate a new tradition in English drama, the idea of the **tragic hero**. Faustus is a character of immense energy and potential, but his inability to curb his desires brings about his inevitable downfall. The play itself seems torn between admiration for Faustus's refusal to

---

Take note

Shakespeare and other later playwrights (including **Christopher Marlowe** – see below) drew on the traditions of the morality plays. The villains in Elizabethan and Jacobean drama, for example, often have Vice-like characteristics.

Checkpoint 1

In which famous theatre were many of Shakespeare's plays first performed?

Links

See pages 116–17 in the chapter on **Shakespeare** for more on the historical context of Elizabethan and Jacobean drama.

Checkpoint 2

What is the literal meaning of the word **renaissance**?

accept constraints on his behaviour, and recognition that in the end men must be subservient to God.

Marlowe's *Edward II* is another groundbreaking work, an historical tragedy in which the hero loses his throne in part because of his homosexuality. The play explores the values and attributes that are necessary for the successful exercise of political power, with the king's refusal to give up his love for his favourite Gaveston helping to bring about his downfall.

John Webster ●●●

John Webster (*c*.1578–*c*.1632) was the author of *The White Devil* and *The Duchess Of Malfi*. Both plays are **revenge tragedies**, an important dramatic tradition initiated by Thomas Kyd's *The Spanish Tragedy* in 1592. The most famous revenge tragedy is Shakespeare's *Hamlet*. Webster's plays have Italian settings and portray corrupt aristocratic courts, in which intrigue, violence and murder are pervasive. Another similarity between Webster's two major works is that both have strong tragic heroines. Vittoria Corombona is the 'white devil', a woman who is both evil and beautiful. A character says of her, *If the devil/Did ever take good shape behold his picture*. Her character is also ambiguous in more complex ways, capable both of extreme cruelty and of guilt and remorse. She also demonstrates great courage, and acquires some nobility at her death. The Duchess Of Malfi is a more virtuous character, and portrayed more sympathetically as a victim of male violence. In both plays there is a **malcontent**, an important figure found in many Elizabethan and Jacobean plays. The malcontent (Flamineo in *The White Devil*, Bosola in *The Duchess Of Malfi*) is typically a cynical, self-interested character with a grievance against society. His acerbic comments on the behaviour of others make him partly a mouthpiece for the playwright's views.

Ben Jonson ●●●

Ben Jonson (*c*.1572–1637) was a **satirist**, who used humour to expose the failings of society. In *The Alchemist* a group of confidence tricksters exploit the greed of others, fleecing a variety of gullible victims by offering them fraudulent charms and spells. *Volpone*, another play about human avarice, concerns a rich man who pretends he is dying in order to obtain gifts from people motivated by the belief they will inherit his fortune.

Checkpoint 3

Do you know the names of any other plays written by **Christopher Marlowe**?

Take note

The initial *c*. before a date stands for *circa*, and indicates that the date is approximate.

Exam preparation   answers: page 109

On page 107 there is an extract from Marlowe's *Edward II*. Examine how Marlowe presents the relationship between King Edward and the barons in this extract.

Restoration drama

Links

For more on the historical context of this period, see pages 154–5.

The period of English history immediately following 1660 is known as the **Restoration** because the monarchy was restored after England had experienced nearly 20 years without a king or queen. Charles II came to the throne, his father Charles I having been deposed in 1642 and executed in 1649.

Overview

During the Interregnum (the period between kings) the Puritans, led by Oliver Cromwell, ruled England. They closed down the theatres, believing they encouraged immorality. The return of the monarchy meant theatrical performances could begin again, but the old Jacobean theatres had either been pulled down or were now derelict. New theatres were built, better equipped but designed to attract a wealthier, more exclusive audience. The types of plays that were performed changed also. There was more emphasis on comedy, and on plays that reflected the social world of the new audiences, with characters who were mostly from the aristocracy. After the years of censorship and attempts to impose high standards of public morality, there was also a new appetite for bawdy, sexually suggestive material.

Restoration comedy was mainly concerned with marriage, sexual desire and infidelity. In many of the plays gullible husbands are duped by their wives and the clever young men they fall in love with. The plays often feature **stock characters**, such as virtuous heroines, unsophisticated country bumpkins and slow-witted servants. They are **comedies of manners**, a genre especially associated with the Restoration and the 18th century. Plays of this kind use clever verbal comedy to examine the attitudes and morals of high society. Many Restoration plays highlight the absurdity of social behaviour. There is also a preoccupation with sexual desire and intrigue, which at the time some found shocking. In 1698, Jeremy Collier wrote an influential pamphlet entitled *A Short View Of The Immorality and Profaneness Of The English Stage*.

William Wycherley

The Country Wife by **William Wycherley** (1641–1715) is generally regarded as one of the best Restoration comedies. The complex, skilfully constructed plot centres around a visit to London by Mr Pinchwife and his wife Margery, for the marriage of his sister Alithea. Another important character is Horner, a pleasure-loving libertine who deliberately encourages a rumour that he is impotent. The ruse means that husbands who would otherwise be suspicious of his intentions are happy to let Horner spend time with their wives. A succession of ladies (including Margery) succumb to Horner's charms, each discovering his secret but revealing nothing. In the final scene the wives learn that Horner has seduced them all, but they have to cover for him to protect themselves from their husbands. When the play was first performed some considered it verged on the obscene, and a revival in the late

Checkpoint 1

What other term was used for those who opposed Charles I during the English Civil War?

Checkpoint 2

Explain what you understand by the term **stock characters**.

Take note

A **libertine** is a person (usually a man) whose approach to life ignores generally accepted rules of morality.

18th century (retitled *The Country Girl*) was a much staider version of the play. Horner's escape at the end of the play has been interpreted as implying approval for his deceitfulness and amorality, though those he dupes generally deserve to suffer, and the play succeeds in exposing the greed and hypocrisy of fashionable society.

William Congreve ●●●

The Way Of The World by **William Congreve** (1670–1729) is often described as the greatest Restoration comedy. Like *The Country Wife* (and many other Restoration dramas) it again has a very intricate plot. The hero Mirabell is a young gentleman in love with Millamant, a niece of Lady Wishfort, whose approval Mirabell has to win if he is to marry Millamant. Mirabell has to overcome a variety of obstacles, including the scheming Mrs Marwood, who has been spurned by Mirabell and in revenge tries to turn Lady Wishfort against him. The play satirises the mercenary values of upper-class society (several characters are driven by the desire for money and property), but also celebrates Mirabell's genuine love for Millamant. The play has a more conventional moral outcome than *The Country Wife*: the decent, virtuous characters triumph and the selfish, hypocritical characters are defeated. Congreve's strengths include witty, incisive dialogue and characterisation which gives the 'types' of Restoration comedy unexpected individuality and depth.

Checkpoint 3

What are **mercenary** values?

Aphra Behn ●●●

Aphra Behn (1640–89) was praised by the 20th century novelist Virginia Woolf for being the first English woman to dedicate her life to writing: *All women together ought to let flowers fall upon the grave of Aphra Behn, for it was she who earned them the right to speak their minds.* Before her success as a playwright and novelist she was a spy in Holland and then, soon after her return to England, was arrested and imprisoned for debt. Upon her release, she was 'forced to write for bread'. Her most successful play was *The Rover*, about the adventures in continental Europe of a group of English cavaliers during Charles II's exile. The hero of the play is Willmore, a sea captain and the 'rover' of the title, but there are also two strong female characters, the sisters Florinda and Hellena, whose intelligence and wit equals that of their male suitors.

Take note

Writers on drama sometimes distinguish between **flat** and **rounded** characters. Flat characters are portrayed in quite a simple, straightforward way and do not change during the course of the play. Rounded characters are more complex and are more likely to change and develop. Restoration comedies often have flat characters.

Exam preparation

'The comic plays of the Restoration often have an underlying seriousness of purpose.' Write an essay in which you discuss this statement, referring closely to one or more plays from the period.

18th and 19th century drama

Our overview of the history of English drama reaches the 18th and 19th centuries.

Overview ●●●

The 18th and 19th centuries were not a strong period for English drama; poetry and the novel were more significant. The taste for light **comedies of manners** (see page 96) continued into the 18th century. However, the cynicism and acerbic wit that characterised much Restoration comedy were toned down and instead there was a trend towards a gentler approach, known as **sentimental comedy**. Plays generally were conventional in both form and content, with stock characters and predictable themes. It was not until the late 19th century that drama began to change significantly, largely owing to the influence of European playwrights such as Ibsen and Chekhov. The Norwegian dramatist **Henrik Ibsen** (1828–1906) is generally regarded as the founder of modern drama. His plays broke new ground by addressing contemporary social and political issues. In *A Doll's House*, for example, he examined the social position of married women, portraying a wife who at the end of the play makes the courageous decision to leave her husband. Ibsen is also associated with **naturalism**, a literary movement of the late 19th century which believed in the realistic portrayal of everyday life in novels and plays.

This period in English Literature does however include a few notable dramatists, whose works are sometimes set for AS/A2 study.

Oliver Goldsmith ●●●

She Stoops To Conquer by **Oliver Goldsmith** (1728–74) can be seen as a reaction against sentimental comedy (see above). The play has a harder edge, ridiculing social pretension and general human foolishness. The plot, like that of many comedies, is built upon mistaken identity. The hero, Marlow, is a young man who travels with a friend to the country to meet the Hardcastle family, because his father has proposed a match between his son and Mr and Mrs Hardcastle's daughter Kate. After losing their way they arrive at the Hardcastles' house, believing it to be an inn. Marlow is attracted to Kate and sets out to seduce her, thinking she is a barmaid. When he meets the 'real' Kate he does not realise she is the same woman and his manner is completely different – he is cripplingly shy and inarticulate. Eventually, after several twists and turns of the plot, the misunderstandings are cleared up and all ends happily. The play is partly a **social satire**, contrasting the values of town and country and showing how Marlow's behaviour is heavily influenced by considerations of social class. It draws upon stock characters, such as the young lovers overcoming barriers to their happiness, but makes them fresh and individual: Kate is a strong, resourceful woman, and Marlow a convincing blend of strengths and weaknesses. Goldsmith was a prolific writer, and also wrote novels (including *The Vicar Of Wakefield*) and poems (notably *The Deserted Village*).

Links

The historical **context** of this period is discussed on pages 154–7.

Checkpoint 1

Can you name any other plays written by **Ibsen**?

Checkpoint 2

Explain what you understand by the term **social satire**.

Richard Brinsley Sheridan ●●○

Richard Brinsley Sheridan (1751–1816) is best known for his comedies *The Rivals* and *The School For Scandal*. Although these plays are entertaining, they also have their darker moments, and as in Goldsmith's *She Stoops To Conquer* beneath the comedy there is serious social comment. In *The Rivals* the wealthy Lydia Languish is a romantic who wants to defy convention and marry a man who is poor. As a result, Jack Absolute, who is in love with her, pretends he is an impoverished soldier. A parallel sub-plot involves two other lovers, Julia and Faulkland, though here it is the man who has a romantic conception of love. Two other important characters are Sir Anthony Absolute (Jack's father) and Mrs Malaprop (Lydia's aunt), and the play examines critically their attempts to control the destinies of the younger generation.

Oscar Wilde ●●○

Oscar Wilde (1854–1900), who was born in Ireland, wrote four successful comedies: *The Importance Of Being Earnest*, *Lady Windermere's Fan*, *A Woman Of No Importance* and *An Ideal Husband*. Of these, *The Importance Of Being Earnest* is usually considered his finest work. The title is a play on words: Jack Worthington leads a double life, known in London as 'Ernest' while telling his ward Cecily, who lives in the country, that he has a disreputable brother with this name. His friend Algy Moncrieff also has a dual identity of sorts, claiming whenever he needs an excuse to get out of an undesirable commitment that he has a cousin ('Bunbury') he has to visit. The play is a romantic comedy, with Algy attracted to Cecily and Jack pursuing Algy's cousin Gwendolen, but it is also a serious study of Victorian attitudes and social behaviour. The 'double life' theme is of relevance to Wilde's own situation as a married man and successful playwright who was also a homosexual, at a time when homosexuality was illegal (this led to Wilde's eventual imprisonment). An important stylistic feature of Wilde's dialogue is his use of polished, epigrammatic phrases and sentences which are witty and perceptive (as in the famous line from *Lady Windermere's Fan*: A man who knows the price of everything and the value of nothing).

Checkpoint 3

What single word of three letters is a term meaning a **play on words**?

Links

Oscar Wilde also wrote the novel *The Picture Of Dorian Gray* (see page 63).

Take note

Wilde's homosexuality is an important element in the **context** of his works.

Take note

Another Irish playwright was **George Bernard Shaw**, who was greatly influenced by the work of Ibsen (see above). His plays often focus on social, political or religious issues. They include *Man And Superman*, *Major Barbara*, *The Doctor's Dilemma*, *Pygmalion* and *Saint Joan*.

Exam preparation

If you have studied a play from this period, write an essay in which you consider whether the play still has relevance to modern audiences.

20th century drama 1

Links

The **historical context** of this period is discussed on pages 158–9.

Checkpoint 1

What is **John Osborne's** most famous play?

Links

See page 92 for a discussion of **Tom Stoppard's** *Professional Foul*.

The next two sections look at 20th century plays, beginning with an **overview of modern drama** and a discussion of **Samuel Beckett** and **Harold Pinter**.

Overview

The main trend in modern drama has been the rejection of conventional attitudes and beliefs, reflected in the abandonment of traditional dramatic forms and conventions.

A key figure in the first half of the 20th century was the German dramatist **Bertolt Brecht**. A typical Brecht play has a series of loosely connected scenes, with songs accompanying the action. Brecht rejected the idea that plays should seek to imitate real life, though his works such as *Mother Courage* are strongly political.

The Theatre of the Absurd was a movement that emerged in the 1950s. It sought to reflect the absurdity of existence in plays that deliberately confounded audience expectations of a recognisable plot and coherent dialogue. Playwrights associated with this movement, or influenced by it, include **Samuel Beckett** and **Harold Pinter**.

In contrast, the emphasis in British **kitchen sink drama** of the 1950s was domestic realism. Reacting against the drawing-room comedies and middle-class drama of post-war English theatre (associated with **Terence Rattigan** and others), dramatists such as **John Osborne** and **Arnold Wesker** focused on the lives of working-class and lower middle-class characters.

Later British drama has continued to address contemporary issues, though from a variety of perspectives. The plays of **Tom Stoppard** reflect an interest in both abstract philosophical concepts and contemporary political issues, such as human rights. **Brian Friel** has written several important plays about Irish history and politics. **Feminist theatre** is another development of the late 20th century. Plays by writers such as **Caryl Churchill** (author of *Top Girls*) and **Pam Gems** celebrate women and challenge the values of patriarchal society.

Although the texts set for AS/A2 study are usually stage plays, most drama is in fact now written for **television** and **film**. Both forms encompass a range of **genres**, including, for example, soap operas, detective dramas and situation comedies (popular television genres) and horror, thrillers and westerns (all established film genres). Early television plays were shot in a studio, but from the 1960s onwards much television drama has been more cinematic. Important writers include **Jeremy Sandford** (who wrote *Cathy Come Home*, a play about homelessness), **Jimmy McGovern**, **Alan Bleasdale** and **Paul Abbott**. Other dramatists, including **Alan Bennett** and **Tom Stoppard**, have written for both stage and screen.

The 20th century also saw the rise of **American drama**, which previously had been of little significance. Writers including **Arthur Miller**, **Tennessee Williams** and **David Mamet** found a large international audience for their plays, though the issues they explore are often of particular relevance to American society. Mamet's 1992 play *Oleanna*, for example, was a controversial response to the vigorous pursuit of political correctness in American universities.

The next few pages look more closely at the work of some of the playwrights mentioned above.

Samuel Beckett ●●○

The main reason for many modern writers rejecting orderly, predictable dramatic structures is that they view life itself as unpredictable and disordered, and want their plays to reflect this. **The Theatre of the Absurd** (see above) is a term used to describe the work of several European and American dramatists writing in the 1950s and 1960s. Their plays are characterised by inconsequential storylines and repetitive, apparently meaningless dialogue, suggesting that the world defies rational explanation. *Waiting For Godot* by **Samuel Beckett** (1906–89) is one of the most influential plays in this tradition. Two tramps, Estragon and Vladimir, spend the play waiting for the mysterious Godot, a character who never arrives. A sense of futility and paralysis pervades the play, each of the two acts ending with the following exchange:

> *Well, shall we go?*
> *Yes, let's go.*

On both occasions this is followed by the stage direction *They do not move*.

Harold Pinter ●●○

The plays of **Harold Pinter** (born 1930) typically portray a closed environment (often a single room) where the social equilibrium is disturbed and threatened by the arrival of outsiders. *The Caretaker* and *The Homecoming* are both examples of this. In *The Caretaker* two brothers share a flat and one of them offers accommodation to a vagrant. The play is built around the interaction between the three characters, as they form shifting alliances and battle for territorial domination. Pinter's **dialogue** and **use of language** are important features of his plays. His dialogue is both close to everyday speech and a heightened, exaggerated version of it. Words are never wasted and the language of his characters is spare, concentrated and intense. At the same time it is lively and colloquial, and has the repetitions, hesitations and disconnectedness of natural speech. Language often has several levels of meaning, as characters use it as a weapon to threaten and intimidate others, or as a mask to conceal the truth.

Checkpoint 2

Explain the term **political correctness**.

Checkpoint 3

Harold Pinter was awarded a celebrated international prize in 2005. What was it?

Links

See page 90 for an example of **Pinter's** dialogue.

Exam preparation

Choose a play that you have studied from the 20th or 21st centuries. To what extent might the play be described as 'a product of its time'?

20th century drama 2

This second section on 20th century drama focuses on the works of four playwrights: **John Osborne, Brian Friel** and the American dramatists **Tennessee Williams** and **Arthur Miller.**

John Osborne ●●●

Look Back In Anger by **John Osborne** (1929–94) was a landmark in the history of drama, bringing a new kind of domestic realism to the English stage. The play takes place in the flat of Jimmy and Alison Porter, a young married couple. Jimmy runs a market stall while Alison is the daughter of an army colonel. Jimmy is very conscious of their social differences, and uses verbal assaults on his wife to attack the class she represents and the values of the British establishment. The term 'Angry Young Men' was loosely applied in the mid-1950s to writers such as Osborne, whose main connection was disillusionment with contemporary society. Other significant plays by Osborne include *The Entertainer*, in which the declining popularity of the music hall as a form of entertainment is a metaphor for Britain's fading imperial power, and *Luther*, an historical drama about the life of the German priest Martin Luther.

Brian Friel ●●●

Brian Friel (born 1929) is from Northern Ireland and several of his most important works explore Irish history. *Translations* is set in Baile Beag, a Gaelic-speaking area of northwestern Ireland, in 1833. A group of English soldiers arrive to carry out an ordnance survey project, creating a map of the area and replacing the old Gaelic place-names with new Anglicised versions. The play shows how colonial power can crush the identity of an occupied community. However, Friel's attitude to colonialism is also more complex and more ambiguous than this. Baile Beag has a rich cultural legacy, but the community is also backward-looking and poverty-stricken. The play explores Ireland's past, but when it was first performed in 1980 it also had clear contemporary relevance, as the nationalist rebellion against British rule in Northern Ireland was at its height. The attitudes that the Irish characters have towards the British (e.g. some favour Irish resistance) are representative of 20th century as well as 19th century views. Friel's play *Making History* goes further back into the past, looking at Anglo-Irish conflict in the late 16th and early 17th centuries, but it is a work that again has contemporary resonance. It is based on an attempt by Hugh O'Neill, the Earl of Tyrone, to bring Ireland and Spain together in a coalition that would force English troops out of Ireland.

Checkpoint 1

Do you know the names of any other writers who were termed **'Angry Young Men'**?

Links

See pages 85, 86 and 92–3 for more on *Translations*.

Tennessee Williams

Tennessee Williams (1911–83), Arthur Miller and Eugene O'Neill are usually regarded as the three most important American playwrights of the 20th century. Williams's plays, such as *A Streetcar Named Desire* and *The Glass Menagerie*, are often about desire, family and marital conflict, and the values of the old American South. *A Streetcar Named Desire* describes the disintegration of Blanche DuBois, who at the beginning of the play has already lost her job, her home and her husband. The play opens with her arrival at her sister's apartment in New Orleans, and ends with her detention in a mental institution. At the centre of the play is a conflict between Blanche and her sister's husband Stanley. Blanche represents the old South, a way of life that is fast disappearing. She comes from a family of once wealthy plantation owners, but the money and the family's mansion, Belle Reve, are now gone. 'Belle reve' means 'beautiful dream' in French, suggesting that the life Blanche tries to cling onto can no longer exist in the real world. Stanley in contrast represents the new America. He is the son of Polish immigrants, working class but confident and aggressive. Both characters are seriously flawed – Stanley is brutal and selfish, while Blanche is manipulative and deceitful – and Williams ensures the audience is not wholly sympathetic towards either of them. The battle between Blanche and Stanley is focused on Stella, who loves her sister but has also embraced the new world by marrying Stanley. During the play her loyalties are divided, but ultimately – and inevitably – she chooses her husband.

Arthur Miller

The plays of **Arthur Miller** (1915–2005) are often about 20th century American family life, with troubled relationships set against a background of economic and social change. In a statement that reflects one of the central preoccupations of his plays, he once said, '*Dislocation . . . is part of our uneasiness. It implants the feeling that nothing is really permanent.*' His first successful work was *All My Sons*, in which the guilty secret of a wartime manufacturer of defective aeroplane parts is revealed when one of his sons decides to marry the fiancée of his dead brother, who was killed when his plane crashed. In *Death of A Salesman*, Biff's discovery of his father Willy Loman's adultery casts a permanent shadow over their relationship. The play also charts Willy's futile, despairing pursuit of a version of the American Dream, which results in his eventual suicide. The play is notable for its fusion of realism and Expressionism, with episodes which arise from Willy's memories and dreams but which are also rooted in the realities of everyday life.

Exam preparation

If you are studying a play by Tennessee Williams or Arthur Miller, write an essay in which you discuss how the play portrays American society.

Links

See page 93 for a practice question on *A Streetcar Named Desire*.

Checkpoint 2

Reference is made here to *All My Sons* and *Death Of A Salesman*. Can you name any other plays written by **Arthur Miller**?

Links

See pages 82–3, 84–5 and 86 for more on *Death Of A Salesman*.

Checkpoint 3

What is meant by **'the American dream'**?

Take note

Expressionism is an approach to art (including drama) that developed in the early 20th century. It aims to communicate the internal, emotional truth of a person or situation rather than the external reality. It contrasts with realism or **naturalism** (see page 84).

Analysing drama extracts

Questions on plays that you have studied sometimes involve the analysis of **extracts**. The type of question that is set varies from one examining board to another, so as with all aspects of your AS or A2 examination it is important that you know the format of the exam paper you will be taking.

Answering the question ●●●

→ As mentioned above, it is important to go into the exam knowing the **kind of question** you are likely to be set. Will you be given an extract from the play to analyse, or will you be expected to find episodes in the play that will support your answer? If you are given an extract, will the question ask you to use the extract as a starting-point for a broader discussion of the play as a whole?

→ You should also go into the exam knowing **how you are going to be assessed**. What **assessment objectives** are relevant to this question? For example, an awareness of alternative interpretations of the text may be important.

→ When you are in the exam, make sure you **answer the question that is set**. This sounds obvious, but students often waste time or lose marks by including irrelevant material in their answers. The question may, for example, direct you towards a particular aspect of the extract, such as the presentation of one of the characters. Also it may not be necessary for you to make much reference to the rest of the play in your answer – some specifications test your knowledge of the play as a whole in a separate question.

Context ●●●

As already mentioned, you should be careful not to write too much about the rest of the play if the question does not require this. Usually you need to focus closely on the specific extract. However, it is always helpful to think about **the importance of the extract in relation to the play as a whole**. The questions to ask are **when**, **where**, **who** and **what**?

→ **When** does the extract take place? Is your understanding of the extract helped by thinking about what happens before – or after – it in the play? Does this extract **develop** the play's plot, characters or themes in any way?

→ **Where** does it take place? Is the setting significant?

→ **Who** is present? This will obviously include the characters who speak, but is anyone else on stage as well? Your knowledge of the text should help you to understand how the characters are being presented at this point in the play. If more than one character is present, you are also likely to have some understanding of the **relationships** that the characters have.

→ **What** is the extract about? On a simple level, what happens during it and what are the characters talking about? On a deeper level, what is the significance of the extract? Why was this passage included in the

Links

See pages 6–7 for more on **assessment objectives**.

Take note

Depending on the assessment objectives for the question (see above), other kinds of **context** (such as when the play was written) may also be important. See pages 148–59.

Checkpoint 1

Knowledge of the whole play will help you to identify if any **dramatic irony** is present. What is dramatic irony?

play? How does it contribute to our understanding of the play's characters and themes (see below)?

Characters

Much of your answer is likely to relate to the presentation of **characters**:

→ What **aspects of the character(s)** are illustrated in the extract? As with the rest of your answer, any points you make should usually be supported by specific **quotations** from the extract.
→ Is the extract important to the **development** of any of the characters? For example, are there attitudes or views expressed that are different from those expressed elsewhere in the play?
→ What kinds of **relationships** do the characters have? Is there conflict, or understanding? Does one character dominate another?

Themes

→ Are any of the **ideas** or **issues** that are important to the play as a whole present in this extract? If so, where and how are they presented?

Language

Questions on extracts often expect you to examine closely the use of **language** in the extract.

→ Look at the **vocabulary** that is used. For example, are any particular words or phrases emotive, powerful, ambiguous? How do we gain a sense of individual characters through the vocabulary that they used? Is there significant use of **imagery**?
→ Think also about **grammatical features**, such as short or long sentences, different types of sentences (questions, commands) etc.
→ Try to use relevant **terminology**, referring, for example, to the use of similes, metaphors, irony etc. However, beware of 'feature-spotting' – identifying language features without commenting on their significance or the effects that they have.

Staging

→ Remember the extract is from a play, not a novel or a poem. Think about how it would be presented **on stage**. For example, would any part of the extract have a particularly striking visual impact?
→ Think also about any use of **lighting**, **music**, **sound effects** etc. – especially if these are referred to in the stage directions.
→ How would an **audience** be likely to respond to the extract? What kind of reaction was the playwright aiming for?

Exam preparation

See pages 93 and 95 for practice questions which involve the analysis of extracts from plays.

Checkpoint 2

Should **quotations** generally be long or short?

Checkpoint 3

List some of the ways in which it might be evident in a piece of dramatic dialogue that one character is more dominant than another.

Take note

If the extract is in **verse**, it will also be relevant to comment on poetic effects, such as the use of rhythm or rhyme.

Practice extracts

Take note

The question for this extract is on page 93.

Examiner's secrets

Think about contrasts between the two characters, and who tends to dominate.

Text A

BLANCHE [*drawing involuntarily back from his stare*]: You must be Stanley. I'm Blanche.

STANLEY: Stella's sister?

BLANCHE: Yes.

STANLEY: H'lo. Where's the little woman?

BLANCHE: In the bathroom.

STANLEY: Oh. Didn't know you were coming in town.

BLANCHE: I – uh –

STANLEY: Where you from, Blanche?

BLANCHE: Why, I – live in Laurel.

[*He has crossed to the closet and removed the whisky bottle.*]

STANLEY: In Laurel, huh? Oh, yeah, in Laurel, that's right. Not in my territory. Liquor goes fast in hot weather. [*He holds the bottle to the light to observe its depletion.*] Have a shot?

BLANCHE: No, I – rarely touch it.

STANLEY: Some people rarely touch it, but it touches them often.

BLANCHE [*faintly*]: Ha-ha.

STANLEY: My clothes're stickin' to me. Do you mind if I make myself comfortable? [*He starts to remove his shirt.*]

BLANCHE: Please, please do.

STANLEY: Be comfortable is my motto.

BLANCHE: It's mine, too. It's hard to stay looking fresh. I haven't washed or even powdered my face and – here you are!

STANLEY: You know you can catch cold sitting around in damp things, especially when you been exercising hard like bowling is. You're a teacher, aren't you?

BLANCHE: Yes.

STANLEY: What do you teach, Blanche?

BLANCHE: English.

STANLEY: I never was a very good English student. How long you here for, Blanche?

BLANCHE: I – don't know yet.

STANLEY: You going to shack up here?

BLANCHE: I thought I would if it's not inconvenient for you all.

STANLEY: Good.

BLANCHE: Travelling wears me out.

STANLEY: Well, take it easy.

[*A cat screeches near the window.* BLANCHE *springs up.*]

BLANCHE: What's that?

STANLEY: Cats . . . Hey, Stella!

STELLA [*faintly, from the bathroom*]: Yes, Stanley.

STANLEY: Haven't fallen in, have you? [*He grins at* BLANCHE. *She tries unsuccessfully to smile back. There is a silence.*] I'm afraid I'll strike you as being the unrefined type. Stella's spoke of you a good deal. You were married once, weren't you?

[*The music of the polka rises up, faint in the distance.*]

BLANCHE: Yes. When I was quite young.

STANLEY: What happened?

BLANCHE: The boy – the boy died. [*She sinks back down.*] I'm afraid I'm – going to be sick! [*Her head falls on her arms.*]

Text B ●●○

Enter KING EDWARD, KENT, LANCASTER, *the elder* MORTIMER, *the younger* MORTIMER, WARWICK, PEMBROKE, *and* Attendants.

KING EDWARD: Lancaster!

LANCASTER: My lord?

GAVESTON: [*Aside*] That Earl of Lancaster do I abhor.

KING EDWARD: Will you not grant me this? [*Aside*] In spite of them
    I'll have my will; and these two Mortimers,
    That cross me thus, shall know I am displeased.

ELDER MORTIMER: If you love us, my lord, hate Gaveston.

GAVESTON: [*Aside*] That villain Mortimer! I'll be his death.

YOUNGER MORTIMER: Mine uncle here, this earl, and I myself,
    Were sworn to your father at his death,
    That he should ne'er return into the realm:
    And know, my lord, ere I will break my oath,
    This sword of mine, that should offend your foes,
    Shall sleep within the scabbard at thy need,
    And underneath thy banners march who will,
    For Mortimer will hang his armour up.

GAVESTON: [*Aside*] *Mort dieu!*

KING EDWARD: Well, Mortimer, I'll make thee rue these words:
    Beseems it thee to contradict thy king?
    Frown'st thou thereat, aspiring Lancaster?
    The sword shall plane the furrows of thy brows,
    And hew these knees that now are grown so stiff.
    I will have Gaveston; and you shall know
    What danger 'tis to stand against your king.

GAVESTON: [*Aside*] Well done, Ned!

LANCASTER: My lord, why do you thus incense your peers,
    That naturally would love and honour you,
    But for that base and obscure Gaveston?
    Four earldoms have I, besides Lancaster, –
    Derby, Salisbury, Lincoln, Leicester:
    These will I sell, to give my soldiers pay,
    Ere Gaveston shall stay within the realm:
    Therefore, if he be come, expel him straight.

Take note

The question for this extract is on page 95.

Take note

Although Gaveston speaks during this extract, he is not seen by the other characters. He was banished from the kingdom by Edward's father, King Edward I, but has returned to England.

Answers
Plays

Plays: study tips

Checkpoints

1 'Historical context' means the background historical influences on a text, especially those related to the period when the text was written. A text may refer directly to historical events and situations, or be more subtly (and perhaps unconsciously) influenced by them. See pages 148–59.
2 Quotations should generally be short – often a single word or phrase, and rarely more than two or three lines at most. This is because the majority of an essay should be devoted to your own argument and analysis. Frequent brief quotation is much better than a small number of long quotations.
3 False. A critic comments on a text, but the comments may be positive or negative. You should not be misled by the everyday meaning of 'criticise', which is of course 'to find fault with'.

Dramatic form and structure

Checkpoints

1 Over-reaching – the excessive pride or self-confidence that precedes, and helps to cause, a tragic hero's downfall.
2 A detailed explanation of something.
4 *A Midsummer Night's Dream*.

Stagecraft 1

Checkpoints

1 Mike Leigh's films include *Vera Drake*, *Secrets And Lies*, *Life Is Sweet* and *Topsy Turvy*.
2 The lighting reinforces the impression that the house is surrounded. A sense of menace and threat (and perhaps Willy Loman's own bitterness and frustration) is suggested by the *angry glow of orange*.
3 Properties.

Stagecraft 2

Checkpoints

1 Queen Elizabeth I and King James I.
2 *Twelfth Night*.
3 New Orleans.

Dramatic dialogue 1

Checkpoints

1 Dialect.
2 An extended speech by a character, heard by the audience but not by the other characters.
3 French.

Exam preparation

Several aspects of the language of this extract help it to resemble genuine speech. The characters speak in short sentences, and use vocabulary that is simple (much of it is monosyllabic) and quite informal (*Hi*, *in a minute* and abbreviated expressions such as *you're* and *don't*). At the same time, notice how the dialogue, despite appearing natural and spontaneous, serves a dramatic purpose. It gives us some early clues about the relationship between Laurence and Beverly, who is quite abrupt towards her husband and has a domineering tone, making accusations (*You're late*), asking questions (*What happened?*) and giving orders (*don't leave your bag on there, please*).

Dramatic dialogue 2

Checkpoints

1 If meaning is 'explicit' it is openly expressed or stated. If it is 'implicit' it is implied or suggested.
2 A series of short, sharp sounds (the term is also used in relation to music).
3 Associations.

Exam preparation

Mick intimidates and unsettles Davies in a variety of ways. He fires a series of questions at him. He interrupts Davies's answers, and makes sudden changes of subject (e.g. from *Sleep well?* to *What bed?* before the first of these questions has been answered). He also unnerves Davies by shouting and speaking rapidly (the stage directions refer to a *violent bellow* and *continuing at great pace*).

Characters in plays

Checkpoints

1 Someone who opposes official policy, especially in an authoritarian state.
2 The direct opposite.
3 Ancient Greece.

Exam preparation

The opening stage direction immediately suggests that Blanche is intimidated by, and retreats from, Stanley's assertive presence: *drawing involuntarily back from his stare*. Stanley continues to dominate by asking Blanche a series of questions, sometimes interrupting her replies. He establishes early on that he sees himself as the master of the household, referring to his wife as *the little woman*. He takes his shirt off, a gesture that asserts his masculinity. He describes himself as *the unrefined type*, and makes no attempt to moderate or disguise this, using language which is occasionally quite coarse: *You going to shack up here?*, *Haven't fallen in, have you?* Some of his remarks probe Blanche's weak spots. He is aware that Blanche has been drinking his whisky, despite her claim to *rarely touch it*, and comments sarcastically, *Some people rarely touch it, but it touches them often*. He also asks about her disastrous marriage: *You were married once, weren't you? . . . What happened?*

In contrast to Stanley, Blanche is a character desperate to retain some dignity by appearing ladylike. She speaks more formally and more politely: *please do, if it's not inconvenient*. Stanley's manner unnerves her, as shown by her hesitant speech (*I – uh –*) and her reaction to the screeching cat. Her emotional fragility is confirmed at the end of the extract, when after responding to Stanley's questions about her marriage she *sinks back down* and exclaims *I'm afraid I'm – going to be sick!*

Elizabethan and Jacobean drama

Checkpoints

1 The Globe theatre.
2 Rebirth.
3 Marlowe's other plays include *Tamburlaine* and *The Jew Of Malta*.

Exam preparation

Edward's barons have opposed the return to England of Edward's favourite, Gaveston. Edward's question to Lancaster early in the extract suggests weakness: *Will you not grant me this?* However, the barons' intransigence angers Edward and he reacts with threats of violence, telling Lancaster a sword shall *hew* (cut down) his knees and *plane the furrows of thy brows*. The barons are superficially respectful towards their king, addressing him as *my lord*. But Younger Mortimer threatens to withdraw his military support for Edward, and the extract closes with Lancaster giving the king a direct order: *if he be come, expel him straight*.

Restoration drama

Checkpoints

1 Roundheads.
2 Standard or stereotypical characters, with very similar characteristics, who appear in a number of different works.
3 A person with 'mercenary values' is motivated by self-interest, especially financial gain. They put the pursuit of this above concern for others.

18th and 19th century drama

Checkpoints

1 Ibsen's other plays include *Ghosts*, *Hedda Gabler*, *The Master Builder*, *Enemy Of The People*.

2 A satire is a work which uses humour or ridicule to make serious criticisms of someone or something. A 'social satire' uses satire to criticise a social class or group.
3 Pun.

20th century drama 1

Checkpoints

1 *Look Back In Anger*.
2 Political correctness means taking steps to avoid giving offence to a social group (e.g. women, the disabled, ethnic minority groups etc.). It is especially used in relation to language, where it means the avoidance of language which is racist, sexist etc. The term tends to have negative connotations and is often used by people who are critical of aspects of political correctness which they consider excessive or unnecessary.
3 The Nobel Prize for Literature.

20th century drama 2

Checkpoints

1 Other writers given this label include Kingsley Amis, Alan Sillitoe, Keith Waterhouse and Colin Wilson.
2 Arthur Miller's other plays include *The Crucible*, *A View From The Bridge* and *The Price*.
3 The traditional ideals of American society: the belief in equality and democracy, and the idea that the opportunity for success and material prosperity is available to all.

Analysing drama extracts

Checkpoints

1 Dramatic irony occurs in plays when something said by a character has an additional meaning or significance, apparent to the audience but not to the character.
2 Short.
3 Possible indications of dominance include: asking questions, issuing orders or commands, interrupting, speaking more than others, initiating and changing topics of conversation, ignoring what other speakers say, speaking more loudly or with a raised intonation. However, always consider the context of this kind of behaviour. Asking questions, for example, might mean that the character is seeking guidance from others.

Revision checklist
Plays

1	Explain the terms 'tragedy' and 'comedy' when used in relation to drama.	Confident	Not confident. **Revise** page 82
2	Outline the traditional three-part structure followed by most plays.	Confident	Not confident. **Revise** page 83
3	Explain the difference between plot and sub-plot.	Confident	Not confident. **Revise** page 83
4	Understand the contribution to a play that might be made by the stage set.	Confident	Not confident. **Revise** page 84
5	Understand the possible kinds of significance stage directions might have in plays.	Confident	Not confident. **Revise** page 85
6	Explain with examples the contribution that might be made to plays by costume, lighting, music and sound effects.	Confident	Not confident. **Revise** pages 86–87
7	List the main possible purposes of dramatic dialogue.	Confident	Not confident. **Revise** page 88
8	Explain the difference between naturalistic and non-naturalistic dialogue.	Confident	Not confident. **Revise** pages 88–89
9	Explain the main purposes that a character might have within a play.	Confident	Not confident. **Revise** pages 92–93
10	Outline five or more important elements when considering how a character is presented in a play.	Confident	Not confident. **Revise** page 93
11	Identify the key features of Elizabethan and Jacobean drama, and major dramatists from this period.	Confident	Not confident. **Revise** pages 94–95
12	Identify the key features of Restoration drama, and major dramatists from this period.	Confident	Not confident. **Revise** pages 96–97
13	Offer an overview of 18th and 19th century English drama.	Confident	Not confident. **Revise** pages 98–99
14	Identify major trends and dramatists in 20th century English and American drama.	Confident	Not confident. **Revise** pages 100–103
15	Approach with confidence the analysis of drama extracts.	Confident	Not confident. **Revise** pages 104–105

The study of a Shakespeare play is a compulsory element in advanced English Literature courses, usually at AS. Of course, you'll have studied Shakespeare before, at GCSE and/or Key Stage 3. As you might expect, the approach at AS/A2 is more demanding. For example, you'll need to have a good knowledge of the *whole* play (before you might just have studied extracts), and will need to examine more closely Shakespeare's use of language. Depending on your examination board, knowledge of the play's historical context or the different ways the play might be interpreted could also be important when your understanding of the play is assessed.

Several of the sections in the first half of this chapter are relevant to all of Shakespeare's plays. For example, there are sections on the contexts of the plays and on aspects of Shakespeare's language. There are then separate sections on different groups of plays: histories, tragedies, comedies and romances. A section on critical approaches should be especially useful if you need to consider different interpretations of the play you are studying. Finally, there is some guidance on tackling questions which involve the analysis of extracts from your set play.

Exam themes

→ Knowledge and understanding of set Shakespeare texts

→ Use of relevant terminology

→ Awareness of relevant contexts and interpretations

Topic checklist

AS ◯ A2 ●	AQA/A	AQA/B	EDEXCEL	OCR	WJEC	CCEA
Shakespeare: study tips	◯	◯	◯	◯	◯	◯
Shakespeare: overview	◯	◯	◯	◯	◯	◯
Shakespeare: contexts	◯	◯	◯	◯	◯	◯
Verse and prose in Shakespeare	◯	◯	◯	◯	◯	◯
Shakespeare's use of rhetoric	◯	◯	◯	◯	◯	◯
Other aspects of Shakespeare's language	◯	◯	◯	◯	◯	◯
Shakespeare: important themes	◯	◯	◯	◯	◯	◯
Shakespeare on stage	◯	◯	◯	◯	◯	◯
Shakespeare's history plays	◯	◯	◯	◯	◯	◯
Shakespeare: comedies	◯	◯	◯	◯	◯	◯
Shakespeare: tragedies 1	◯	◯	◯	◯	◯	◯
Shakespeare: tragedies 2	◯	◯	◯	◯	◯	◯
Shakespeare: romances	◯	◯	◯	◯	◯	◯
Critical approaches to Shakespeare	◯	◯	◯	◯	◯	◯
Analysing Shakespeare extracts	◯	◯	◯	◯	◯	◯
Practice extracts	◯	◯	◯	◯	◯	◯

Shakespeare: study tips

This section gives you some initial advice about studying a Shakespeare play.

First reading

The aim of your **first reading** of the play is simply to gain a very broad understanding of what happens in the play (the **plot** or storyline) and of who the **characters** are. It is almost inevitable that you will find parts of the play difficult to follow. Here is some advice on how to make this first reading easier:

→ It might help to read a **summary of the plot** before you read the play itself. Study guides on the play (see 'Other tips' below) usually contain these, or you might find your edition of the play has one. They are also in many encyclopaedias and reference books. Of course the disadvantage of this is that it may 'spoil the story', but if you try reading the play and can't understand what is happening in any case, there isn't much to lose!

→ Before you start reading, it is also helpful to know the **genre** of the play. Shakespeare wrote **tragedies**, **histories**, **comedies** and **romances**, and the plays within each of these categories tend to have certain features in common. If you have some idea of what to expect – of the conventions associated with the genre, and of the general 'shape' or form the play is likely to have – this should help.

→ The main barrier to understanding Shakespeare is the **language** that he uses. Inevitably there will be phrases, sentences and perhaps even whole speeches that you cannot understand. Initially you should try not to let this slow you down too much. You might want to make occasional reference to the explanatory notes that are probably included in your edition of the play, but you could also simply skim over particularly difficult passages, returning to them when you begin studying the play in more depth.

Second reading

Second and subsequent readings are when you study the play more closely. In carrying out this more detailed examination of the text, it is essential to know the relevant **assessment objectives** for this component of your AS or A2 course. For example, it might be important to know about the play's **context**, or different **critical interpretations** of the text. If it is an examination text, you should also find out the **type of question** you will need to answer. Will you need to analyse an extract, or write an essay – or answer a two-part question that involves both?

Whatever the particular requirements of your specification, your study of the play is likely to include a strong focus on these five elements:

→ **The plot** It's important to grasp the storyline, but remember that when writing about the play you should never simply 'tell the story'. Instead, you should look at how the development of the plot reveals

Take note

Study guides and editions of the play often include not just a plot summary for the whole play, but individual summaries for each scene. Reading these as you are going along can help you follow the development of the plot in more detail.

Checkpoint 1

Explain the term **genre**.

Checkpoint 2

Can you name one Shakespeare play from each of these four categories?

Links

For more on the genres of Shakespeare's plays, see pages 114–15 and 128–37.

character, conveys themes or ideas, and generates certain kinds of response from the audience. Also you should consider the purposes and effects of any **sub-plots**.

→ **The characters** You obviously need detailed knowledge and understanding of the play's central characters, but you should also think about the roles played by more minor characters. What do they contribute to the play, and why did Shakespeare include them?

→ **The themes** What are the main ideas or issues running through the play? Is there any 'moral' or message that can be drawn from how the play ends?

→ **The language** An especially important aspect of language is **imagery**. Often there are **patterns** in the use of imagery, with certain images occurring repeatedly – *Othello*, for example, is full of references to light, darkness and animals.

→ **Stagecraft** Never forget that Shakespeare wrote his plays to be performed on stage. As you read the text, try to **visualise** what is happening, and how each scene might be staged. Clearly it will help if you are able to see a performance of the play.

Other tips ●●●

→ As mentioned above, you should try to see a **performance** of the play. Alternatives are watching a film/television version, or listening to an audio recording. Remember though that you are watching an **interpretation** of the play. A good performance should clarify and illuminate aspects of the play, but you may still want to disagree with the way certain characters or events are presented.

→ Keep an organised set of **notes**. You will probably need notes on each scene, on the five elements of the play mentioned above, and (depending on the relevant assessment objectives) on such additional aspects as contexts and critical interpretations. If you are allowed to, make some notes in the text itself, though for books taken into the exam there are limits on the amount of permissible annotation.

→ Carry out relevant **wider research** (e.g. into the context of the play), especially if this is needed to fulfil the assessment objectives. Study guides will often point you in the right direction, and can also be of more general help when studying the play. Remember though that not all study guides are written for AS/A2 students, so they need to be used with care. Also you should not expect them to cover all that you need to know. Finally, make full use of the introduction, notes etc. that are probably included in your edition of the play.

Links

Some common themes that are found in many of Shakespeare's plays are discussed on pages 124–5.

Checkpoint 3

How would you define the term **imagery**?

Links

See pages 118–23 for more on Shakespeare's language.

Links

There is more on stagecraft in the section 'Shakespeare on stage' (pages 126–7).

Exam preparation

After your first reading of the Shakespeare play you are studying, write a summary in your own words of the plot (i.e. the storyline). Aim to write about 300 words.

Take note

A plot summary is sometimes known as a **synopsis**.

Shakespeare: an overview

This section gives you an overview of Shakespeare's life and also includes a list of his plays grouped by genre.

Shakespeare's life

Shakespeare was born in Stratford-upon-Avon in 1564. His father was a glovemaker and a prominent local citizen, holding several civic offices in Stratford, though he later fell badly into debt. It is thought that Shakespeare's parents may have had a secret allegiance to the Catholic faith, which at the time was outlawed in England. When he was 18 William married Anne Hathaway, who was pregnant with the first of their three children (none of whom survived into adulthood). He moved to London, where he began working in the theatre, initially as an actor. He became the most successful playwright of his day, and by the time of his retirement to Stratford in 1612 was very wealthy. He came out of retirement twice, writing *Henry VIII* and *The Two Noble Kinsmen* (collaborations with John Fletcher). He died in 1616.

Shakespeare's works

Shakespeare wrote 37 plays, as well as some poetry (including a collection of **sonnets**). His plays are shown in the box opposite. They are loosely grouped by **genre** (**histories**, **tragedies**, **comedies** and **romances**), though the differences between these groupings are sometimes blurred and problematic (see below). Approximate dates of composition are also given.

Sub-groups and mixed-genre plays

Although Shakespeare's plays can roughly be divided and grouped as shown opposite, there are not rigid differences between the groups and several plays could be placed in more than one category. Each of the genres listed has conventions associated with it in terms of plot, characters and themes, but Shakespeare often breaks these conventions or mixes the genres. For example, *Richard III* is a history play that has many elements of tragedy, exploring the weaknesses of its central character and how these contribute to his downfall. Similarly, *Antony And Cleopatra* is usually considered a tragedy, but it is also in many respects a history play.

Antony And Cleopatra also illustrates how plays can be divided into smaller sub-groups. Together with *Julius Caesar*, *Coriolanus* and *Titus Andronicus*, it forms a group known as the **Roman plays**. Another grouping is made up of plays known as **problem plays** (or **problem comedies**). These are plays where comedy is present but overshadowed by darker, more disturbing elements. The plays in this category are *Measure For Measure*, *All's Well that Ends Well* and *Troilus And Cressida*.

Checkpoint 1

What was the name of the Oscar-winning film about Shakespeare's life in London as an actor and playwright?

Take note

Shakespeare also collaborated with John Fletcher in the writing of *Cardenio*, a copy of which has never been found.

Take note

Shakespeare's plays were not placed in these categories until after his death. The *First Folio*, a collection of his plays published in 1623, divided them into histories, comedies and tragedies. The fourth category – romances – was not used until the 19th century.

Checkpoint 2

What are **conventions**?

Links

The **genres** of Shakespeare's plays are also discussed on pages 128–37.

The plays

HISTORIES	COMEDIES
Henry VI Part One (1589–90)	The Comedy Of Errors (1592–94)
Henry VI Part Two (1590–91)	The Taming Of The Shrew (1593–94)
Henry VI Part Three (1590–91)	The Two Gentlemen Of Verona (1594)
Richard III (1592–93)	Love's Labour's Lost (1594–95)
King John (1594–96)	A Midsummer Night's Dream (1595–96)
Richard II (1595)	The Merchant Of Venice (1596–97)
Henry IV Part One (1596–97)	The Merry Wives Of Windsor (1597)
Henry IV Part Two (1598)	Much Ado About Nothing (1598–99)
Henry V (1599)	As You Like It (1599)
Henry VIII (1612–13)	Troilus And Cressida (1601–02)
	Twelfth Night (1601–02)
	All's Well That Ends Well (1602–03)
	Measure For Measure (1604)

TRAGEDIES	ROMANCES
Titus Andronicus (1593–94)	Pericles (1607–08)
Romeo And Juliet (1595–96)	Cymbeline (1609–10)
Julius Caesar (1599)	The Winter's Tale (1610–11)
Hamlet (1600–01)	The Tempest (1611)
Othello (1604)	
King Lear (1605)	
Macbeth (1606)	
Antony And Cleopatra (1606–07)	
Coriolanus (1607–08)	
Timon Of Athens (1607–08)	

Checkpoint 3

Two monarchs ruled England during the period Shakespeare wrote his plays. Who were they?

Exam preparation

To what genre does the Shakespeare play you are studying belong? Does it have any features associated with *other* genres? Make a list of these. (For more on the characteristics of the various genres, see pages 128–37.)

Shakespeare: contexts

Links

See pages 148–59 for more advice on what writing about the **contexts** of a text involves.

Take note

Examples of words which make their first recorded appearance in Shakespeare are *assassination, accommodation, barefaced* and *obscene*.

Checkpoint 1

What does **quintessential** mean?

It is important to know about the historical and literary **contexts** of the books that you study. Shakespeare wrote in the late 16th and early 17th centuries, and gaining some knowledge of this period will help your understanding of his plays.

The Renaissance

Shakespeare lived during the **Renaissance**, a period of European history which roughly extends from the 14th to the 17th centuries. 'Renaissance' means rebirth or renewal, and the period is given this name because it was a time of transition between the medieval and the modern world. It was an era of dynamic change: power shifted from the church to the state, new lands were discovered, trade and commerce multiplied. Increased contact with other nations and cultures, and the intense interest in new ideas, caused language itself to develop and expand: thousands of new words poured into English. Shakespeare made full use of this dramatically enlarged vocabulary: the first recorded use in English of over 2000 words is in Shakespeare's plays. Scientific discoveries and a spirit of restless intellectual enquiry meant that while confidence in a divinely ordered universe diminished, confidence in the energy and potential of the individual increased. Hamlet, a Shakespearean hero who contemplates the nature of existence and questions the values and assumptions of the society he lives in, is in many respects a quintessential Renaissance figure.

Political and historical context

When Shakespeare wrote his plays England was ruled by **Elizabeth I** (who was queen from 1558 to 1603) and **James I** (who reigned from 1603 to 1625). At this time the monarch was still the centre of political power, but during James's rule in particular there was increasing **tension between parliament and the crown**. Eventually this would lead to the Civil War of 1642 and the execution of James's successor, Charles I. **Religion** was another source of division: England was officially a Protestant country but many wanted to restore it to Catholicism. It was a period of plots and conspiracies, including the rebellion led by the Earl of Essex in 1601 and the gunpowder plot of 1605.

This political turbulence is mirrored in the world of Shakespeare's plays, where **order is repeatedly under threat**. The succession from Elizabeth to James was not a smooth transition: Elizabeth did not marry or have children, and in the later years of her reign there was much uncertainty about the future of the throne. Significantly, *Hamlet* is a play in which there is a troubled succession, and *King Lear* begins with a monarch deciding who should inherit his kingdom.

An important concept at the time was **the divine right of kings**, the belief that the king derived his authority from God, and in effect was God's chosen representative on earth. Shakespeare appears in some of his plays to endorse this doctrine, but he also exposes the weaknesses of those who exercise political power: his kings are not figures of godlike wisdom and authority but flawed individuals, plagued by fears and insecurities and acting in ways that are morally questionable.

Elizabethan and Jacobean drama ●●●

The Renaissance was a period of great artistic achievements. In England, this was especially evident in **literature**. Shakespeare was the most notable in a group of Elizabethan and Jacobean playwrights who, over a period of approximately 50 years straddling the 16th and 17th centuries, created what is usually considered English drama's golden age.

Shakespeare's works include numerous features which are typical of the drama of his day. For example, **revenge** was a recurring theme in the plays of Shakespeare's contemporaries, and is an important element in plays such as *Hamlet* and *Othello*. Hamlet in particular has many of the features associated with revenge tragedies of the time, including a ghost, death by poisoning and madness. A stock figure in Jacobean tragedy was the **malcontent**, an embittered character who offers cynical commentaries on the actions of others. Iago in *Othello* is clearly a character in this tradition.

How plays were performed ●●●

The **theatres** of Shakespeare's time differed in many important respects from their modern equivalents. Although a few theatres were enclosed, most (like the **Globe Theatre**, where many of Shakespeare's plays were first performed), were open to the sky. Performances took place during the daytime and there was no artificial lighting. There was also no stage curtain and very little in the way of scenery or props. The actors did however wear rich, elaborate costumes. The rectangular stage jutted out into the body of the theatre and was partially protected from the elements by a canopy. Some of the audience stood around the three exposed sides of the stage; other spectators paid extra to sit in one of the three covered tiers or galleries.

The **audience** for the plays is likely to have been socially very mixed, from the **'groundlings'** who paid a penny to stand to the more affluent seated spectators. The design of the theatres also meant that the actors were physically very close to the audience, and it is important to remember this when considering some of the dramatic techniques employed by Shakespeare – for example, his use of **soliloquies**.

Checkpoint 2

Can you name any other playwrights from this period?

Links

There is more discussion of the **dramatic conventions** of Shakespeare's theatre in the section 'Shakespeare on stage' (pages 126–7). Knowledge of conventions such as these helps our understanding of the plays, but it is of course the use that Shakespeare makes of them that is important – and the ways in which he breaks with tradition.

Checkpoint 3

What is a **soliloquy**?

Exam preparation

In what ways is the historical context of Shakespeare's plays reflected in the play that you are studying? Write an essay explaining and justifying your response.

Shakespeare's language: verse and prose

The next few sections consider some important aspects of Shakespeare's **language**, beginning with the basic distinction in his plays between the parts that are written in **verse**, and the parts written in **prose**.

Blank verse ●●●

All of Shakespeare's plays are mostly written in **verse**. The particular form of verse Shakespeare favours is known as **blank verse**. This consists of unrhymed lines of poetry, with an arrangement of stressed and unstressed syllables known as the **iambic pentameter**. This means there are five pairs of syllables, with the second syllable in each pair stressed – as in these lines from *A Midsummer Night's Dream*:

> Four _days_ will _quickly_ _steep_ them_selves_ in _night;_
> Four _nights_ will _quickly_ _dream_ a_way_ the _time_

Blank verse was the usual medium for Elizabethan and Jacobean drama, and was the commonest metre in English poetry for several hundred years. Shakespeare often uses the pattern of stressed syllables to place **emphasis** on important or emotive words. In the following example from *Othello*, the strength of Iago's contempt for Cassio (who has been promoted to lieutenant when Iago thinks the position should have gone to him) is underlined by the metrical stress on the first syllables of _prattle_ and _practice:

> Mere _prattle_ without _practice_
> Is all his soldiership.

Varying the metre ●●●

If Shakespeare kept rigidly to a strict iambic pentameter his plays would sound repetitive and monotonous. Instead, he includes **variations** on the metre. One way of varying the metre is to **alter the expected pattern of stressed and unstressed syllables**. In this line from *Hamlet*, extra stressed syllables help to convey Hamlet's desperation as he wishes that he were dead:

> _O_ that this _too_ _too_ _sullied_ _flesh_ would _melt_

Another variation is to **alter the expected number of syllables**, by having more or less than ten. This line from *Othello* has 12:

> Heaven is my judge, not I for love and duty

Shakespeare also sometimes breaks the regularity of the metre by **dividing a single line between two or more speakers**, as in this example (also from *Othello*):

> EMILIA: *Why, would not you?*
> DESDEMONA: *No, by this heavenly light!*

Checkpoint 1

As well as plays, Shakespeare also wrote **poems**. His best-known poems are examples of what particular type of poem?

Take note

Note how in this quotation from *Othello*, alliteration (the repeated 'p' sounds) further emphasises Iago's scorn.

Checkpoint 2

Using your own words, explain what Iago is saying about Cassio here.

Take note

This line from *Hamlet* has a powerful beginning as it opens with a stressed syllable, immediately reversing the usual pattern. It also has three successive stressed syllables in the middle of the line, before ending with two standard pairs of unstressed–stressed syllables.

Note how the arrangement of the words on the page (Desdemona's speech begins over to the right) indicates that these speeches make up a single line of verse rather than two lines of prose. When this happens it usually means that the second speaker responds immediately to the first. In this case, Emilia is asking Desdemona whether she would commit adultery if the prize was *all the world*, and Desdemona's quick reponse shows how strongly she rejects the idea.

Prose

Parts of Shakespeare's plays are written in **prose**. You can tell when Shakespeare switches from verse to prose because the layout of the words on the page changes – lines continue to the edge of the page, and are no longer set out as lines of poetry. There is little prose in Shakespeare's earliest plays, where the language tends to be quite formal and artificial. The later plays are still mostly in verse, but passages of prose are also quite frequent.

Broadly speaking, there is a tendency for the **aristocratic characters** who feature in the main plots of the plays to speak **verse**, while the **lower class characters**, who are usually involved in the less important **sub-plots**, speak **prose**. In *Measure For Measure*, Angelo, Isabella, Claudio and the Duke usually speak in verse, while Pompey, Mistress Overdone, Elbow, Lucio and Froth usually speak in prose. Prose also tends to be used for **comic scenes** and **informal conversations**, while verse is used for scenes that are more serious and dramatic.

There are though no absolute rules regarding when Shakespeare uses verse and when he uses prose. Within the same scene, Shakespeare will often move freely from verse to prose and back again, and the same characters can sometimes be speaking prose one minute and verse the next. Iago in *Othello* is a good example of a character who uses both kinds of language. The ease with which he switches from one to the other might be said to reflect his intelligence and verbal dexterity. Prose is also suited to Iago because the attitudes and opinions he expresses often have a robust, down-to-earth quality.

The key to understanding why verse or prose is being used in a specific scene or extract usually lies in the **context**: ask yourself why it might be appropriate for these particular characters to speak in verse or prose in this particular situation.

Checkpoint 3

Comment on the **imagery** in Desdemona's line – how is it appropriate to her character, and to what she is saying?

Take note

In some instances, dividing a line between speakers may create a sense of excitement, speed or tension, or make a passage of conversation seem more natural and spontaneous.

Exam preparation

In your Shakespeare text, find two passages of ten or more lines each which are prose rather than verse. With close reference to the language of the two extracts, explain why you think Shakespeare has chosen to use prose, and comment on the effects that are achieved.

Shakespeare's language: rhetoric

Rhetoric is the art of speaking or writing persuasively. From the 12th century onwards books on literary composition were written, advising writers on literary conventions and techniques they should use. Shakespeare and his contemporaries were very much aware of these techniques, and made use of them in their works.

Rhetoric

The difference between Shakespeare and many other writers of his time is that whereas they often appear to have included rhetorical devices for the sake of it – as if they were merely following the rules of fine writing – Shakespeare (especially in his middle and later plays) *used* the techniques because they served his artistic purpose.

Some of the main rhetorical techniques used by Shakespeare include:

Wordplay

As the term itself suggests, **wordplay** involves playing around with the sounds or meanings of words. Wordplay involving meaning produces **puns**, as in this exchange between Kent and Gloucester in the opening scene of *King Lear* (the characters are discussing Gloucester's illegitimate son Edmund):

> KENT: *I cannot conceive you.*
> GLOUCESTER: *Sir, this young fellow's mother could; whereupon she grew round-wombed, and had indeed, sir, a son for her cradle ere she had a husband for her bed.*

Here Kent's line means 'I cannot understand you', but Gloucester makes a pun out of the word *conceive*, using it to mean 'become pregnant'. The wordplay is humorous, but it is also revealing, as we see that Gloucester talks about Edmund (who is present during the conversation) in a disparaging and derogatory way.

Antithesis

This is the contrasting of direct opposites. This example is from *Romeo And Juliet*:

> Why then, O brawling love, O loving hate,
> O any thing, of nothing first created:
> O heavy lightness, serious vanity

Hyperbole

This is the use of exaggeration. In this example from *Othello* Cassio announces that Desdemona has arrived safely in Cyprus, despite encountering a violent storm at sea during her journey from Venice. He says the natural elements have held back their usual deadly ferocity in order to let *the divine Desdemona* pass safely through the storm:

Checkpoint 1

You may have come across the words **rhetoric** and **rhetorical** used in other (though related) ways. What does it mean if a speech by a politician is dismissed as 'empty rhetoric'? What are 'rhetorical questions'?

Checkpoint 2

Explain the famous play on words that occurs at the beginning of *Richard III*:
*Now is the winter of our discontent
Made glorious summer by this son
of York.*

Tempests themselves, high seas, and howling winds,
The guttered rocks and congregated sands,
Traitors ensteeped to enclog the guiltless keel,
As having sense of beauty, do omit
Their mortal natures, letting go safely by
The divine Desdemona.

Sound

Several rhetorical techniques involve the use of sound. Examples
include **alliteration**, **assonance** and **onomatopoeia**. They are especially
common in poetry, but are also found in prose. Alliteration (the
repetition of sounds, especially at the beginnings of words) is
present in the opening speech of *Antony And Cleopatra*:

> *his captain's heart,*
> *Which in the scuffles of great fights hath burst*
> *The buckles on his breast*

In this example, the repetition of hard 'b' sounds helps to convey
Antony's strength and energy as a soldier. The idea of Antony's
superhuman *heart* – his courage and determination – bursting the
buckles on his armour is also **hyperbole**.

Parallelism

Rhetorical techniques often involve some kind of **repetition** – of sounds
(see above), individual words or grammatical constructions. When
grammatical constructions are repeated, this is known as **parallelism**.
The device involves giving phrases or whole sentences a similar pattern
or structure. This example is from Shylock's famous speech in *The
Merchant Of Venice*, where he condemns Christians for their prejudice
against Jews, arguing that Jews and Christians share a common
humanity:

> *If you prick us, do we not bleed? If you tickle us, do we not laugh? If
> you poison us, do we not die?*

The parallelism here creates a repetitive rhythm which adds power and
emphasis to Shylock's words.

Checkpoint 3

What does this extract suggest about
Cassio's attitude towards Desdemona?

Links

These techniques are discussed more
fully on page 21.

Take note

If you come across examples of rhetorical
techniques in the play you are studying,
you should always look for how
Shakespeare *uses* them to present
characters or ideas, or to create particular
effects. Shakespeare was aware that
rhetorical devices could seem artificial
and contrived, and in some of his plays
he parodied those who used them
excessively. He also grew less dependent
on conventional rhetorical techniques as
his career developed, though he never
abandoned them completely.

Take note

Parallelism occurs here because each
of the three sentences has a similar
grammatical structure. One way to spot
this kind of patterning is to look for
phrases or sentences with a similar
number of words, with some of the
words repeated.

Exam preparation

In your Shakespeare text, try to find one example of each of these rhetorical
techniques: wordplay, antithesis, hyperbole, alliteration and parallelism.
Comment on the effects created by the use of these techniques.

Shakespeare's language: other aspects

This final section on Shakespeare's language looks at some other important features of his style.

Checkpoint 1

There are five terms that can be used for images that appeal to the five different senses. For example, a **visual image** appeals to our sense of sight. Do you know the terms for the four other types of image?

Take note

In this case, Iago's *poison* image confirms that he is a malign, destructive influence, the enemy of order and goodness.

Take note

Images of blood also recur in *Macbeth*, helping to create the violent world of the play.

Imagery

In its broadest sense, **imagery** refers to writing which appeals to any of our five senses. More specifically, it refers to language which is **figurative** rather than **literal** – that is, language which involves the use of **similes** and **metaphors**. An **image** is therefore usually a comparison.

When Othello, planning to kill his wife Desdemona, tells Iago *Get me some poison* he is speaking literally, but when earlier in the play Iago urges Roderigo to wake up Brabantio and *poison his delight*, the word *poison* is used metaphorically. In writing about images you should consider their effect – what do they add to our understanding of the play's characters, themes and ideas?

As well as considering the effect of individual images, you should look for **patterns** in the imagery of the play you are studying. It is likely that certain images are repeated. It may be that a **character** is strongly associated with a particular kind of image. In *Othello*, Iago often uses animal imagery when describing the other characters, emphasising his contempt for humanity.

Repeated (or **recurring**) images can also reflect important **themes** in the play. Images of darkness recur in *Macbeth*, suggesting the evil that overtakes Scotland after Macbeth's murder of Duncan. In *Antony And Cleopatra*, images relating to 'the world' or 'the earth' recur. Antony is described as *The triple pillar of the world* (the Roman Empire at the time had three joint leaders), and when he dies Cleopatra says, *The crown o'the earth doth melt*. Caesar uses the following image when he claims he would like to settle his dispute with Antony:

> Yet, if I knew
> What hoop should hold us staunch from edge to edge
> O'the world, I would pursue it.

The recurrence of this kind of imagery in *Antony And Cleopatra* has a variety of effects. It emphasises the size and scale of the Roman Empire, and the enormous power exercised by its leaders. The specific association of several of these images with Antony suggests also that there is a particular greatness about him that the other characters lack. At the same time, the descriptions applied to Antony sometimes seem overblown, suggesting that some characters (and perhaps Antony himself) idealise him, overlooking his human flaws and limitations. After Antony's death, Cleopatra says of him:

> His legs bestrid the ocean, his rear'd arm
> Crested the world.

She then asks Dolabella, a follower of Caesar, whether *there was, or might be* such a man as this. His reply is telling: *Gentle madam, no.*

Dramatic irony

Dramatic irony occurs when what a character says has an additional significance because of something that happens elsewhere in the play. The audience recognises this hidden significance, but the characters themselves are unaware of it. An example is Othello's declaration of love for Desdemona:

> Perdition catch my soul
> But I do love thee! And when I love thee not,
> Chaos is come again.

Othello means here that if he ever stopped loving Desdemona it would be as if the world had returned to the chaos that existed before Creation. What Othello does not realise (though the audience do) is that Iago is about to destroy his love for Desdemona. By the end of the scene Othello has indeed descended into mental and emotional chaos.

Repetition of key words

As well as recurrent images (see above), in any Shakespeare play there are likely to be certain **words** that occur with unusual frequency. In *Othello*, for instance, the words *lie*, *honest* and *jealous* occur repeatedly. Often, as here, the words have a clear link to the central themes of the play. During the course of a play a word can acquire different associations and shades of meaning as it is repeated. An example is the word *nothing* in *King Lear*. The word is first batted back and forth between Lear and his daughter Cordelia, when she refuses to make a public declaration of love for her father in order to gain a share of the kingdom:

LEAR:	*What can you say to draw*
	A third more opulent than your sisters? Speak.
CORDELIA:	*Nothing, my lord.*
LEAR:	*Nothing?*
CORDELIA:	*Nothing.*
LEAR:	*Nothing will come of nothing: speak again.*

Later Lear himself is reduced to a different kind of 'nothing' when he loses all his power and possessions, vindicating the Fool's observation *I am better than thou art now; I am a Fool, thou art nothing.* But it is only after losing the superficial trappings of wealth and status that Lear gains true wisdom and insight.

Checkpoint 2

The word **irony** can also be used on its own. It can have a range of meanings. Explain some of them.

Links

See page 87 for more on **dramatic irony**.

Take note

Othello's words here are also an example of **prefiguring** – which occurs when something is said that anticipates later events.

Checkpoint 3

Which character in *Othello* is often described by other characters as *honest*?

Exam preparation

Identify the patterns of imagery in the Shakespeare play that you are studying. What kinds of images are repeated, and why?

Shakespeare: important themes

Any single Shakespeare play will of course have its own particular set of themes and ideas, but certain themes are found in several of the plays, and clearly were of particular interest to Shakespeare. Some of these are discussed here.

Order vs. disorder ●●●

In many of Shakespeare's works **order breaks down** in some way. Typically, a sense of order exists at the beginning of the play, though there is usually from very early on hints that this order is threatened. Order then collapses, before being restored at the end of the play.

This theme is presented in a variety of ways and can operate at different levels. For example, it may be a family, society or country that is plunged into disorder, an individual, or a combination of these. Leontes in *The Winter's Tale* and Othello are examples of individuals who lose their composure and self-control. In both cases passion or emotion overcomes their reason (another recurring idea in Shakespeare's plays), and others suffer as a result. By the end of *The Winter's Tale* Leontes has learned from the terrible consequences of his actions, and is reunited with his wife Hermione and his friend Polixenes. Othello dies, but in his final speech regains his earlier dignity and restraint.

In *Macbeth*, the whole of Scotland is thrown into turmoil by Macbeth's assassination of the rightful king, Duncan. This relates to the Elizabethan concept of a **divinely ordered society**, in which the king was God's chosen ruler, and the murder of a king a sin.

Within the plays, there are often certain characters or groups of characters who are the **agents of disorder**. In *Othello*, for example, Iago delights in the creation of chaos. The idea of order and disorder can also be presented through characters with **opposing sets of values** (see below), and linked to **contrasting societies or locations**. In *Antony And Cleopatra*, Rome is associated with order and emotional control, while Egypt is associated with disorder and emotional abandonment.

Broadly speaking, the plays favour order and stress the dangers of disorder. This is another reflection of Elizabethan attitudes, as when Shakespeare lived there was a widespread fear of civil conflict, and uncertainty about England's future when Queen Elizabeth died. However, Shakespeare's attitude is often **ambiguous**. Thus in *Antony And Cleopatra* the emotional freedom of Egypt is in many ways more attractive than the cold efficiency of Rome. For more on this, see 'Opposing sets of values' and 'Ambiguous endings' below.

Opposing sets of values ●●●

The plays often feature characters or sets of characters with **contrasting values and approaches to life**. In *King Lear*, Lear's daughter Cordelia has a genuine, selfless love for her father, while her sisters Goneril and Regan pretend to care for him but in reality are motivated by ambition and greed. In the same play, a similar contrast exists between Gloucester's sons Edgar and Edmund.

Take note

In *Macbeth*, Duncan's death is presented as a violation of nature: on the night of his murder, violent winds blow down chimneys, and there are reports that the earth *did shake*.

Checkpoint 1

What was the name of the king who succeeded Queen Elizabeth?

The **language** of the plays often reflects the idea of opposition, with **contrasting images** of darkness and light, heaven and hell and so on. At a very basic level, conflicts of this kind might be described as 'good versus evil', but Shakespeare's plays are not as simple as that. We usually have reservations about his 'good' characters, while the 'evil' characters often have attractive qualities or redeeming features. In a play such as *Antony And Cleopatra* (see above) there is the sense of an **unresolved antithesis** – two opposing and irreconcilable ways of life have been presented and explored, one of which has conquered the other, but we are left with the sense that Shakespeare has avoided committing himself to either side. He has shown us the merits and failings of both, and left us to arrive at our own judgements.

Ambiguous endings ●●●

As *Antony And Cleopatra* illustrates, many of Shakespeare's plays have **ambiguous** or **paradoxical endings**. Superficially, order is usually restored and 'good' triumphs, but we are often left with a sense of unease. *The Merchant Of Venice* ends happily for the 'good' Christians, the 'evil' Jewish moneylender Shylock having been roundly defeated. But for many members of the audience (especially in the modern day) disquiet at the vicious prejudice experienced by Shylock lingers. Shakespeare's plays often end on this kind of note: superficial resolution but underlying irresolution and doubt. Of course this helps to explain why they have endured for so long, and why they are such rewarding texts to study – because they challenge us to think.

Appearance and reality ●●●

In the world of the plays, characters often find it difficult to distinguish between **appearance and reality**. At a simple, literal level, the wearing of disguises is a recurrent feature. There are also characters who deliberately deceive others about their inner selves: Iago in *Othello*, Goneril, Regan and Edmund in *King Lear*. Some characters are the innocent victims of others' misjudgements: Leontes in *The Winter's Tale* and Othello both mistakenly believe their wives have committed adultery. In Othello's case, this is because Iago malevolently sets out to turn Desdemona's 'virtue' into 'pitch', inverting the truth by giving a grotesquely distorted account of Desdemona's character, which he persuades Othello to accept. **Imagery** suggestive of false appearance runs through the plays: in *Macbeth*, for example, Lady Macbeth urges her husband to *look like the innocent flower,/But be the serpent under't*.

Checkpoint 2

What is an **antithesis**?

Checkpoint 3

What is a **paradox**?

Take note

Hamlet is another play with an ambiguous ending. Fortinbras gains the throne of Denmark at the end of the play, replacing Claudius, who had become king by murdering his brother. Fortinbras is an effective man of action (unlike Hamlet) and as an outsider is untainted by the corruption and 'rottenness' of the Danish court. But he is also a ruler *'puffed'* with *'ambition'*, prepared to send *'twenty thousand men'* to their deaths in order to gain *a little patch of ground/That hath in it no profit but the name*.

Take note

An example of disguise is the Duke pretending he is a friar in *Measure For Measure*, so he can move about Venice undetected.

Exam preparation

Choose one of the above themes and write an essay in which you consider its relevance to the Shakespeare play that you are studying.

Shakespeare on stage

It is important to remember that Shakespeare wrote his plays to be performed on stage. This section looks at some of the performance elements of Shakespeare's works.

The role of language

As explained on page 117, theatres in Shakespeare's time did not have artificial lighting and also made only limited use of scenery or props. In contrast, today's dramatists can if they choose achieve effects through the use of lighting and elaborate stage sets, as well as technological devices such as revolving stages, back-projection and computer-generated images. Because these resources were not available to Elizabethan dramatists, **language** was crucial to the creation of mood, atmosphere and a sense of location.

In *Macbeth*, the speeches of Duncan and Banquo when they arrive at Macbeth's castle evoke an atmosphere of natural beauty and tranquillity:

DUNCAN: *This castle hath a pleasant seat; the air*
Nimbly and sweetly recommends itself
Unto our gentle senses.
BANQUO: *This guest of summer,*
The temple-haunting martlet, does approve
By his loved mansionry that the heaven's breath
Smells wooingly here; no jutty, frieze,
Buttress, nor coign of vantage, but this bird
Hath made his pendent bed and procreant cradle;
Where they most breed and haunt I have observed
The air is delicate.

Stage conventions

It is helpful to be aware of certain **dramatic conventions** of Shakespeare's time, which would have influenced the writing and staging of his plays. These include:

→ The occasional use of **prologues** and **epilogues** to begin and end plays.
→ The use of **soliloquies** and **asides**. The closeness of spectators to the stage meant that characters could share jokes with the audience, and give the impression of confiding in them. The soliloquy, a lengthy speech delivered by a character who is usually alone on stage and who appears to be thinking aloud, is especially important in Shakespeare's plays. It is a device used to reveal characters' innermost thoughts and can help us to trace the development of a character over the course of a play. The soliloquies and asides of Shakespeare's villains (such as Richard III and Iago) often have an ambiguous effect, exposing the moral wickedness of the characters but also encouraging the audience to identify with them, making us feel like their accomplices or fellow conspirators.

Checkpoint 1

Why is Duncan's praise of Macbeth's castle ironic?

Take note

A *martlet* is a type of bird (a martin).

Take note

Romeo And Juliet is an example of a play with a **prologue**.

Checkpoint 2

Explain the difference between a **soliloquy** and an **aside**.

→ The use of **blank verse** and **rhetoric** (see pages 118–21). Unlike
the dialogue in many modern plays, speeches were generally not
intended to appear realistic.

→ The use of certain stock **character types**, such as the tragic hero,
the revenger and the malcontent. Shakespeare drew on tradition and
convention here, but still created characters who are individuals
rather than stereotypes.

→ The **absence of act or scene divisions**. These did not exist in the
versions of Shakespeare's plays printed during his lifetime. The
divisions inserted by later editors mark natural breaks in the action,
but contemporary productions of Shakespeare's plays would have
been faster and more free-flowing than we are used to today.

→ The exclusive use of **male actors**, even for female roles. It is thought
that women's parts were usually played by apprentice actors in their
early teens (though mature characters such as Hamlet's mother
Gertrude and Cleopatra were probably played by older actors).

Visual and aural effects ●●●

Although Elizabethan theatres made limited use of scenery, visual
effects could still be achieved by the characters' **costumes** and by their
actions. Shakespeare's plays are often enlivened by dramatic events
such as swordfights, battle-scenes, dances and processions. Sometimes
actions are understated but still powerful, as in the chilling moment
when Othello and Iago kneel together and commit themselves to
vengeance on Desdemona and Cassio. The main sound effect was
the use of **music**. In *The Tempest*, music helps to create the magical
atmosphere of the island where the play is set.

Staging and interpretation ●●●

Although you should try to imagine how the play you are studying
would first have been presented, you should also think about the effects
achieved by more recent productions. Try to see a performance of the
play, ideally in a theatre but alternatively on film. You should consider
how the producer and the actors have **interpreted** the play, and
particular roles within it. Shakespeare's plays contain many passages
that are **ambiguous**, where the nature of what occurs, or the response
Shakespeare intended us to have, is open to debate.

More broadly, a producer can aim for specific effects by setting
the play in a particular historical period (including the present day)
or by emphasising particular aspects of it (this can sometimes involve
re-ordering the text, or deleting parts of it).

Checkpoint 3

Can you name any characters from
Shakespeare's plays who might be called
revengers or **malcontents**?

Take note

Orsino is listening to music at the
beginning of *Twelfth Night*, and the play
begins with the famous line *If music be
the food of love, play on.*

Take note

Trevor Nunn's 2005 production of *Richard
II* (with the American actor Kevin Spacey
in the title role) was an example of a
modern dress version of a Shakespeare
play, complete with machine guns,
television cameras and scenes set in
night clubs. Richard and his followers
wore business suits, and the fast pace
of the production helped to create an
atmosphere of intrigue and ruthless
power politics. The effect was to suggest
parallels between Richard's court and
modern-day governments.

Exam preparation

Choose a scene from the Shakespeare play you are studying which you think
is especially effective when performed on stage. Write an essay justifying your
choice.

Shakespeare's history plays

The next few sections examine the four main genres of Shakespearean drama, beginning with the **history plays**.

Overview

Most of Shakespeare's history plays can be grouped into two **tetralogies** (a tetralogy is a group of four plays). Each tetralogy depicts a cycle in English history; taken together the eight plays cover a period of almost a hundred years, from the end of the 14th century through to 1485.

One tetralogy consists of *Richard II*, *Henry IV Parts 1* and *2*, and *Henry V*. This sequence begins with the overthrow of Richard by Bolingbroke, a cousin of Richard and the son of John of Gaunt, the Duke of Lancaster. Bolingbroke becomes Henry IV, and when he dies the crown passes to his son, Henry V.

The other tetralogy comprises *Henry VI Parts 1*, *2* and *3*, and *Richard III*. These plays focus on the Wars of the Roses, a prolonged struggle for power between two opposing family groups, the Houses of **York** and **Lancaster**. Power shifts from the Lancastrian to the Yorkist dynasty when Henry VI is murdered and Edward IV becomes king. When Edward dies his brother, Richard III, seizes the throne. The sequence ends with Richard defeated by the Earl of Richmond, who as Henry VII becomes the first **Tudor** king, his marriage to a Yorkist princess uniting the Houses of York and Lancaster.

Although Shakespeare wrote his plays more than a hundred years after the events portrayed in them occurred, these events would still have seemed interesting and relevant to Elizabethan audiences. Queen Elizabeth was herself a Tudor monarch, and Henry VII was her grandfather.

Certain **themes** recur in the history plays, especially **order** and **kingship**. In all of the plays there are threats to order, usually from within the kingdom. The plays examine how kings respond to these threats, looking at the characteristics of an effective monarch and at the human strains and burdens kingship imposes on the individual ruler. As with his other plays, Shakespeare's treatment of these themes is open to a variety of interpretations. Some critics argue that Shakespeare promotes what has become known as the **Tudor myth**, a version of history associated with the 16th century historians who provided the source material for Shakespeare's plays. This version of events stresses the importance of order, and celebrates the achievements of the Tudor dynasty in bringing lasting peace and stability to an England racked by years of civil strife. There is certainly much in the plays to support this interpretation, but other critics have identified aspects of the plays which contradict it. Shakespeare shows us the brutal realities of political infighting, and none of his monarchs have unblemished characters. Moreover, the opponents of order in the plays are often portrayed sympathetically, and the arguments Shakespeare gives them telling and forceful.

Take note

As explained on page 114, although Shakespeare's plays can be divided into groups, the differences between them should not be overstated. Shakespeare's history plays often contain elements of **comedy** and **tragedy**.

Take note

Although it is helpful to arrange the plays into these sequences, Shakespeare did not actually write the plays in this order.

Take note

Shakespeare's history plays would also have seemed relevant to contemporary audiences because doubts about who would succeed Elizabeth meant that there were parallels between the past and the present in plays about monarchs who faced threats to their position.

Take note

Shakespeare's main source for his history plays was **Holinshed's** *Chronicles of England, Scotland and Ireland*, first published in 1577.

Take note

Shakespeare's other history plays are *King John* and *Henry VIII*. He also wrote **Roman history plays** (such as *Coriolanus* and *Antony and Cleopatra*), though these are usually classified as **tragedies**.

Richard II

In Shakespeare's time there was a belief in the **divine right of kings**. According to this belief the universe was divinely ordered, and the rightful king was an integral part of this. In effect, he was God's representative on earth, which meant that overthrowing him would be an offence against God. This is what happens in *Richard II*, when Richard is deposed by Bolingbroke. Shakespeare recognises Richard's claim to divine authority, and the years of turmoil that follow Bolingbroke's accession (chronicled in the *Henry IV* plays) are partly seen as divine retribution. However, the play also presents Richard as weak and uncertain, and Bolingbroke as a stronger, more effective ruler. After Richard loses the throne he becomes a more sympathetic character, and the self-knowledge he gains through his downfall gives the play a tragic dimension.

Henry IV Parts 1 and 2

The two *Henry IV* plays focus on the growth to maturity of Henry's heir, Prince Hal. The young prince initially spends much of his time with a bunch of riotous, disreputable characters, led by Sir John Falstaff. The Prince's eventual rejection of Falstaff is seen as a necessary political act if the Prince is to assume the responsibilities of kingship, but Shakespeare does not disguise its human callousness. Falstaff's anarchic behaviour and scepticism towards authority represent an important challenge to the values of the political establishment within the play.

Henry V

Much of *Henry V* is devoted to Henry's successful war against France. He besieges and captures Harfleur, then has a second triumph at Agincourt. The play's patriotism (expressed, for example, in Henry's inspirational speeches to his troops) is highlighted by some critics; others argue that the play is more subversive, presenting Henry less flatteringly as a ruler who is ruthless and calculating.

Richard III

Richard III is presented as a sinister, frighteningly evil character, in accordance with the orthodox Elizabethan view of him as a villainous king whom the Tudors justifiably deposed. However, he is also clever, witty and energetic; his compelling soliloquies encourage a conspiratorial closeness between the character and the audience.

Take note

The rest of this section looks briefly at some individual history plays that are frequently set for AS or A2 study.

Checkpoint 1

What is **divine retribution**?

Checkpoint 2

Falstaff was such a popular character with Elizabethan audiences that Shakespeare included him in another play. What was it called?

Checkpoint 3

What does the word **'orthodox'** mean here?

Exam preparation   answers: page 144

Text A on page 142 is an extract from *Richard III*. It is a soliloquy by Richard after he has attempted to win Lady Anne's love. With close reference to Shakespeare's use of language, consider how Shakespeare presents Richard in this extract.

Shakespeare's comedies

We now look at Shakespeare's **comedies**, with particular reference to those plays most commonly set for AS/A2 study.

Overview

Shakespeare wrote a large number of comedies. While the tone and content of individual plays can vary considerably, there are also strong links between them. Generally they can be described as **romantic comedies**, in that the plays focus on love relationships. Many of the plays follow a similar pattern. Young people meet each other and fall in love, but have to overcome obstacles before their love can be fulfilled. Often the plot involves several **parallel relationships** of this kind. The play then ends happily, usually with each of the couples united in marriage. Certain **comic devices** are also found in many of the plays. These include, for example, the wearing of disguises, mistaken identities, coincidences and characters eavesdropping or playing tricks on one another.

Although Shakespeare's comedies are obviously intended to create laughter, they also have **serious themes**. Often these are similar to those found in his other plays (see pages 124–5). For example, Shakespeare's preoccupation with the tension between the forces of **order and disorder** (both within society and within individual characters) is very evident. In the comedies order is disrupted by the power of love and the exuberance of youth. Youthful passion causes characters to act irrationally and to defy parental authority. As is so often the case with Shakespeare, his presentation of this theme is **ambiguous**. Some commentators regard Shakespeare as essentially **conservative** in outlook, ending his plays with order restored and with his characters conforming to social convention by entering into marriage. Others see Shakespeare as more **subversive**, deliberately bringing chaos into the world of his plays by releasing the forces of anarchy and disruption, and contriving endings in which love overcomes repressive authority.

There is a similar division of critical opinion in relation to the issue of gender within the plays. The comedies often have strong female characters, who rebel against the wishes of their parents or adopt a male role through the wearing of disguise. Some commentators argue that the endings of the plays, in which disguises are cast aside and the women marry, symbolise a final acceptance of male authority. Others believe Shakespeare's emphasis on the intelligence and independence of these characters implicitly questions the values of a patriarchal (male-dominated) society.

In a few of Shakespeare's comedies more serious elements are especially prominent. *Measure For Measure*, *Troilus And Cressida* and *All's Well That Ends Well* are sometimes known collectively as **problem plays** (or **problem comedies**). Although these plays have 'happy' endings, the mood at the close is decidedly mixed, and the plays as a whole are generally darker and more disturbing than the other comedies. Another difference is that whereas most of the other

Checkpoint 1

What does the phrase **parallel relationships** mean here?

Take note

As explained on page 82, originally the term **comedy** simply meant that a play had a happy ending – it was not necessarily funny!

Checkpoint 2

What do the words **conservative** and **subversive** mean here?

Checkpoint 3

What term is sometimes used for plays which are a blend of **tragedy** and **comedy**?

comedies are set in a make-believe world, in these plays the settings are more harshly realistic.

Some of these general points about Shakespeare's comedies can now be illustrated by looking more closely at two specific plays.

Measure For Measure ●●●

As mentioned above, *Measure For Measure* is one of the **problem plays**. On the one hand, it has several of the **elements associated with more traditional comedies**, including for instance the wearing of disguise: Vincentio, the Duke of Vienna, asks Angelo to deputise for him while he is away from the city, then remains in Vienna disguised as a friar to observe what happens. Central to the later development of the plot is the playing of another trick: the so-called 'bed-trick', which leads Angelo to sleep with Mariana, a woman he has previously rejected. He believes she is Isabella, who he has tried to blackmail into having sex with him by threatening her brother Claudio with execution. As in traditional comedies, the play also has an apparently happy ending, with male and female characters paired off, a character (Claudio) who was presumed dead revealed to be alive, and another character (Angelo) spared execution.

However, **the play's conclusion has several unsettling elements**. Although the Duke declares his love for Isabella at the end of the play, Isabella herself is strangely silent and does not necessarily return the Duke's feelings. The pairing of Angelo and Mariana (on the Duke's orders) is also unsatisfactory, as Angelo had earlier cast her aside. Angelo's life is spared but another character, Lucio, is to be hanged. Moreover, throughout the play Shakespeare has caused us to **question the morality of all the central characters**, including the notional hero and heroine, Vincentio and Isabella.

Much Ado About Nothing ●●●

Much Ado About Nothing centres upon the development of **two parallel love relationships**, both of which have to overcome difficulties before happiness can be achieved. Claudio falls in love with Hero, but the malevolent Don John convinces him of Hero's unfaithfulness. The other lovers, Beatrice and Benedick, have to overcome their own inability to understand their feelings for each other, and much of the play's comedy derives from their verbal sparring. As in several of Shakespeare's comedies, a central theme is **the growing maturity and self-awareness of the young lovers**. All ends happily, but (again as with other comedies) the play has its more **disturbing aspects**, including Don John's attempts to destroy Claudio's happiness, and Beatrice's demand that Benedick prove his love for her by killing Claudio. A distinctive feature of the language of the play is its extensive use of prose rather than verse.

Take note

Although not classed as one of the problem plays, *The Merchant Of Venice* is another dark comedy. The Jewish moneylender Shylock is the villain of the play, who threatens the life of Antonio, a Venetian merchant. But Shakespeare also makes clear the vicious prejudice Shylock experiences at the hands of the Christians of Venice, including Antonio. The play concludes like other romantic comedies with the coming together of several pairs of lovers, but the togetherness excludes not only Shylock but also Antonio himself: Shakespeare hints that he has an unrequited homosexual love for his friend Bassanio, and he is a lonely figure at the end.

Exam preparation

If you are studying one of Shakespeare's comedies, write an essay in which you consider the proposition that the play is entertaining but also has a serious purpose.

Shakespeare's tragedies 1

The next two sections consider Shakespeare's **tragedies**. The general features of Shakespearean tragedy are outlined, then four plays are looked at in more detail.

Overview ●●●

As explained on page 82, when Shakespeare wrote his plays tragedy had already existed as a dramatic genre for many hundred years. It was first defined by the Greek philosopher **Aristotle** in the fourth century BC. According to classical tradition, a tragic play will usually have these elements:

→ There is a **tragic hero** who reaches a pinnacle of happiness and/or worldly success.
→ He then **falls** from this height and the play ends with his **death**.
→ His fall may be due to inner weakness (known as a **tragic flaw**), external circumstances (**fate**) or a combination of these.
→ The character has qualities that are **admired** by the audience, so that although his downfall may appear inevitable and even deserved, it also leaves us with a **sense of loss**.

Although the above inevitably simplifies what happens in the plays, Shakespeare's major tragedies do broadly follow this pattern. His tragic heroes all have inner weaknesses (Macbeth cannot control his ambition, Othello is gripped by jealousy), and these flaws precipitate their downfall. But the cruelty and malevolence of others also plays a part: Lady Macbeth urges her husband to achieve their ambitions by murdering Duncan, Iago convinces Othello that Desdemona is unfaithful.

Shakespeare's heroes, despite their flaws, also have qualities that the audience can admire. In fact there is a **polarity** in that the plays explore the human potential for evil but also for greatness. There is terrible wickedness (as exemplified by the characters of Iago in *Othello* and Lear's daughters Goneril and Regan in *King Lear*), and this wickedness has horrific consequences, often involving the deaths of those who are pure and innocent (Desdemona in *Othello*, Lady Macduff and her children in *Macbeth*). But at the same time, Shakespeare's tragic heroes develop as human beings through the plays, acquiring both self-knowledge and a deeper understanding of life itself and of what it means to be human. This understanding is expressed in famous, memorable speeches: Lear asking *Is man no more than this?*, Macbeth reflecting that *Life's but a walking shadow*.

Aristotle also argued that at the end of a tragedy the audience are purged of pity and fear, and feel a sense of peace (an emotional state he called **catharsis**). All of Shakespeare's tragedies end with the restoration of order: terrible destruction has taken place, but the evil have been punished and a fresh start can be made. Usually there is a final sombre speech which laments what has happened but also looks to the future. However, as is typical of many of Shakespeare's plays, his

---

Take note

Shakespeare's four major tragedies are *Hamlet, Macbeth, King Lear* and *Othello*. They all date from the middle of his career as a dramatist. Earlier tragedies (such as *Romeo And Juliet*) are impressive plays but are usually considered to lack the power and complexity of these later works. In addition, certain of the English history plays (e.g. *Richard III*) are tragedies, as are the Roman history plays, notably *Antony And Cleopatra* and *Coriolanus*.

Checkpoint 1

As mentioned above, *Antony And Cleopatra* and *Coriolanus* are two Roman history plays that can be described as tragedies. Can you name any other **Roman history plays**?

Take note

Romeo And Juliet is an example of a tragedy in which **fate** plays an important part. Shakespeare's later tragedies (such as the ones discussed here) tend to place more emphasis on the hero's own weaknesses.

Checkpoint 2

What does **polarity** mean?

---

tragedies often have **ambiguous endings**, so that hope for the future is undermined by uncertainty.

Othello ●●●

A summary of the plot of *Othello* shows how it corresponds to the basic pattern for tragic drama outlined above. Othello experiences great personal happiness when he marries Desdemona. The opening scenes of the play also emphasise his high professional standing, as Venice's most respected military general. His world begins to collapse when the villainous Iago persuades him that Desdemona has committed adultery. He murders Desdemona, then when he learns that she was innocent commits suicide. Othello's principal **flaws** are that he is **credulous** (too ready to believe others) and capable of extreme sexual **jealousy**.

However, in some respects *Othello* differs from other Shakespeare tragedies. In particular, **not all critics would agree that Othello gains self-knowledge by the end of the play**. He certainly discovers the truth about Iago, and realises that he should not have trusted him. In his final speech he also regains the dignity and composure he displayed at the beginning of the play. But it can be argued that this speech is deluded and self-justifying. Blind to the extent of his own guilt, he describes himself as *one that loved not wisely, but too well*.

If you are studying one of Shakespeare's tragic dramas, in addition to exploring those elements which make the play a tragedy you also need to consider other themes and ideas that are present in the text. For example, **race** and **gender** are important issues in *Othello*. Othello is respected in Venice for his military capabilities, but as a Moor (from North Africa) he is socially an outsider. Desdemona's father (Brabantio, a Venetian senator) entertains Othello at his house but does not want him as a son-in-law and violently opposes the marriage. Other characters make pejorative references to Othello's race, speaking of his *sooty bosom* and referring to him as *the thick-lips*. Othello's sense of social inferiority gives rise to an insecurity which is exploited by Iago, who presents himself as an experienced man of the world, who is familiar with the ways of Venetian women.

The play has three female characters, all of whom experience some kind of abuse or ill-treatment at the hands of men. The play portrays a society in which women clearly have a subordinate role, but they respond to this in different ways. Desdemona is generally loyal and submissive (despite her husband's misjudgement of her), but Emilia (Iago's wife) has a speech – remarkable for its time – in which she tells Desdemona that women should not be so accepting of male authority.

Checkpoint 3

Name the character who gives the final speech in any one Shakespearean tragedy.

Take note

At the close of the play Emilia demonstrates her belief that there should be limits to a wife's obedience when she reveals her husband's guilt: *'Tis proper I obey him, but not now.*

Exam preparation answers: page 145

Text B on page 142 is an extract from *Othello*, in which Desdemona and Emilia are discussing adultery. Consider Shakespeare's presentation of the two characters in this extract, including the contrasts between them.

Shakespeare's tragedies 2

This second section on Shakespeare's tragedies looks at *King Lear*, *Hamlet* and *Antony And Cleopatra*.

King Lear ●●●

The tragic events of *King Lear* are set in motion by the aged king's abdication and the division of his kingdom between his daughters Goneril and Regan. This act of folly **destroys the unity of the kingdom** and prepares the way for **future conflict and uncertainty**. Lear's other **error of judgement** is to banish his daughter Cordelia for her refusal to pander to his desire for flattery, while handing over power to her cruel, self-serving sisters. Disaster follows on two levels: the kingdom is soon plunged into civil strife, and Lear personally bears the brunt of his daughters' inhumanity as his family disintegrates. In a **parallel sub-plot**, Gloucester is tricked into banishing his son Edgar by Edgar's villainous half-brother Edmund. In the closing scenes of the play Lear is reunited with Cordelia, and Gloucester with Edgar. But Lear, Gloucester and Cordelia all die, and the play has been described as having the bleakest ending of all Shakespeare's tragedies. The main sources of hope in the play are **the goodness of Cordelia and Edgar**, and **Lear's ability to learn from his mistakes** and grow in wisdom and humanity.

King Lear was first performed in 1606. A few years earlier, Queen Elizabeth had been succeeded by James VI of Scotland, who became James I of England. As Elizabeth was childless, the future of the throne had for some time been uncertain. In 1605 a group of conspirators had attempted to blow up parliament in the Gunpowder Plot. The play, it could be argued, reflects these aspects of its historical context in its portrayal of a society in which there is a troubled succession and threats to the order and unity of the state.

Hamlet ●●●

Hamlet is set in Denmark rather than *King Lear's* ancient Britain, but again there is a **problematic succession** and a **disunited family**. Old Hamlet, Hamlet's father and the former king, is dead but the throne has passed not to his son but to his brother Claudius, who has also married Hamlet's mother. Hamlet's resentment of his uncle turns to murderous hatred when he learns from his father's ghost that Claudius poisoned his brother to gain the throne.

That Denmark is a **troubled kingdom** is established in the play's first scene, which opens with a tense, nervous exchange between guards who on previous nights have seen the king's ghost. Horatio believes the ghost's appearance *bodes some strange eruption to our state*, and Marcellus's account of the country's urgent preparations for war increases the sense of political unrest. Another important function of this scene is to suggest the nature of the old order which existed in Denmark when Hamlet's father was alive, an order which has been superseded by a very different set of values now that Claudius is on the throne. *Valiant Hamlet* emerges as a man of honour who settled disputes such as that with Fortinbras (the elder) of Norway by personal combat. Claudius, in contrast, governs with ruthless self-interest.

Links

For more on the relationship between **plots** and **sub-plots** in plays, see page 83.

Checkpoint 1

The political instability in England eventually led to what important event, some 35 years later?

Links

Political instability is also an important element in Shakespeare's **history plays** (see pages 128–9).

Take note

Claudius is able to succeed his brother because Denmark had an elective system of kingship, which meant that power did not pass automatically to the king's son.

Hamlet is usually said to be **indecisive**. Commanded by the ghost to avenge his father's death he delays and procrastinates, allowing Claudius to protect his position and move against him. However, it is in his lengthy reflections on his situation that we find Hamlet's most penetrating insights into the human condition and the moral choices he must make. Moreover, when Hamlet finally becomes a brutal and effective man of action, **some commentators feel that he adopts standards of behaviour his better nature has previously rejected**. With Claudius-like cunning he arranges for his treacherous friends Rosencrantz and Guildenstern to be executed, and feels no remorse: *They are not near my conscience.*

Hamlet belongs to the genre of **revenge tragedy**, popular in Shakespeare's time. In revenge tragedies the hero seeks vengeance, often spurred on by the ghost of a murdered relative or loved one. Typical elements of the genre that are present in *Hamlet* include a play-within-the-play, madness (both feigned and real), and a scene set in a graveyard.

Antony And Cleopatra

Antony And Cleopatra, one of Shakespeare's **Roman history plays**, is a **tragedy of love**: Antony's downfall is caused by his relationship with Cleopatra. Within the play, **Egypt and Rome represent opposing sets of values**: Egypt is associated with emotional indulgence and the pursuit of personal fulfilment, Rome with efficiency, self-discipline and emotional repression. **Antony is unable to reconcile the two**, abandoning his responsibilities as a Roman triumvir in order to continue his relationship with Cleopatra, Queen of Egypt. Shakespeare offers us contrasting evaluations of this relationship. The play opens with the Roman view, Philo preparing us for Antony's entrance by declaring that we are about to see a great general *transform'd/Into a strumpet's fool*. But moments later Antony is on stage with Cleopatra, asserting that *the nobleness of life/Is to do thus*. Using evidence from the rest of the play, a convincing argument could be constructed to support either viewpoint – and this is perhaps Shakespeare's point: he shows us Antony's dilemma, but does not pretend that it can be resolved.

Checkpoint 2

Can you name any other **revenge tragedies** from this period?

Checkpoint 2

What was a **triumvir**?

Exam preparation   answers: page 145

Text C on page 143 is the opening of *Antony And Cleopatra*. With close reference to Shakespeare's use of language, consider the significance of this extract in relation to the play as a whole.

Shakespeare's romances

The final plays we shall look at in this chapter are the four plays that are often called **romances**.

Overview

The four Shakespeare plays commonly known as **romances** were all written towards the end of his career as a playwright: *The Winter's Tale*, *The Tempest*, *Pericles* and *Cymbeline*. The first two of these are the plays most often set for AS or A2 study.

The plays are not called romances because they are about love (although love is an important element in all four plays), but because they tell stories which involve **magical and mysterious events**. Characters and settings are less realistic than in earlier works, and combine with bizarre, miraculous plot developments to give the plays a fairy-tale quality.

Shakespeare's romances have also been described as tragicomedies, because they establish situations where there is the **potential for tragedy**, then **end happily in an atmosphere of harmony, order and reconciliation**. Another link between the plays is that they usually focus on a **family which is divided** in some way, then **re-united** at the close of the play. The **younger generation**, who often find themselves in conflict with their elders, are seen as the **agents of regeneration and renewal**, and there is an emphasis in the plays on children making up for the wrongs committed by their parents.

Shakespeare's approach to **characterisation** is different in these plays. As mentioned above, the characters are less believable and they lack the complex individuality of Shakespeare's tragic heroes. This was clearly intentional, and it seems that Shakespeare was more interested in what these characters represented than in presenting them as credible, fully rounded people. He often seems to be striving in the romances for clarity and simplicity, and characters and events are used more explicitly than before to symbolise particular feelings and values.

The Winter's Tale

The Winter's Tale is very much a play of two halves, in which **winter** contrasts with **spring**, **tragedy** with **comedy**, and **death** with **rebirth**. In the first half of the play, Leontes's irrational jealousy has tragic consequences, some real and some only apparent. He is the king of Sicilia and in the opening scene begins to suspect his wife Hermione of adultery with his lifelong friend Polixenes, the king of Bohemia. He imprisons Hermione and tries unsuccessfully to engineer Polixenes's death. Hermione is pregnant; Leontes is convinced the child is not his, and when his daughter is born he orders that she be taken to a remote spot and left to die. Leontes's young son Mamillius, who has been forcibly separated from his mother, falls ill and dies, and Hermione collapses on hearing the news. Leontes is told she is dead and suddenly comes to his senses, acknowledging Hermione's innocence and vowing to spend the rest of his life mourning his dead wife and son. His baby daughter Perdita has already been taken away and she is abandoned on the shores of Bohemia.

Links

As explained in a 'Take note' on page 114, these four plays were not in fact classified as **romances** until the 19th century. It was felt that these plays were 'different' from Shakespeare's other plays, and did not comfortably fit into the other categories (history, tragedy, comedy).

Checkpoint 1

Name one or more Shakespeare **tragedy** in which, as in the romances, **family division** is an important theme.

Checkpoint 2

Can you name five of Shakespeare's **tragic heroes**?

Sixteen years pass, and we move into the second phase of the play. The emphasis now is on **regeneration** and **hope**, and there is much more **comedy**. Perdita, who has been brought up by a shepherd, has met and fallen in love with Florizel, the son of Polixenes. We see them at a sheep-shearing feast, where the joy and exuberance of rural life contrast strongly with the deadly hatred and suspicion of Leontes's court. However, the lovers have to flee to Sicilia when Polixenes opposes their relationship. There Perdita's true identity is discovered. Leontes is joyfully reunited with his long-lost daughter, and with his estranged friend Polixenes, who now welcomes his son's marriage to Perdita. In a magical ending to the play, Leontes also learns that his wife Hermione is alive. He is shown a 'statue' of her, which is revealed to be the living Hermione, who has remained hidden from him since her apparent death. Leontes has atoned for his wrongdoings and has grown through his suffering. His family, and the courts of Sicilia and Bohemia, have been reunited by the love of Perdita and Florizel, who as the younger generation represent new hope and new life.

The Tempest ●●●

Family divisions are also **healed by the younger generation** in *The Tempest*, Shakespeare's last play as sole author. The play is set on a remote, mysterious island where Prospero has lived for 12 years with his daughter Miranda. Before arriving on the island he had been ousted from his position as the Duke of Milan by his brother Antonio. When a ship sails close to the island, carrying Antonio, King Alonso of Naples (who had helped to overthrow Prospero) and Alonso's heir Ferdinand, Prospero uses magic powers to conjure up a storm and the ship is wrecked on the island. His former enemies are now at his mercy. Ferdinand has been separated from his companions and they presume he has drowned. He and Miranda fall in love, and at the close of the play Prospero forgives his brother and reunites Alonso and his lost son.

Many recent commentators on the play have examined the theme of **colonisation**, drawing parallels between the island setting and the new lands discovered and settled in Shakespeare's time. Prospero has enslaved the island's sole native inhabitant, Caliban, a strange, barely human creature who is the son of a witch. It could be argued that Shakespeare uses the relationship between Prospero and Caliban to explore the morality of colonial exploitation.

Checkpoint 3

The second half of the play has a strong **pastoral** element. What does this mean?

Take note

As is often the case with Shakespeare, the play's 'happy ending' is somewhat ambiguous. In particular, there is some doubt about the extent to which Hermione forgives Leontes.

Take note

As explained on page 114, after writing *The Tempest* Shakespeare collaborated with John Fletcher in the writing of *Henry VIII* and *The Two Noble Kinsmen*.

Exam preparation

If you are studying one of Shakespeare's romances, write an essay in which you consider the contribution that magic and mystery make to the play.

Critical approaches to Shakespeare

Take note

Make sure you know whether your examining board specification identifies awareness of different interpretations as a specific **assessment objective** for your Shakespeare module.

Watch out!

Remember **'criticism'** in this context simply means writing which analyses and interprets literature – the critic's view is not necessarily 'critical' in a negative sense.

Links

For more on different critical approaches to literature, and advice on how to make use of them in answers, see pages 162–5.

Checkpoint 1

Explain the meaning of the term **status quo**.

When you write about the Shakespeare play you have studied, it might be important for you to show an awareness of how the play as a whole, or particular aspects of it, might be **interpreted** in different ways. Traditionally, the main approach to the plays has involved looking closely at the **characters**, but a major shift in criticism occurred in the closing decades of the 20th century, when there began to be a strong emphasis on the **social, political and historical contexts** of the plays.

Traditional criticism

Since they were first performed, Shakespeare's plays have been interpreted by critics in many different ways. Notable pre-20th century critics of Shakespeare include **Samuel Johnson** in the 18th century and **Samuel Taylor Coleridge** in the 19th. Johnson tended to look for a positive **moral purpose** in the plays, arguing for example that the ending of *King Lear* was 'contrary to the natural ideas of justice'. The major critic of the early 20th century was **A.C. Bradley**, whose approach was very much **character-based**. In his book *Shakespearean Tragedy* (originally a series of university lectures) he wrote sympathetically about Shakespeare's tragic heroes, stressing their nobility of spirit and trying to identify the tragic flaws or weaknesses that led to their downfall. Like Johnson, Bradley drew **moral lessons** from the plays, interpreting them from an essentially Christian perspective. His approach (sometimes known as **character criticism**) has remained influential, but the main weaknesses of it are that there is a danger of writing about the characters as if they were real people, and other important aspects of the plays (such as ways in which they might reflect the attitudes and values of Shakespeare's time) tend to be ignored.

New historicism and cultural materialism

New historicism and **cultural materialism** are recent (late 20th century) schools of criticism that emphasise the importance of **historical contexts**, identifying connections between the plays and political events and documents of Shakespeare's time.

New historicist criticism is mostly American and usually regards Shakespeare as essentially a supporter of the status quo, writing plays which stress the importance of order within society and oppose those who threaten it. Shakespeare's history plays, for example, are viewed by most new historicist critics as reinforcing the Tudor version of England's recent history (Elizabeth was a Tudor monarch). At a time of potential political instability, they argue, the plays also warn of the dangers of rebellion.

Cultural materialism is associated with a group of British critics. It focuses more on how the plays demonstrate the vulnerability of those in power, and the existence of resistance to the authority of the state.

It also looks at how changes in society cause Shakespeare's plays to be understood and interpreted in different ways.

Feminist criticism ●●●

Another critical movement that emerged in the late 20th century was **feminism**. Feminist approaches to Shakespeare focus on the portrayal of women characters, and on whether the plays reinforce or subvert traditional gender roles. Elizabethan and Jacobean society was strongly **patriarchal** (male-dominated) and women had limited status and power. Some critics argue that Shakespeare's plays reflect and endorse the view that women are inferior. Other feminist commentators believe Shakespeare is more sympathetic to women, and more critical of traditional sexist attitudes.

A feminist reading of *Antony And Cleopatra*, for example, would consider closely Cleopatra's role in the play, including her relationships with male characters such as Antony and Caesar, and with other female characters, especially her handmaidens. There is also Caesar's sister Octavia, who is used as a political pawn by both Caesar and Antony. Another relevant aspect of the play is the Roman concept of masculinity: Antony's passionate relationship with Cleopatra is considered unmanly by most of the Roman characters, and Lepidus's sensitivity, and affection for Antony, are ridiculed on the same grounds.

Psychoanalytic criticism ●●●

Psychoanalytic criticism developed out of psychoanalysis, an approach to the understanding of human behaviour pioneered in the first half of the 20th century by Sigmund Freud. He explored how an individual's personality is influenced by unconscious psychological factors, such as repressed memories or desires. A psychoanalytic approach to a play would consider the unconscious motives of characters (and perhaps of the author). Psychoanalytic critics have for example argued that certain of Shakespeare's characters, such as Iago in *Othello* and Antonio in *The Merchant of Venice*, have a latent homosexuality. They also look for evidence of classic psychoanalytic conditions, such as the Oedipus complex (a son's suppressed desire to displace his father as the sexual partner of his mother).

> **Checkpoint 2**
>
> What does *'subvert'* mean here?

> **Checkpoint 3**
>
> Which one of Shakespeare's tragic heroes is often said to suffer from an Oedipus complex?

> **Exam preparation**
>
> Choose one of the following critical approaches and explain how it might be used to interpret the Shakespeare play you are studying: new historicism; feminist criticism; psychoanalytic criticism.

Analysing Shakespeare extracts

Examination questions on Shakespeare often involve the analysis of extracts from the plays. Here is some advice on tackling this kind of question.

Watch out!

Shakespeare extract questions take different forms, depending on the examining board specification. For example, sometimes analysis of an extract is a starting-point for a more general essay on the play as a whole. Make sure you know the kind of question you will be set.

Watch out!

'Context' here does not mean the broader context (social, historical etc.) of the text.

Checkpoint 1

Name another Shakespeare play which has two contrasting locations.

Context

Usually a good way to get started is to consider the **context** of the extract in relation to the play as a whole. Ask yourself *When*, *Where*, *Who* and *What*:

→ **When** in the play does the extract occur? What has led up to it? Is this some kind of turning-point in the play? In broad terms, how is the extract important to the development of the play's plot, characters or themes?

→ **Where** is the extract set? This is not necessarily significant, but it may be. In *Othello*, for example, there are important differences between the two locations of Venice and Cyprus. Venice is associated with order and restraint, whereas in Cyprus there is disorder and violence.

→ **Who** is speaking? Use your knowledge of the characters to help your understanding of the extract. If more than one character speaks, what kind of relationship do the characters involved have? Are there characters who do not speak but who are also present?

→ **What** is the extract about? You obviously need to understand what is going on at a very simple level (e.g. 'Caesar has received a letter from Egypt and responds to the news it contains about Antony'), but you also need to consider the extract's deeper meaning and significance (see 'Content' below).

Content

→ How does the extract develop our understanding of **characters and their relationships**, and of the **themes** in the play? Don't just 'tell the story'. You need to **comment** on the characters' words and actions.

→ Consider the **dramatic effect** that an extract has. Note that 'dramatic' here doesn't have its everyday sense of exciting and out of the ordinary. It refers to the effects that are achieved when the play is performed in front of an audience.

→ If the extract is a passage of **dialogue**, how do the characters **interact**?

→ If it is a **soliloquy**, what is revealed about the character's innermost thoughts?

→ **Make connections with the rest of the play**, especially if the question you are answering specifies that you should do this. Look for similarities and contrasts with other parts of the play, and think about the significance of the extract in relation to what has preceded it and what happens later.

→ Are any aspects of the extract open to **alternative interpretations**? For example, some commentators argue that Othello's final speech demonstrates the nobility of his character, while others believe it confirms that he has a deluded view of himself. Showing an awareness of alternative readings – as well as giving your own response – will gain you credit.

→ As explained above, it is important to consider the **context** the extract has within the play as a whole. However, it may also be relevant (and for some exam board specifications it will be essential) to refer to the play's broader political, historical or literary contexts (see pages 116–17).

Language ●●●

Questions usually specify that you should look closely at the **language** of the extract. The guidance given on pages 118–23 is relevant here. Points to consider include:

→ Is the extract **prose** or **poetry**, or a mixture of the two? You may be able to comment on the likely reason for this (see pages 118–19).
→ If **blank verse** is used, does the metre cause significant words to be stressed? Is the metre disturbed or altered at any point, and if so why does this happen? If the metre is steady and regular, why might this be appropriate?
→ How does the **vocabulary** that is used reflect the attitudes and feelings of the characters who are speaking?
→ What **imagery** (similes/metaphors) is present? What effect does it have? Are there links between any of the images that are present and the imagery found elsewhere in the play?
→ What about the effects achieved by **individual words**? What connotations do particular words have? Are they emotive, shocking, evocative, powerful? Are any **key words** present – words that are important because they occur repeatedly in the play as a whole (e.g. the word *nothing* in *King Lear*)?
→ Are any **rhetorical** devices used, such as repetition, antithesis, wordplay and hyperbole?
→ Is the **sound** of the words important at any point? Are any devices such as alliteration, onomatopoeia, assonance and sibilance used? (Remember you should only mention these if you are confident they have a particular effect, and you can explain what this effect is.)

Staging ●●●

How would the extract be **presented on stage**? Try to visualise it (if you have seen a performance or watched a video of the play, this will obviously help). Try to identify specific aspects of the extract that would be enhanced by a live performance.

Take note

Make sure you know whether knowledge of alternative interpretations is one of the specific **assessment objectives** for your Shakespeare question (see pages 6–7).

Checkpoint 2

Give one reason why Shakespeare sometimes uses **prose** rather than poetry.

Checkpoint 3

Explain what is meant by **blank verse**.

Exam preparation

See pages 129, 133 and 135 for practice questions on Shakespeare extracts.

Practice Shakespeare extracts

Take note

The extracts below are for use with the practice exam questions for this chapter.

Take note

The question for this extract is on page 129.

Examiner's secrets

Think about how an audience might respond to this speech by Richard.

Text A

Was ever woman in this humour woo'd?
Was ever woman in this humour won?
I'll have her, but I will not keep her long.
What, I that kill'd her husband and his father:
To take her in her heart's extremest hate,
With curses in her mouth, tears in her eyes,
The bleeding witness of her hatred by,
Having God, her conscience, and these bars against me –
And I, no friends to back my suit at all;
But the plain devil and dissembling looks –
And yet to win her, all the world to nothing!
Ha!
Hath she forgot already that brave prince,
Edward, her lord, whom I, some three months since,
Stabb'd in my angry mood at Tewkesbury?
A sweeter and a lovelier gentleman,
Fram'd in the prodigality of Nature,
Young, valiant, wise, and no doubt right royal,
The spacious world cannot again afford.
And will she yet debase her eyes on me,
That cropp'd the golden prime of this sweet prince,
And made her widow to a woeful bed?
On me, whose all not equals Edward's moiety?
On me, that halts and am misshapen thus?
My dukedom to a beggarly denier,
I do mistake my person all this while!
Upon my life, she finds – although I cannot –
Myself to be a marvellous proper man.
I'll be at charges for a looking-glass,
And entertain a score or two of tailors
To study fashions to adorn my body:
Since I am crept in favour with myself,
I will maintain it with some little cost.
But first I'll turn yon fellow in his grave,
And then return, lamenting, to my love.
Shine out, fair sun, till I have bought a glass,
That I may see my shadow as I pass.

Take note

The question for this extract is on page 133.

Text B

DESDEMONA: Wouldst thou do such a deed for all the world?
EMILIA: The world's a huge thing: it is a great price for a small vice.
DESDEMONA: In troth, I think thou wouldst not.
EMILIA: In troth I think I should, and undo't when I had done it. Marry,
I would not do such a thing for a joint ring, nor for measures of lawn,
nor for gowns, petticoats, nor caps, nor any petty exhibition. But for all
the whole world! Ud's pity, who would not make her husband a cuckold,
to make him a monarch? I should venture purgatory for't.

DESDEMONA: Beshrew me, if I would do such a wrong for the whole world!

EMILIA: Why, the wrong is but a wrong I'th'world; and having the world for your labour, 'tis a wrong in your own world, and you might quickly make it right.

DESDEMONA: I do not think there is any such woman.

EMILIA: Yes, a dozen: and as many to th'vantage as would store the world they played for.

But I do think it is their husbands' faults
If wives do fall. Say that they slack their duties,
And pour our treasures into foreign laps;
Or else break out in peevish jealousies,
Throwing restraint upon us; or say they strike us,
Or scant our former having in despite –
Why, we have galls, and though we have some grace,
Yet have we some revenge. Let husbands know
Their wives have sense like them: they see and smell,
And have their palates both for sweet and sour
As husbands have. What is it that they do,
When they change us for others? Is it sport?
I think it is. And doth affection breed it?
I think it doth. Is't frailty that thus errs?
It is so too. And have not we affections,
Desires for sport, and frailty, as men have?
Then let them use us well: else let them know
The ills we do, their ills instruct us so.

Text C ●●●

PHILO: Nay, but this dotage of our general's
O'erflows the measure: those his goodly eyes,
That o'er the files and musters of the war
Have glow'd like plated Mars, now bend, now turn
The office and devotion of their view
Upon a tawny front: his captain's heart,
Which in the scuffles of great fights hath burst
The buckles on his breast, reneges all temper,
And is become the bellows and the fan
To cool a gipsy's lust.
[Flourish. Enter ANTONY, CLEOPATRA, her Ladies, the Train, with Eunuchs fanning her.]
                    Look, where they come:
Take but good note, and you shall see in him
The triple pillar of the world transform'd
Into a strumpet's fool: behold and see.

Take note

The question for this extract is on page 135.

Examiner's secrets

Think about how Antony is described, and the language used to refer to Cleopatra.

Answers
Shakespeare

Shakespeare: study tips

Checkpoints

1 A genre is a *type* of writing, music, film etc. Drama is a literary genre, but within this there are other smaller genres, including, for example, comedies and tragedies.
2 See page 115 for a list of Shakespeare's plays, grouped by genre.
3 The broad definition of 'imagery' is any aspect of a text that appeals to the reader's senses. The term is also used to refer more specifically to the use in literature of similes and metaphors.

Shakespeare: an overview

Checkpoints

1 *Shakespeare In Love.*
2 The features, techniques, customs etc. normally associated with each genre.
3 Queen Elizabeth I and King James I.

Shakespeare: contexts

Checkpoints

1 Containing the essence of something; a perfect example.
2 Other notable playwrights of the period include Christopher Marlowe, John Webster and Ben Jonson.
3 An extended speech by a character, heard by the audience but not by the other characters.

Shakespeare's language: verse and prose

Checkpoints

1 The sonnet.
2 He means that Cassio knows the theory of soldiership and can talk about it, but lacks practical military skills and experience.
3 The image reflects Desdemona's innocence and moral purity.

Shakespeare's language: rhetoric

Checkpoints

1 'Empty rhetoric' implies the speech uses techniques that are calculated to impress an audience, but lacks sincerity or depth of meaning. A 'rhetorical question' is a question that does not seek or expect an answer.
2 The play on words involves the similar sound of 'son' and 'sun'. The king, Edward IV, is a 'son' of York, but the image of summer is suggested by the word's similarity to 'sun'.
3 Cassio idealises Desdemona. He speaks reverently of her and appears in awe of her beauty.

Shakespeare's language: other aspects

Checkpoints

1 Imagery can be visual (appealing to our sense of sight); auditory (hearing); tactile (touch); gustatory (taste); olfactory (smell).

2 Irony can mean stating the opposite of what is meant. It can also refer to an event having consequences that are the opposite of those expected or intended.
3 Iago.

Shakespeare: important themes

Checkpoints

1 King James I.
2 An idea, situation, character etc. that is the direct opposite of another.
3 A statement, situation etc. which appears contradictory but which is nevertheless true.

Shakespeare on stage

Checkpoints

1 Because it is while he is staying at Macbeth's castle that he is murdered.
2 A 'soliloquy' is a lengthy speech delivered by a character who is often alone on stage. It is heard by the audience but not by other characters. 'Asides' are much shorter. A character turns away mid-conversation and says something that only the audience hear.
3 Hamlet is a revenger. Iago and Richard III might be described as malcontents (characters who are dissatisfied with their situation and deliberately incite trouble as a result).

Shakespeare's history plays

Checkpoints

1 Punishment by God for some wrongdoing.
2 *The Merry Wives Of Windsor.*
3 Traditional or conventional; approved of by those in positions of established authority.

Exam preparation

As Richard himself points out, he has wooed Lady Anne despite having *kill'd her husband and his father*. In claiming to love her, he is guilty of a monstrous deception, but it is difficult for an audience not to find his delight in his own success engaging: *Was ever woman in this humour wooed?* He is aware that he has triumphed against all the odds: as well as murdering her husband and father-in-law, his misshapen appearance contrasts with that of her husband, a *sweet prince* who died in his *golden prime*. Richard's self-deprecating humour is seen when he jokes that he must be more attractive than he thought, and should get himself a looking-glass and some new clothes. But his ruthless self-interest is also evident: his active mind is already thinking ahead, and he says with casual brutality, *I'll have her, but I will not keep her long.*

Shakespeare's comedies

Checkpoints

1 Relationships which have strong similarities and which tend to develop in similar ways.

2 'Conservative' implies conventional, conforming to traditional views and attitudes; generally opposed to change. 'Subversive' implies rebellious, though in an underhand way; undermining society, established attitudes etc. from within.

3 Tragicomedies.

Shakespeare's tragedies 1

Checkpoints

1 Other Roman history plays include *Julius Caesar* and *Titus Andronicus*.

2 'Polarity' means having opposite ideas, attitudes, characteristics etc.

3 Final speeches in Shakespeare's major tragedies are delivered by: Escalus, Prince of Verona (*Romeo And Juliet*); Fortinbras (*Hamlet*); Lodovico (*Othello*); Albany (*King Lear*); Malcolm (*Macbeth*); Octavius Caesar (*Antony And Cleopatra*); Aufidius (*Coriolanus*).

Exam preparation

Desdemona's purity and innocence are apparent in this extract. She cannot believe there are women who would betray their husbands: *I do not think there is any such woman*. She would never be unfaithful herself: *Beshrew me, if I would do such a wrong for the whole world*. Emilia contrasts strongly with Desdemona. In her discussion of women's behaviour she shows she is more experienced and more realistic. When Desdemona expresses her belief that there cannot be wives who would be unfaithful, she replies, *Yes, a dozen*. Her attitude to morality is practical and down to earth: she says she would consider being unfaithful if the reward were high enough. When Desdemona asks, *Wouldst thou do such a deed for all the world?* she says, *The world's a huge thing: it is a great price for a small vice*. In her important speech at the end of the extract, Emilia goes on to argue that if women are unfaithful it is usually their husbands' fault. If husbands are themselves unfaithful (if they *pour our treasures into foreign laps*), or if they are jealous or hit their wives (clearly references to Othello), their wives are entitled to *revenge*. She calls upon husbands to recognise that their wives have the same feelings and desires as them, and are tempted to stray just as they are. She issues a warning: men should remain faithful, or their wives will follow their example: *Then let them use us well: else let them know/The ills we do, their ills instruct us so*. This early expression of a belief in sexual equality strikes a chord with modern audiences. At the same time, we imagine that marriage to Iago has hardened Emilia's attitude towards men.

Shakespeare's tragedies 2

Checkpoints

1 The English Civil War.

2 Other notable revenge tragedies from the period include *The Spanish Tragedy* (Thomas Kyd); *The Jew Of Malta* (Christopher Marlowe); *The Revenger's Tragedy* (of disputed authorship, but usually attributed to Thomas Middleton).

3 For a period in ancient Rome, governing power was divided between three men, each of whom was known as a 'triumvir'.

Exam preparation

Philo's speech presents a Roman view of Antony and his relationship with Cleopatra. There is admiration for Antony's military prowess, evident in the comparison with *Mars*, which presents him as a godlike figure, and the suggestion of superhuman strength and energy, created through the use of alliteration: *his captain's heart,/Which in the scuffles of great fights hath burst/The buckles on his breast*. However, in his relationship with Cleopatra, Antony is guilty of physical and emotional self-indulgence, a lack of self-restraint: his passion for her *O'erflows the measure* and his heart *reneges all temper* (rejects all self-control). The relationship humiliates him: a great Roman triumvir, a *triple pillar of the world*, has been reduced to a *strumpet's fool*. The rest of the play presents us with other characters who support Philo's view, and with some evidence to justify it. However, set against the values of Rome are those of Egypt, where personal fulfilment is placed above the demands of political power and military honour. Shakespeare makes plain the emotional sterility of Rome, and the play as a whole contains much to challenge Philo's view.

Shakespeare's romances

Checkpoints

1 *King Lear*; *Hamlet*; *Romeo And Juliet*.

2 Hamlet; Othello; King Lear; Macbeth; Antony; Romeo; Coriolanus.

3 'Pastoral' means associated with country life, especially if the life of the countryside is romanticised or idealised.

Critical approaches to Shakespeare

Checkpoints

1 The status quo is the established state of affairs, especially in relation to politics.

2 To subvert is to undermine from within, often in a hidden or secretive way.

3 Hamlet.

Analysing Shakespeare extracts

Checkpoints

1 In *Antony And Cleopatra* there are contrasts between Rome and Egypt.

2 Prose is often used for lower class characters, comic scenes or informal conversations.

3 Blank verse consists of unrhymed iambic pentameter lines of poetry. 'Iambic pentameter' means there are five pairs of syllables in each line, with the second syllable in each pair stressed.

Revision checklist
Shakespeare

By the end of this chapter you should be able to:

1 List and briefly explain the four genres into which Shakespeare's plays are traditionally grouped.	Confident	Not confident **Revise** pages 114–15
2 Understand the key elements of the literary and historical contexts relevant to the study of Shakespeare.	Confident	Not confident **Revise** pages 116–17
3 Explain why and how Shakespeare makes use of both verse and prose in his plays.	Confident	Not confident **Revise** pages 118–19
4 List six or more rhetorical techniques commonly used by Shakespeare.	Confident	Not confident **Revise** pages 120–21
5 Explain and illustrate the importance of recurring imagery in Shakespeare's plays.	Confident	Not confident **Revise** page 122
6 List and explain four or more key themes that often appear in Shakespeare's plays.	Confident	Not confident **Revise** pages 124–25
7 List and explain six or more Elizabethan stage conventions that are important to an understanding of Shakespeare's plays.	Confident	Not confident **Revise** pages 126–27
8 Identify the main characteristics of Shakespeare's history plays.	Confident	Not confident **Revise** page 128
9 Identify the main characteristics of Shakespeare's comedies.	Confident	Not confident **Revise** pages 130–31
10 Identify the main characteristics of Shakespeare's problem plays.	Confident	Not confident **Revise** pages 130–31
11 Identify the main characteristics of Shakespeare's tragedies.	Confident	Not confident **Revise** pages 132–33
12 Identify the main characteristics of Shakespeare's romances.	Confident	Not confident **Revise** page 136
13 Offer an overview of how critical approaches to Shakespeare have changed and developed.	Confident	Not confident **Revise** page 138
14 Explain in relation to Shakespeare the terms 'traditional criticism', 'new historicism', 'cultural materialism', 'feminist criticism' and 'psychoanalytic criticism'.	Confident	Not confident **Revise** pages 138–39
15 Approach with confidence the analysis of an extract from one of Shakespeare's plays.	Confident	Not confident **Revise** pages 140–41

Contexts and interpretations

This chapter has two main elements. Most of the sections relate to the **contexts** of literary texts. The term 'contexts' essentially means the background influences on a text. As explained in the opening section, there are various kinds of context, including, for example, the historical period when the text was written and relevant aspects of the author's life. Most of the remaining sections on contexts cover different historical periods, from medieval times up to the 20th century. Knowledge of contexts will help your understanding of all of the texts that you are studying, but it is especially important in relation to certain specified texts (your teacher will tell you which ones, or you can check your exam board specification to find out).

The rest of the chapter is about **interpretations**. As with contexts, this has particular relevance to certain of the texts you study. You will be expected to show an awareness of different readings of these texts. This chapter explains what this involves, and the kinds of interpretation that might be relevant.

Exam themes

→ Understanding how contexts influence literary texts

→ Knowledge and understanding of different interpretations of literary texts

Topic checklist

AS ○ A2 ●	AQA/A	AQA/B	EDEXCEL	OCR	WJEC	CCEA
Types of context	○●	○●	○●	○●	○●	○●
Medieval contexts	○	○●	●	○●	●	○●
Renaissance contexts	○●	○●	○●	○●	○●	○●
Restoration, Augustan and Romantic contexts	○●	○●	○●	○●	○●	○●
Victorian contexts	○●	○●	○●	○●	○●	○●
20th century contexts	○●	○●	○●	○●	○●	○●
Using critical interpretations	○●	○●	○●	○●	○●	○●
Critical approaches 1	○●	○●	○●	○●	○●	○●
Critical approaches 2	○●	○●	○●	○●	○●	○●
Practice extracts	○●	○●	○●	○●	○●	○●

Types of context

Take note

For some of the books you study at AS or A2, an understanding of the text's context is a specific requirement (see 'Writing about contexts' at the end of this section).

Take note

The example of Shakespeare's history plays also illustrates another kind of period context: factors relevant to **the period when the text is set**. Your understanding of *Richard III*, for example, would be helped by an outline knowledge of major historical events during the period covered by the play.

Checkpoint 1

In particular, Dickens's novels about childhood are usually seen as partly autobiographical. Can you name any of these?

Context is a very broad term covering a variety of **background influences** on a text. Many of these relate to the **period** when the text was written, but there are other kinds of context as well. Some of the main types of context are listed below, arranged into four broad categories.

Period contexts

This is often the most significant type of context. It includes **historical**, **political**, **social** and **cultural** aspects of **the period when the text was written**. Sometimes the relevance of this kind of context is obvious: if you are studying First World War poetry, it would clearly be helpful to have some knowledge of how the war started, what people thought about it at the time, what conditions were like for soldiers fighting in the war and so on. With other texts, the relevance of contemporary circumstances is not so evident. Shakespeare's history plays, written at the end of the 16th century, describe events that occurred more than a hundred years earlier. However, many critics believe Shakespeare uses the plays to comment indirectly on the political situation in England during his own time.

Social conditions and contemporary **attitudes** can be important. Oscar Wilde's novel *The Picture Of Dorian Gray* gives a vivid sense of the gulf between rich and poor that existed in Victorian London, while the book's veiled references to homosexuality reflect a time when homosexuality was illegal.

Author contexts

Aspects of the **author's life** might be reflected in the text. As mentioned earlier (see page 66), there are often autobiographical elements in Charles Dickens's novels. A writer's **attitudes** might change over time, and this can be reflected in contrasts between early and later works. The **gender**, **social class** or **race** of the writer is significant, especially when viewed in relation to their wider social background: Anne Bronte's *The Tenant Of Wildfell Hall* is regarded as an early feminist novel by a woman writer working within a patriarchal society.

Literary contexts

There are several kinds of **literary context**:

→ The context of an extract in terms of its **relationship to the rest of the text**. The full significance of a chapter in a novel, for instance, can only be understood if the rest of the book is taken into account.
→ The context of a text in terms of its **relationship to other texts**. These might be texts by the same author or by other writers. For example, Chaucer's *Canterbury Tales* often have connections to each other, so that it is sometimes possible to see one Tale as a response to another. A text might be influenced by another writer's work, or might deliberately parody another text.

→ The **genre** of a text. The main literary genres are poetry, prose and drama, but within these broad groupings there are more specific genres: the sonnet is a particular kind of poem, tragedy a particular kind of play. Each of these genres has its own traditions and conventions, which a writer may follow or intentionally subvert.

→ **Literary movements** Keats and Blake, for example, are **Romantic** poets, and if you are studying these writers you should find out about the ideas and attitudes associated with Romanticism.

→ The **language** of the text in relation to the ways literary language has changed and developed. Traditional poetry has a metre based on the iambic pentameter, but this is much less common in contemporary poetry.

Checkpoint 2

What does **'subvert'** mean here?

Checkpoint 3

What is the **iambic pentameter**?

Reader/audience contexts ●●●

These kinds of context are partly to do with **how readers and audiences receive or experience a text**. For instance, it is important to know that Chaucer's poems would usually have been read out to audiences, and that Dickens's novels were originally serialised and published in instalments. The **identity** of an audience can also be important. Who was Shakespeare writing for – who attended his plays, and what kinds of beliefs, attitudes and prejudices would they have been likely to have? Texts can also mean different things to different readers. A feminist approach to a text will be different from a psychoanalytic or Marxist approach. Readers and audiences change over time as well, and this will inevitably affect the way a text is interpreted.

Take note

In the same way, if you are studying a play, you should obviously try to imagine how it would be performed (and preferably see a production).

Links

This aspect of context is also relevant to the requirement for some texts that you consider how texts can be interpreted differently by different readers. For more on different critical approaches to literature, and alternative interpretations of texts, see pages 160–5.

Writing about contexts ●●●

Here is some advice on writing about contexts:

→ Knowledge of contexts can help your understanding of any text, but it will be **a specific requirement for some of the texts you are studying** – make sure you know what they are.

→ At AS you need to show **'understanding'** of contexts; at A2 you are expected to **'evaluate the significance'** of contextual influences. In other words, at A2 you should try to deal with contexts in a more sophisticated way, assessing their importance.

→ Remember **your primary focus should always be the text itself**. Explain how a knowledge of contexts increases your understanding of it: never write about an author's life, or historical events that occurred when a text was being written, unless you can convincingly show that factors such as these have **influenced the text**.

Exam preparation

Choose a text you are studying which has knowledge of context as a syllabus requirement. Work through the types of context listed above, identifying which are especially relevant to an understanding of the text.

Medieval contexts

The period of European history known as the **Middle Ages** runs roughly from the 12th to the 15th centuries. (The period from the fifth to the 11th centuries is known as the **Dark Ages**, but is also sometimes referred to as the **early Middle Ages**.) If you are studying a writer from this period it will almost certainly be **Geoffrey Chaucer** (*c.*1340–1400), and this section focuses on the social, historical and literary contexts of Chaucer's works.

Overview

Chaucer wrote at a time when English society was still **feudal**, with the landowning nobility at the top of the social hierarchy and the peasants, who worked the land and were almost completely dependent on their masters, at the bottom. The group of pilgrims assembled for the *Canterbury Tales* gives us an idea of the structure of Chaucer's society, with the Knight having the highest status, followed by senior members of the Church and characters such as the Merchant from the newly emerging middle class. The lower class are represented by figures such as the Miller and the Plowman.

Although the *General Prologue* in particular suggests the rigid, hierarchical nature of medieval society, during Chaucer's lifetime there was great **social and political turbulence**. Outbreaks of plague are thought to have wiped out between a third and a half of England's population. This had far-reaching social consequences, including a shortage of labour which encouraged agricultural and other workers to push for higher wages and better conditions. The Peasants' Revolt of 1381 had many causes, and not all of those involved were peasants, but oppressive labour laws and punitive taxation were two of the main grievances. There was also growing disillusionment with the Church, a huge and powerful institution tainted by greed and corruption.

Chaucer's attitude towards all of this unrest is not entirely clear. He moved in royal circles, sets many of his Tales in the world of the aristocracy and makes only a brief, passing reference to the Peasants' Revolt. Given his background it would not be surprising if his outlook was essentially conservative, though there are moments in the Tales when the established social order seems to be challenged, as when the Miller refuses to wait his turn to speak. Chaucer is more outspoken about the Church, using portraits of pilgrims such as the Monk and the Friar to expose the self-interest and lax morality of many ecclesiastics. He also makes it clear that for some of the pilgrims the pilgrimage itself is very much a social occasion rather than an act of worship.

Chaucer's attitude towards the **role and position of women** is also ambiguous. In medieval society men were traditionally dominant, in social and political institutions and also within marriage. Some critics argue that Chaucer supports this, but the Tales also feature several assertive women (notably the Wife of Bath).

Chaucer wrote in **Middle English**, a blend of Old English (or Anglo-Saxon) and newer French words, which entered the language in the centuries following the Norman Conquest of 1066. As explained on

Checkpoint 1

Can you name any other texts or writers from the medieval period?

Checkpoint 2

Why was Canterbury a place of pilgrimage during Chaucer's time?

page 24, Chaucer's exploitation of the differences between these two kinds of vocabulary is an important stylistic feature of the Tales. He also shows a mastery of **rhetoric**, the medieval art of fine writing and effective speaking. Rhetoric was widely taught and studied, and specified a range of stylistic devices that writers might use. Rhetorical features are plentiful in Chaucer's works, but he also on occasion mocks rhetorical techniques by exaggerating or parodying them.

It is important to note that Chaucer was writing within an **oral** tradition. Literature was generally read aloud, as a form of entertainment at social gatherings, especially in royal, aristocratic and other prosperous households.

Take note

An example of a rhetorical technique often used by Chaucer is the **digression**, a deviation from the main narrative of a story.

Checkpoint 3

List some of the ways in which poetry (such as that written by Chaucer) might be influenced by the fact that it was intended to be read aloud.

Timeline (1330–1400) ●●●

	EVENTS	CHAUCER'S LIFE
1330		
	1337 Hundred Years' War (England v. France) begins	
1340		*c.***1340** Chaucer's birth
	1348–49 Plague (the Black Death) kills up to 50% of England's population	
1350		**1350s** Enters royal service
		1359–60 Military service in France. Imprisoned but released after ransom is paid.
1360		**1360s/1370s** Diplomatic missions in Europe
	1362 English becomes the language of Parliament	*c.***1366** Marries Philippa de Roet, lady-in-waiting to the Queen
		1368 Writes *The Book Of The Duchess*
1370		
		1374 Appointed Comptroller of Customs for the port of London
	1377 Death of King Edward III. Richard II becomes king.	**1380** A charge of rape against Chaucer is withdrawn
1380	**1381** The Peasants' Revolt	**1382** Writes *The Parlement Of Fowles*
	1380s First English translations of the Bible (e.g. *The Wycliffe Bible*)	**1380s** Writes *Troilus and Criseyde*
		1380s Begins *Canterbury Tales*
		1389 Appointed Clerk of the King's works
1390		**1391** Appointed deputy forester in Somerset
		1394 Awarded a pension by King Richard II
	1399 King Richard II is forced to abdicate Henry IV becomes king	**1399** Awarded another pension by King Henry IV
1400	**1400** Richard II, imprisoned in Pontefract Castle, is murdered there	**1400** Chaucer dies. Buried in Westminster Abbey

Exam preparation   answers: page xx

If you are studying a medieval text (such as one of Chaucer's *Canterbury Tales*), write an essay in which you consider some of the ways in which the text reflects aspects of medieval society.

Renaissance contexts

The period of European history from the 14th to the 17th centuries is known as the **Renaissance**. The term means 'rebirth' and is appropriate both because the period in many ways marks the beginning of the modern world, and because there was a revival of interest in ancient Greek and Roman philosophy, literature and art. In relation to English literature, the most important years are at the end of the 16th century and the beginning of the 17th. This was the age of Shakespeare, other Elizabethan and Jacobean dramatists such as Christopher Marlowe and John Webster, and the Metaphysical poets.

Overview

The **English Renaissance** was a time of enormous **religious and political upheaval**. In 1534 Henry VIII broke with the Catholic Church in Rome, establishing the Protestant Church of England. This was part of a wider movement against the Catholic Church in Europe (known as the **Reformation**), led by figures such as the German monk Martin Luther. A more questioning attitude towards established beliefs developed, though within England many people (possibly including Shakespeare's parents) maintained a secret allegiance to Catholicism.

Politically, England enjoyed a period of relative stability during the reign of Elizabeth I (1558–1603), and the country's emergence as the most powerful nation in Europe (symbolised by the defeat of the Spanish Armada in 1588) created a mood of national self-confidence. But there was a growing refusal to accept traditional authority: the reign of James I (1603–25) was more troubled, and the struggle for power between parliament and king after his son Charles succeeded to the throne eventually resulted in the **English Civil War**, and the execution of Charles in 1649.

Writers, artists and explorers during the Renaissance are characterised by a restless intellectual energy, and a passion for experimentation and discovery. New lands (especially in the Americas) were found and conquered, and developments in science meant ideas about the nature of the universe were radically altered.

In England, a surge in artistic creativity was especially noticeable in **drama**. England's first theatre was built in 1576, and in the decades that followed Elizabethan and Jacobean playwrights produced many important works. The most significant of these dramatists was of course **William Shakespeare** (1564–1616), whose plays reflect many aspects of his age, from the mirroring of political tensions in the history plays to the exuberance of the comedies. The other important literary genre was **poetry**. Sir Thomas Wyatt, Sir Philip Sidney and Edmund Spenser were important 16th century poets, while **metaphysical poetry** emerged in the early 17th century. This term is used for a group of poets (including John Donne and George Herbert) whose works were usually experimental, notable for their surprising images and for the way intellectual reasoning is applied to emotional experience.

Checkpoint 1

Can you name any plays written by **Christopher Marlowe** and **John Webster**?

Checkpoint 2

Can you name any of the theatres in which **Shakespeare's** plays were first performed?

Links

See pages 116–17 for more on the **contexts** of Shakespeare's plays.

Checkpoint 3

What is **Edmund Spenser's** most famous work?

152

Timeline (1500–1660)

	ENGLISH MONARCHS	EVENTS	LITERATURE
1500			
	1509–47 Henry VIII	1521 Martin Luther excommunicated by the Pope	**Poets** Sir Thomas Wyatt (1503–42) Edmund Spenser (1552–99) Sir Philip Sidney (1554–86)
		1534 Henry VIII breaks with Catholic church, establishes Protestant Church of England	
	1547–53 Edward VI		
1550			
	1553–58 Queen Mary I		
		1584 Virginia, first British colony in America, established	**Elizabethan/Jacobean dramatists**
	1558–1603 Elizabeth I	1588 Defeat of the Spanish Armada	William Shakespeare (1564–1616) Christopher Marlowe (1564–93) Ben Jonson (1572–1637) John Webster (1580–1625)
1600			
	1603–25 James I	1605 Gunpowder Plot (Guy Fawkes and other Catholic conspirators attempt to blow up Parliament)	**Metaphysical poets** John Donne (1572–1631) George Herbert (1593–1633) Andrew Marvell (1621–78)
		1611 Authorised version of the Bible (the 'King James' bible) published	
	1625–49 Charles I	1642–48 English Civil War (royalist supporters of Charles I v. parliamentary forces led by Oliver Cromwell)	John Milton (poet) (1608–74)
		1649 Execution of Charles I During the Interregnum Britain is a republic under Cromwell's leadership	
	1649–60 Interregnum		
1650			
	1660–85 Charles II	1658 Cromwell dies 1660 Parliament invites Charles I's son to return from France – he becomes Charles II	

Exam preparation

answers: page 168

'The Good-morrow', a poem by the Metaphysical poet John Donne is shown on page 42 as Text B. In what ways does a consideration of contexts help your understanding of this poem?

Links

See pages 148–9 for a list of the types of context that might be relevant to this question.

Restoration, Augustan and Romantic contexts

In 1660, 11 years after the execution of Charles I, the monarchy was restored when Parliament invited Charles's son to return from France. He became Charles II, and the period immediately following his accession is known as the **Restoration**. The first half of the 18th century is termed the **Augustan** period, because many English writers of the time identified with the classical writers of ancient Rome, especially poets such as Ovid and Virgil who flourished during the reign of the emperor Caesar Augustus. **Romanticism** was a broad cultural movement that developed in Western Europe and America in the late 18th and early 19th centuries.

Overview

Although England again had a king, the monarchy had lost much of its power. Parliament was more dominant, and within Parliament two major political parties emerged, the Whigs and the Tories. There was no appetite for another revolution or civil war, and instead a desire for order and stability. Literature correspondingly became less challenging and less experimental. **Restoration dramatists** such as William Congreve and William Wycherley wrote clever, witty comedies about the values of upper-class society.

The **Augustan** period is associated with a strong belief in the power of reason. **Poetry** often dealt with public themes, and compared with the first half of the 17th century there is less exploration of personal experience and a greater preoccupation with society, manners and morals. The commitment to order and control is reflected in the extensive use of the **heroic couplet**, a verse form comprising pairs of neatly balanced iambic pentameter lines. This period also saw the rise of the **novel**, with works by Daniel Defoe, Henry Fielding and others contributing to the development of the genre. **Language** itself became more regularised during the 18th century, with the publication of numerous books on English grammar, and of Samuel Johnson's Dictionary, which did much to standardise word meanings and make spelling more consistent.

The **Romantic** period, which runs roughly from 1789 (the year of the French Revolution) to the middle of the 19th century, can be seen partly as a reaction against the attitudes and values of the Augustan age. Writers and philosophers associated with the Romantic movement rejected narrow rationalism; instead, inspired by political revolutions in France and America, they stressed the value of emotional and intellectual freedom. **Poets** such as Wordsworth, Blake and Keats celebrated nature, the individual consciousness and the power of the imagination. The **gothic novel** was a genre that depicted bizarre, irrational settings and events in order to evoke a sense of mystery and terror.

Checkpoint 1

Explain the term **iambic pentameter**.

Checkpoint 2

What is Daniel Defoe's most famous novel?

Checkpoint 3

Can you name any **Gothic novels**?

Timeline (1660–1830)

	EVENTS	LITERATURE
1660	**1660** Restoration of the monarchy **1665** Great Plague **1666** Great Fire of London	**Poets** John Milton (1608–74) John Dryden (1631–1700) John Wilmot, Earl of Rochester (1648–80)
1700		**Restoration dramatists** William Wycherley (1640–1716) Aphra Behn (1640–89) William Congreve (1670–1729) George Farquhar (1678–1707)
	1707 Act of Union unites England and Scotland, creates United Kingdom **1755** Samuel Johnson's *Dictionary of the English Language* published **1769** Richard Arkwright establishes first spinning mill **1775** James Watt invents the steam engine **1776** American Declaration of Independence **1789** French Revolution	**Augustan poetry** Alexander Pope (1688–1744) **Novelists** Daniel Defoe (1660–1731) Samuel Richardson (1689–1761) Henry Fielding (1707–54) Laurence Sterne (1713–68) Jane Austen (1775–1817) Mary Shelley (1797–1851)
1800	**1803–15** Napoleonic Wars **1814** George Stephenson invents the railway engine **1815** Napoleon defeated at Waterloo **1819** Peterloo massacre (violent suppression of a demonstration for workers' rights in Manchester)	**Romantic poets** William Blake (1757–1827) William Wordsworth (1770–1850) Samuel Taylor Coleridge (1776–1849) Lord Byron (1788–1824) Percy Shelley (1792–1822)
1830		John Keats (1795–1821)

Exam preparation

answers: page 168

Text A on page 166 is 'The Schoolboy', a poem by the Romantic poet William Blake. In what ways does a consideration of contexts help your understanding of this poem?

Take note

See pages 148–9 for a list of the types of context that might be relevant to this question.

Victorian contexts

Queen Victoria reigned from 1837 to 1901, though the term **Victorian age** is sometimes used more broadly to refer to the period from 1830 to the end of the 19th century. This is so that the period includes important events which helped to shape it, such as the 1832 Reform Act (see below).

Overview

The 19th century was a time of great **social change**, driven by **industrial development** and **economic advancement**. The population of England more than doubled between 1830 and the end of the century. Much of this population growth was centred on cities such as Manchester and Birmingham, where the effects of increasing industrialisation were most obviously apparent. The term **Industrial Revolution** is used for the technological developments which began in the 18th century and continued into the 19th. Hundreds of factories were built, the railway network was extended across Britain and people increasingly lived in densely populated urban conurbations.

Conditions in the factories were harsh, with long working hours, low wages and unsafe machinery. Children worked alongside their parents, and accidents were common. Life outside work was equally unpleasant, with cramped and unhealthy housing. Attempts to improve the lot of the poor met with some success, though progress was slow. Parliament passed a series of Factory Acts, mostly to regulate the working conditions of women and children. The Poor Law Amendment Act of 1834 established workhouses to accommodate those who were homeless and destitute. However, the intention behind the Act was partly to discourage people from becoming a burden upon society, by deliberately making conditions within the workhouses harsh and unpleasant. The early chapters of Charles Dickens's *Oliver Twist* give a vivid impression of what these workhouses were like.

There was also slow **political reform**. The 1832 Reform Act addressed some of the corruption and inequity of the parliamentary system. It gave parliamentary representation to some areas of the country that had not previously had it, and made the rules governing the entitlement to vote more consistent. However, women were still denied the vote, as were approximately 80% of the male population, because the right to vote was only given to those who owned a certain amount of property.

Britain became the **dominant world power** during the 19th century, with continued expansion of its empire overseas. The Great Exhibition of 1851, attended by over 6 million people, reflected Britain's industrial supremacy: over half of the 100,000 exhibits were from Britain or the British Empire. In 1876 Queen Victoria was proclaimed 'Empress of India'. There were some misgivings about the idea of colonial exploitation, reflected for example in Joseph Conrad's novella *Heart Of Darkness* (1902).

The most important literary genre in the Victorian age was the **novel**, which many critics believe enjoyed its finest period during the

Take note

The Factory Act of 1847, for example, limited children's working time in factories to ten hours a day. The 1874 Factory Act raised the minimum working age to ten.

Take note

The 1918 Representation of the People Act gave the vote to all men over 21 and women over 30.

Checkpoint 1

What is a **novella**?

19th century. The works of writers such as Charles Dickens, George Eliot and Thomas Hardy reflect the mixed feelings that many had about the nature and the pace of the changes that were taking place. Dickens, for example, attacks the effects of industrialisation in *Hard Times* (1854), while Hardy's *Under The Greenwood Tree* (1872) portrays an agricultural community undergoing change.

Timeline (1830–1901)

	EVENTS	LITERATURE
1830		**Novelists**
	1832 First Reform Act	Elizabeth Gaskell (1810–65)
	1833 Abolition of slavery in the British Empire	Charlotte Bronte (1816–55)
		Emily Bronte (1818–48)
	1834 Poor Law Amendment Act	George Eliot (1819–80)
	1837 Reign of Queen Victoria begins	Charles Dickens (1812–70)
	1845–46 Irish famine at its height	Thomas Hardy (1840–1928)
	1848 'Year of Revolutions' – many revolutions in continental Europe	
		Poets
	1848 *The Communist Manifesto*, written by Karl Marx and Friedrich Engels, published	Elizabeth Browning (1806–61)
		Alfred, Lord Tennyson (1809–92)
1850		Robert Browning (1812–89)
	1851 Great Exhibition held in London	Christina Rossetti (1830–94)
	1853–56 Crimean War	W.B. Yeats (1865–1939)
	1857–58 Indian mutiny. Britain establishes direct rule over India.	**Dramatists**
	1858 Darwin's *On the Origin of Species* published	Oscar Wilde (1856–1900)
		George Bernard Shaw (1856–1950)
	1861–65 American Civil War	
	1868 Disraeli and Gladstone both become Prime Minister for first time	
	1868 Trades Union Congress founded	
	1872 Ballot Act introduces secret voting	
	1876 Queen Victoria declared Empress of India	
	1888 'Jack the Ripper' murders in London's East End	
	1899–1902 Boer War	
1900	**1900** Labour Representation Committee formed (beginning of Labour party)	
	1901 Death of Queen Victoria	

Checkpoint 2

Can you name any novels written by **George Eliot**?

Checkpoint 3

Thomas Hardy eventually stopped writing novels and devoted himself to another genre of literature – which one?

Exam preparation   answers: page 168

Text B on pages 166–7 is an extract from *Hard Times* by Charles Dickens, published in 1854. In what ways might a consideration of the historical context of this extract help your understanding of it?

20th century contexts

This final section on contexts moves closer to our own time with a survey of the 20th century.

Overview

The 20th century is dominated by two **World Wars**. The **First World War** (1914–18) was a completely new kind of conflict, drawing in more countries and inflicting more casualties than any previous war. Some 700,000 Britons died; in France, Germany and Russia, the numbers killed were even higher. The war had a profound effect on how people viewed the world, resulting in feelings of pessimism, disillusionment and uncertainty. The **Second World War** (1939–45) had its own horrors, with the killing of millions of Jews and the dropping of atomic bombs on Japan. The sense of dislocation and alienation that runs through much 20th century literature is clearly linked to some of these events.

In terms of domestic politics, a major development was the **rise of the Labour party**, which displaced the Liberal party as the main opposition to the Conservatives. The party was formed to represent the industrial working class at the beginning of the century, and was first elected to power in 1924. The Labour government of 1945–51 established the Welfare State, but the second half of the century was dominated by Conservative administrations, including those led by Margaret Thatcher in the 1980s. The search for electoral success caused Tony Blair to distance Labour from its trade union roots and from 1997 the party achieved a series of election victories.

Britain **declined sharply as an international power** after the Second World War, and the British Empire gradually disintegrated as former colonies became independent. In contrast, the power and influence of the United States grew, and following the break-up of the Soviet Union in 1991 it became the world's only superpower.

In western countries, including Britain, the 20th century was marked by a dramatic rise in living standards, with a sharp increase in property ownership and the consumption of goods and services. There were periodic reversals, however, notably the Great Depression of the 1930s, which began in the United States. In the closing decades of the century Britain's identity as an industrial nation was weakened by the widespread closure of factories and coal mines, though other sectors of the economy (such as financial services) prospered.

The main artistic movement in the first half of the century was **Modernism**, which deliberately broke away from traditional approaches to literature and other art forms. Writers such as the novelist James Joyce and the poet T.S. Eliot produced experimental works which challenged conventional expectations of order and coherence. Later 20th century works which extend and develop modernist approaches are sometimes called **postmodernist**. Culture in general was transformed by the rise of the mass media (notably film and television). Some commentators lamented the division between popular and highbrow culture, but many practitioners tried to bridge the gap by creating works that were both serious and popular.

Checkpoint 1

Which Conservative leader lost the General Election of 1945, and which Labour leader won it?

Checkpoint 2

Who wrote *The Grapes Of Wrath*, an American novel about the Depression of the 1930s?

Checkpoint 3

Can you name **T.S. Eliot's** most famous poem?

Timeline (1900–2003)

	EVENTS	LITERATURE
1900		
	1901 Death of Queen Victoria	**First World War poets**
	1906 First Labour MPs elected to Parliament	Siegfried Sassoon (1886–1967)
	1914–18 First World War	Wilfred Owen (1893–1918)
	1916 Easter Rising in Ireland	
	1918 Representation of the People Act: married women over 30 given the vote	**Other poets**
		Thomas Hardy (1840–1928)
	1922 Irish Free State established. Six counties of Northern Ireland remain British	W.B. Yeats (1865–1939)
		T.S. Eliot (1888–1965)
	1924 First Labour government	W.H. Auden (1907–73)
	1926 General Strike	Philip Larkin (1922–85)
	1928 Representation of the People Act: equal voting rights for men and women	Ted Hughes (1930–98)
		Sylvia Plath (1932–1963)
	1929 Wall Street Crash. Beginning of Great Depression.	Seamus Heaney (1939–)
		Carol Ann Duffy (1955–)
	1933 Adolf Hitler gains power in Germany	
	1939–45 Second World War	**Novelists**
	1945 Atomic bombs dropped on Japan	E.M. Forster (1879–1970)
	1945–51 Labour government. Major industries nationalised; National Health Service established.	James Joyce (1882–1941)
		D.H. Lawrence (1885–1930)
		George Orwell (1903–50)
		William Golding (1911–93)
	1947 India gains independence	Ian McEwan (1948–)
1950		
	1956 Suez crisis	**Dramatists**
	1961 Building of the Berlin Wall	G.B. Shaw (1856–1950)
	1962 Cuban missile crisis	Samuel Beckett (1906–89)
	1963 Assassination of President Kennedy	John Osborne (1929–94)
	1970 Voting age lowered from 21 to 18	Brian Friel (1929–)
	1979–90 Conservative governments led by Margaret Thatcher	Harold Pinter (1930–)
		Tom Stoppard (1937–)
	1989 Collapse of communism in Eastern Europe	**US novelists**
	1997 Labour Party, led by Tony Blair, wins power	F. Scott Fitzgerald (1896–1940)
		John Steinbeck (1902–68)
		Joseph Heller (1923–99)
2000		
	2001 Terrorist attacks on New York. US invasion of Afghanistan.	**US dramatists**
		Tennessee Williams (1911–83)
	2003 US-led forces invade Iraq	Arthur Miller (1915–2005)

Exam preparation

Choose a text you are studying that was written after 1900. In what ways does the text reflect the period of its composition?

Opinions and interpretations

The next three sections look at how you might tackle the AS/A2 requirement that you consider different **interpretations** of some of the texts that you are studying.

What you need to do

All of the examining boards have the following as an **assessment objective** at both AS and A2: *'articulate independent opinions and judgements, informed by different interpretations of literary texts by other readers'*. This assessment objective will be specifically linked to certain of the texts that you are studying, and obviously you need to be sure you know what these are. It means that as well as presenting your own arguments about these texts, you need to be aware of other possible readings.

How interpretations differ

Interpretations can differ in a variety of ways and for a range of reasons:

→ Different readings might be possible for a specific **part of a text**. For example, a single line (or a single word) in a poem might be **ambiguous** and open to more than one interpretation.
→ More broadly, different views might be expressed about **the whole text** – about its meaning, its artistic value, the author's intentions and so on.
→ Interpretations might differ **over time**. Readers from different periods in history might focus on different aspects of a text. Changing attitudes in relation to race and gender, for instance, might have produced new views and responses.
→ The **experience of the reader** might result in different interpretations. Readers may not necessarily be from different historical periods, but if they are from **different social or cultural backgrounds** they may not respond to a text in the same way.
→ Readers may approach a text from **different perspectives**. In recent years several different 'ways of reading' a text have emerged, including, for example, feminist, political and psychoanalytical approaches. These are discussed more fully on pages 162–5.

Discovering other interpretations

The AS/A2 objective referred to at the beginning of this section states that you need to know about *'different interpretations . . . by other readers'*. How do you find these out? There are two main ways:

→ **Research** This involves seeking out interpretations by reading what critics and commentators have said about the text. This should be a useful exercise which also helps your overall understanding of the text, but don't overdo it: your essays should still be mostly based on **your own arguments** about the text, and not filled with great wads of undigested information. Your teacher will probably point you in the right direction, and might well provide you with relevant extracts

Take note

In fact it is a good idea with *all* of your texts to show an awareness of alternative interpretations, because this will demonstrate that you have thought about what you have read, and realise that different responses are possible. However, with some texts it is a specific requirement and you will lose marks if you ignore it.

Checkpoint 1

The term **polysemy** is relevant here. What does it mean?

Checkpoint 2

Another useful word is **contemporaneous**. Do you know what it means?

Checkpoint 3

Can you think of any specific texts where changing attitudes to **race** or **gender** might have caused the texts to be viewed or interpreted in different ways?

from critics. Study guides on set texts often include a 'Critical approaches' section which summarises the main critical positions. There is also your school, college or public library and the Internet (but be discriminating as much Internet material may be unsuitable or of poor quality). Remember that you're looking for **different interpretations** – think about how critics' opinions differ from each other, and from your own views.

→ **Thinking about the text** Students often don't realise that they can think of their own alternative interpretations. As you work through a text, there will probably be numerous occasions when you come across a line or an episode that can be interpreted in more than one way. Most great literature is **ambiguous** and can suggest different meanings to different readers. If you discuss the text in class, you might well find that different students offer different interpretations, either of parts of the text or of the whole text. Obviously some of these views may be unsustainable, because they are based on misunderstandings or misreadings. But others will be valid. Keep a note of these for future use. You can also try to imagine how other readers would respond to the text. When the text was written, would readers of the time have responded differently to readers of today – if so, how and why? If you approach the text from one of the perspectives outlined on pages 162–5 (e.g. from a feminist or psychoanalytical perspective), does this suggest different ideas about the text?

Writing about interpretations ●●●

Within an essay, there are four main ways you can **show an awareness of different interpretations** (a strong answer might well include all four of these):

→ You can refer to how aspects of **the text as a whole** might be interpreted (e.g. by writing things like '*Although much of the The Nun's Priest's Tale is comic, some critics argue that it has a serious purpose*').
→ You can explain how **specific parts of the text** might be interpreted in different ways.
→ You can refer to the views of specific **named critics**.
→ You can discuss how **different types of reader** might interpret the text in different ways (e.g. readers from different historical periods, or readers approaching the text from different critical perspectives).

Examiner's secrets

In order to demonstrate your awareness of alternative interpretations, it is a good idea to include in your answer expressions such as *Some critics argue that . . .*, *Others might believe that . . .*, *One approach to the text is to . . .* and so on.

Examiner's secrets

Remember the assessment objective also states that you need to '*articulate independent opinions and judgements*'. In other words, an essay should primarily be an expression of **your own understanding of the text**. In presenting your own views, phrases such as the following are useful: *I share the view that . . .*, *My own view is that . . .*, *I agree/disagree with this interpretation because . . .*

Exam preparation   answers: page 169

Text C on page 167 is a sonnet by Shakespeare, *My mistress' eyes are nothing like the sun*. How might the overall purpose of the poem, and the attitudes expressed within it, be interpreted in different ways?

Critical approaches 1

The next two sections outline some important **schools of criticism** – specific ways of approaching literary texts. Although these approaches are different, **they are not necessarily incompatible**. As explained in the previous section, it is useful to **approach a text from a variety of angles**, in order to uncover different aspects of it, and different possible interpretations.

Liberal humanism

Older, traditional approaches to the study of literature are sometimes grouped together under the broad heading **liberal humanism**. The term began to be used (often pejoratively) in the 1970s, when newer approaches emerged (such as those discussed in the next few pages). Liberal humanism is strongly associated with the 19th century critic Matthew Arnold, and with critics from the first half of the 20th century such as A.C. Bradley (who wrote extensively on Shakespeare) and F.R. Leavis. There are important differences between individual critics who have been labelled liberal humanists, but they tend to have the following in common:

→ They **focus strongly on the text itself** and **tend to ignore wider contexts**, such as historical, political and social influences.
→ They are interested in the **moral values** expressed in a text, and value texts which have a **positive moral purpose**. As a result, they pay close attention to the **meaning** and **content** of a text, and less attention to matters such as a text's form and structure.

Traditional approaches to texts are more accessible than some of the newer approaches, and although some recent critics have sought to discredit liberal humanism, in practice much of your work on the texts that you study is probably essentially liberal humanist in its approach.

New Criticism

New Criticism was a branch of literary studies that emerged in the United States in the 1930s and 1940s, heavily influenced by the work of earlier British critics, especially I.A. Richards and William Empson. T.S. Eliot, the American poet and critic, who spent most of his life in England, is also associated with this approach. New Criticism also has links to liberal humanism in that it usually **disregards political, social or other contextual influences on a text**. Its main feature is its emphasis on **language**, on the **'close reading'** of texts. A literary composition such as a poem is approached as a self-contained piece of work, and analysed with little or no reference to the author's identity or the period when the text was written. In closely scrutinising the language of a text, New Criticism is particularly alert to the existence of features such as **ambiguity** and **irony**. If you are studying a writer who uses language in an especially concentrated or complex way (e.g. a writer such as the 17th century Metaphysical poet John Donne) this approach has undoubted merits.

Checkpoint 1

What does *'pejoratively'* mean here?

Links

For more on A.C. Bradley's approach to Shakespeare, see page 138.

Checkpoint 2

Define the terms **ambiguity** and **irony**.

Political approaches ●●●

Several more recent approaches to literature can be loosely grouped together as **political approaches**. In contrast to the approaches outlined above, they all stress the importance of the **historical context** of a text. They include:

→ **Marxism** Marxism is a political and economic philosophy based on the work of Karl Marx and Friedrich Engels, who together wrote the *Communist Manifesto*, published in 1848. Marxists believe that society develops as a result of the **struggle between different social classes**, and that modern industrial capitalism is based on the exploitation of the working class by those who own the means of production within a society. The aim of Marxism is to hasten the arrival of a classless society, in which the means of production are in common ownership. Marxist criticism of literary texts usually relates them in some way to their **economic and historical contexts**. This approach can be applied to individual texts or, more broadly, to literary genres: the increasing popularity of the novel in the 18th century, for example, has been linked to the growth of the middle class during that time. Marxist critics also examine **how texts portray different social classes**, and the relationships between them.

→ **New historicism** New historicism developed in the 1980s, and is mainly associated with American critics such as Stephen Greenblatt (who gave the movement its name). It is clearly influenced by earlier Marxist criticism. A new historicist approach to a text usually involves looking at other (frequently non-literary) **texts of the same historical period**, including, for example, letters, government documents, political pamphlets, legal records and so on. The focus is on texts containing subject matter which is linked in some way to the literary text. The work of new historicist critics has a **political dimension** in that they are especially interested in how literary and non-literary texts reflect and reinforce the power of the state, and the position within society of established institutions and social groups.

→ **Cultural materialism** Cultural materialism is sometimes described as the British counterpart of new historicism, as there are several similarities in the two approaches. One difference is that cultural materialists often look at how the works of individual authors **challenge** the established power of the state and the dominant ideology. Another is that cultural materialists are interested in how texts are viewed at different periods in history.

Take note

Marxist approaches to Jane Austen's novels, for example, see them as depicting a society built upon the exploitation of the working class, whose lives are largely ignored by both the author and the middle- and upper-class characters she creates.

Take note

The new historicist approach has been applied to a variety of periods and texts, but is particularly associated with criticism of the Renaissance and Romantic periods. This includes much new historicist work on Shakespeare's plays.

Checkpoint 3

What is an **ideology**?

Take note

A cultural materialist approach to Shakespeare's plays might consider how responses to them today are shaped by such factors as contemporary stage and film versions, and the central position Shakespeare occupies in the teaching of literature in schools and colleges.

Exam preparation

Choose a text you are studying and consider how a **political** approach to it (e.g. a Marxist or cultural materialist approach) might throw light on its meaning.

163

Critical approaches 2

This second section on critical approaches considers three other recent and influential schools of literary criticism: **feminist, psychoanalytic** and **postcolonial** criticism.

Feminist criticism ●●●

Feminist literary criticism rose to prominence in the 1960s, when it was part of a wider feminist movement, aimed at challenging traditional attitudes towards women and exposing social inequality. It has remained an important and influential approach to the interpretation of literary texts. Aspects of feminist criticism include the following:

→ Much feminist criticism is concerned with the **representation** of women in literature. In other words, it looks at **how literary texts portray women**, especially in terms of their position within society and their relationships with men. For example, in many 19th century novels the main goal of women characters is to find a suitable husband; they are economically dependent on others and are not seen as capable of leading independent lives.

→ A feminist approach to a text might also look at the **portrayal of personal relationships**, including those between women and men. Who is dominant within a relationship, and why? Does the man exercise authority, and the woman submit to it? Or is the relationship more complex – for example, does the man have one kind of power (perhaps economic) and the woman another?

→ Feminist critics are also interested in the extent to which texts reflect and reinforce the **norms, attitudes and values** of society. Do texts support, or challenge, the conventions of a **patriarchal** (male-dominated) society?

→ The works of **women writers** receive particular attention. This includes the re-discovery of obscure and neglected writers from the past. Feminist critics also look at whether the works of individual women writers imitate the literary style and the moral and social attitudes of male writers, or have a separate, distinctive approach.

Psychoanalytic criticism ●●●

Psychoanalytic criticism applies to literature the approaches associated with **psychoanalysis**, a way of studying and interpreting human behaviour developed by the psychologist **Sigmund Freud** (1856–1939). Freud was primarily concerned with the influence on an individual's personality of the **unconscious** – suppressed memories, desires and anxieties. Early childhood experiences, relationships with parents and sexual desires or fantasies are especially important. A psychoanalytic approach to a text seeks to discover the **unconscious motives of characters**, and possibly of the **author** as well. Psychoanalytic criticism has often been applied to Shakespeare's plays. Freud himself, for example, argued that Richard III, who is physically deformed, had suffered from birth from 'an unjust disadvantage'. This helped to explain his villainy but also gained

Take note

Not all 19th century novels follow this pattern. For example, in Ann Bronte's *The Tenant Of Wildfell Hall*, Helen Graham leaves her brutal husband and starts a new life with her young son (though she does so in a house owned by her brother).

Take note

Writers, including literary authors, were of course interested in aspects of human psychology before Freud developed his theories. For example, Robert Louis Stevenson in *The Strange Case Of Dr Jekyll And Mr Hyde*, and Oscar Wilde in *The Picture Of Dorian Gray* (both written in the 19th century), were clearly interested in the idea of a divided personality.

him sympathy from the audience because 'we all demand reparation for early wounds to our narcissism, our self-love'.

Psychoanalytic critics identify classic **psychoanalytic conditions or behaviours** in the **actions of characters**. An example is the **Oedipus complex**, the unconscious desire of a male infant to replace his father as the sexual partner of his mother. This has been used to argue that Hamlet delays taking revenge on Claudius (who murdered Hamlet's father) because Claudius has in fact fulfilled Hamlet's subconscious wish to see his father eliminated.

Another element in Freudian psychology is the idea that **objects** (which might, for example, appear in people's dreams) can have **sexual connotations**. Applied to literature, this approach invests objects and symbols which appear in texts with **hidden psychological significance**. In the second chapter of Emily Bronte's *Wuthering Heights*, for instance, the narrator Lockwood leaves Thrushcross Grange, where he is staying, to visit the Heights, where his landlord Heathcliff lives. Just before his departure, a servant-girl at Thrushcross Grange *extinguished the flames of the fire*, in order to clean the grate. A few paragraphs later, Lockwood enters the main room at Wuthering Heights, which *glowed delightfully in the radiance of an immense fire*. These descriptive details could be interpreted as reinforcing Wuthering Heights's association with sexual passion, and Thrushcross Grange's contrasting association with the control and suppression of desire.

Postcolonial criticism

⬤⬤⬤

Like other critical approaches discussed in this section, **postcolonial criticism** developed in the late 20th century. It argues that Western culture has for centuries had a bias towards white, **Eurocentric** (European centred) attitudes, assumptions and values. Other cultures (especially those of countries which have been occupied and colonised) are regarded as inferior. A postcolonial approach to a text would examine its **representation of other cultures**, and the attitude towards such issues as **colonisation** and **imperialism**. With some texts this approach has obvious relevance: Joseph Conrad's *Heart Of Darkness*, published in 1902 and set in the Belgian Congo, clearly addresses these themes. The approach can also be fruitfully applied to less obvious cases. In an essay on Jane Austen's *Mansfield Park*, the critic Edward Said deliberately 'foregrounds the background', by examining the significance to the novel of Sir Thomas Bertram's estate in Antigua, the source of his wealth and – given the time the novel was set – an estate which would have employed slave labour.

Checkpoint 1

Sigmund Freud's name is the origin of the expression *'a Freudian slip'*. What does this mean?

Checkpoint 2

Another psychoanalytic condition or behaviour is **projection**. What is 'projection'?

Checkpoint 3

In Shakespeare's *Hamlet*, what is the name of Hamlet's mother?

Take note

Wuthering Heights has many such symbols. The fierce, unruly dogs which are kept at the Heights are often seen as another symbol of unrestrained passion.

Exam preparation

Choose a text you are studying and consider what aspects of it might be emphasised in a **feminist** reading of the text.

Practice extracts

The extracts below are for use with the practice exam questions for this chapter.

Text A

Take note

The question for this poem is on page 155.

I love to rise in a summer morn,
When the birds sing on every tree;
The distant huntsman winds his horn,
And the skylark sings with me.
Oh! what sweet company.

But to go to school on a summer morn,
Oh! it drives all joy away;
Under a cruel eye outworn,
The little ones spend the day
In sighing and dismay.

Ah! then at times I drooping sit,
And spend many an anxious hour,
Nor in my book can I take delight,
Nor sit in learning's bower,
Worn through with the dreary shower.

How can the bird that is born for joy
Sit in a cage and sing?
How can a child, when fears annoy,
But drop his tender wing,
And forget his youthful spring?

Oh! father and mother! If buds are nipped,
And blossoms blown away,
And if the tender plants are stripped
Of their joy in the springing day,
By sorrow and care's dismay,

How shall the summer arise in joy,
Or the summer's fruits appear?
Or how shall we gather what griefs destroy,
Or bless the mellowing year,
When the blasts of winter appear?

Text B

Take note

The question for this extract is on page 157.

It was a town of red brick, or of brick that would have been red if the smoke and ashes had allowed it; but as matters stood it was a town of unnatural red and black like the painted face of a savage. It was a town of machinery and tall chimneys, out of which interminable serpents of smoke trailed themselves for ever and ever, and never got uncoiled. It had a black canal in it, and a river that ran purple with ill-smelling dye, and vast piles of building full of windows where there was a rattling and a trembling all day long, and where the piston of the steam-engine worked monotonously up and down like the head of an elephant in a state of melancholy madness. It contained several large streets all very like one another, and many small streets still more like one another, inhabited by people equally like one another, who all went in and out at the same hours, with the same sound upon the same pavements, to do the same work, and to whom every day was the same as yesterday and tomorrow, and every year the counterpart of the last and the next.

. . . You saw nothing in Coketown but what was severely workful. If the members of a religious persuasion built a chapel there – as the members of eighteen religious persuasions had done – they made it a pious warehouse of red brick, with sometimes (but this is only in ornamental examples) a bell in a birdcage on the top of it. The solitary exception was the New Church; a stuccoed edifice with a square steeple over the door, terminating in four short pinnacles like florid wooden legs. All the public inscriptions in the town were painted alike, in severe characters of black and white. The jail might have been the infirmary, the infirmary might have been the jail, the town-hall might have been either, or both, or anything else, for anything that appeared to the contrary in the graces of their construction. Fact, fact, fact, everywhere in the material aspect of the town; fact, fact, fact, everywhere in the immaterial. The M'choakumchild school was all fact, and the school of design was all fact, and the relations between master and man were all fact, and everything was fact between the lying-in hospital and the cemetery, and what you couldn't state in figures, or show to be purchaseable in the cheapest market and saleable in the dearest, was not, and never should be, world without end, Amen.

Text C

My mistress' eyes are nothing like the sun;
Coral is far more red than her lips' red:
If snow be white, why then her breasts are dun;
If hairs be wires, black wires grow on her head.
I have seen roses damask'd, red and white,
But no such roses see I in her cheeks;
And in some perfumes is there more delight
Than in the breath that from my mistress reeks.
I love to hear her speak, yet well I know
That music hath a far more pleasing sound:
I grant I never saw a goddess go –
My mistress, when she walks, treads on the ground:
   And yet, by heaven, I think my love as rare
   As any she belied with false compare.

Take note

The question for this poem is on page 161.

Answers
Contexts and interpretations

Types of context

Checkpoints

1 Examples include *Great Expectations*, *David Copperfield* and *Oliver Twist*.
2 To 'subvert' is to challenge or undermine from within. Often the word is used in the context of undermining the authority of an established institution, government etc.
3 A line of poetry with five pairs of syllables, in each of which the first is unstressed and the second stressed.

Medieval contexts

Checkpoints

1 Other medieval writers include William Langland (who wrote *Piers Plowman*), John Gower, Sir Thomas Malory and the *Gawain* poet (the author of *Gawain And The Green Knight*, whose identity is unknown).
2 Canterbury Cathedral was where Thomas a Becket, an archbishop of Canterbury, was murdered in 1170. In 1172 he was declared a saint.
3 There might be features which depend on the sounds of words, such as onomatopoeia, alliteration and assonance. Rhythmic effects might also be important. There might be passages which directly address the audience.

Renaissance contexts

Checkpoints

1 Christopher Marlowe's plays include *Dr Faustus*, *Edward II*, *The Jew Of Malta* and *Tamburlaine*. John Webster's plays include *The White Devil* and *The Duchess Of Malfi*.
2 Theatres include the Globe, the Rose and the Swan.
3 *The Faerie Queene*.

Exam preparation

This poem is discussed on pages 44–45. It has several features typical of Metaphysical poetry, especially the use of unusual imagery, including images drawn from contemporary science and learning (references to the *new worlds* discovered by explorers and astronomers, the two *hemispheares* and the idea that decay results from the incorrect balancing of the elements that make up a physical entity – *What ever dyes, was not mixt equally*). Also typical are the sense of a strong speaking voice (especially at the beginning of the poem), and the complexity of the arguments expressed in the poem and of some of Donne's vocabulary.

Restoration, Augustan and Romantic contexts

Checkpoints

1 Blank verse.
2 *Robinson Crusoe*.
3 Gothic novels include Mary Shelley's *Frankenstein*, Horace Walpole's *The Castle Of Otranto*, William Beckford's *Vathek* and Jane Austen's *Northanger Abbey*.

Exam preparation

This is a poem from the Romantic period. It has several of the features associated with Romantic poetry, in terms of both style and content. These include: interest in childhood; belief in individual freedom; opposition to established institutions; use of natural imagery; use of language that is simple and direct (especially appropriate here because it helps to suggest the voice of a child).

The narrator of the poem is a child whose natural joy and spontaneity are crushed by school (biographical context is also relevant here – Blake himself did not receive a formal education). The first stanza expresses the child's love of life and delight in nature. The natural imagery that runs through the poem helps to suggest that the forced education of children is *un*natural. In contrast, the second stanza portrays school as a joyless place where children toil under the eye of a *cruel* teacher. Ironically, as becomes evident in the third stanza, the boy is eager to learn. He longs to take *delight* in his books and to sit in *learning's bower*, a metaphor which suggests the bliss of private, solitary learning – in contrast to the misery of enforced, institutionalised education.

The second half of the poem is a series of rhetorical questions, addressed to the child's parents and to the reader. More natural images are used: the child is like a caged bird, or a young plant not allowed to grow and flourish. Passive verbs present the boy as a helpless victim (*buds are nipped*, *tender plants are stripped*). In the closing stanza, parallelism (the repetition of *Or . . .* and *How shall . . .*) gives the questioning increased intensity. The poem argues that if we do not have the freedom to enjoy life when we are young, we shall be unhappy in later life: unable to cope with loss (*gather what griefs destroy*) and unable to accept and embrace the passing of time (*bless the mellowing year*). In this last verse the changing of the seasons is used to represent the cycle of life.

Victorian contexts

Checkpoints

1 A short novel – longer than a short story, but not long enough to be described simply as a novel.
2 George Eliot's novels include *The Mill On The Floss*, *Middlemarch*, *Silas Marner*, *Adam Bede*, *Daniel Deronda*.
3 Poetry.

Exam preparation

This extract shows Dickens's misgivings about the effects of industrialisation, which led in the 19th century to the building of hundreds of factories, and the growth of towns (especially in northern England) that were almost exclusively devoted to industry. Dickens based Coketown in *Hard Times* on Preston, which he visited in 1854. In this description he creates the impression of a town dominated by industry, which has polluted the town and reduced its inhabitants to a monotonous, robotic existence. The visual details in the description contribute to this impression: the soot-covered buildings, the continually smoking chimneys, the black canal and the purple river. The ceaseless, repetitive movement of the piston, the sameness of the streets and the endless routine of the people's lives suggest a dreary way of life. In the second paragraph Dickens's target is utilitarianism, a philosophy developed by Jeremy Bentham (1748–1832). This was the belief that the purpose of all legislation should be 'the greatest happiness for the greatest number'. Associated with this belief was the idea of judging things according to the extent to which they served a practical, measurable function. Everything in Coketown was *severely workful*, and the result is a society in which there is no room for imagination or independence of thought, a society based from cradle to grave – *between the lying-in hospital and the cemetery* – on hard, material *fact*.

20th century contexts

Checkpoints

1 Winston Churchill was leader of the Conservative Party, which lost the election. The Labour Party leader was Clement Atlee.
2 John Steinbeck.
3 *The Waste Land*.

Opinions and interpretations

Checkpoints

1 The term is used for words or phrases that have several possible meanings.
2 'At the same time as' – for example, Christopher Marlowe and William Shakespeare were contemporaneous, because they lived and wrote during the same historical period.
3 Changing attitudes towards race have influenced interpretations of Shakespeare's *Othello* and *The Merchant Of Venice*. Changing attitudes towards women have influenced interpretations of several of

Shakespeare's female characters, such as Cleopatra and Lady Macbeth.

Exam preparation

The poem consists of a series of comparisons, all of which are rejected as *not* applicable to the woman described. These comparisons are generally conventional romantic images of Shakespeare's time (cheeks like roses, walking like a goddess etc.). Shakespeare's rejection of these images can be interpreted in a variety of ways: 1. The woman is not conventionally attractive, but he still loves her. 2. He loves her for her inner qualities, implying this is more important than physical beauty. 3. He is mocking the traditional love poetry of his time, emphasising that the romantic cliches included in the poem are unrealistic.

It is important to note the element of humour in the poem, and also how the sonnet form is used in the final couplet, where the poet reveals that despite all that has been said earlier he thinks the woman is *rare* or special.

Critical approaches 1

Checkpoints

1 In a negative way.
2 'Ambiguity' means having more than one possible meaning. 'Irony' can mean stating the opposite of what is meant, or an event having consequences that are the opposite of those expected or intended.
3 A set of ideas or beliefs.

Critical approaches 2

Checkpoints

1 A remark or action which unintentionally reveals hidden, possibly subconscious thoughts, desires etc.
2 This occurs when we attribute our own faults to others.
3 Gertrude.

Revision checklist
Contexts and interpretations

By the end of this chapter you should be able to:

1	List the main types of context that might be relevant to an understanding of a literary text.	Confident	Not confident. **Revise** pages 148–49
2	Offer an overview of the context in which medieval texts were written.	Confident	Not confident. **Revise** pages 150–51
3	Offer an overview of the context in which texts from the Renaissance period were written.	Confident	Not confident. **Revise** pages 152–53
4	Offer an overview of the contexts in which texts from the Restoration, Augustan and Romantic periods were written.	Confident	Not confident. **Revise** pages 154–55
5	Offer an overview of the context in which texts from the Victorian period were written.	Confident	Not confident. **Revise** pages 156–57
6	Offer an overview of the context in which texts from the 20th century were written.	Confident	Not confident. **Revise** pages 158–59
7	Understand the examination requirement that for certain texts you show knowledge and understanding of different interpretations.	Confident	Not confident. **Revise** pages 160–61
8	Explain the main features of liberal humanism.	Confident	Not confident. **Revise** page 162
9	Explain the main features of New Criticism.	Confident	Not confident. **Revise** page 162
10	Understand how Marxist critics approach literature.	Confident	Not confident. **Revise** page 163
11	Understand how new historicist critics approach literature.	Confident	Not confident. **Revise** page 163
12	Understand how cultural materialist critics approach literature.	Confident	Not confident. **Revise** page 163
13	Outline the main characteristics of feminist criticism.	Confident	Not confident. **Revise** page 164
14	Outline the main characteristics of psychoanalytic criticism.	Confident	Not confident. **Revise** pages 164–65
15	Outline the main characteristics of postcolonial criticism.	Confident	Not confident. **Revise** page 165

This chapter offers some final information and advice to help you complete your AS or A2 course successfully. Most of your written work (whether for homework, coursework or exams) will involve writing essays, and there are two sections on essay writing skills. There's also a section on tackling coursework, followed by two sections that relate specifically to elements of the A2 course: one on approaches to the comparison of texts, and another on the analysis of unseen texts. The chapter ends with some concluding tips.

Exam boards

It is useful to have a copy of your exam specification. You can obtain one from the board's publications department or by downloading the specification from the board's website. The boards also supply copies of past exam papers (depending on the board, these might also be available online).

AQA
Publications Department, Stag Hill House, Guildford, Surrey
GU2 5XJ
www.aqa.org.uk

EDEXCEL
Edexcel Publications, Adamsway, Mansfield, Nottinghamshire
NG18 4FN
www.edexcel.org.uk

OCR
1 Hills Road, Cambridge CB2 1GG
www.ocr.org.uk

WJEC
245 Western Avenue, Cardiff CF5 2YX
www.wjec.co.uk

CCEA
29 Clarendon Road, Clarendon Dock, Belfast BT1 3BG
www.ccea.org.uk

Topic checklist

AS ○ A2 ●

	AQA/A	AQA/B	EDEXCEL	OCR	WJEC	CCEA
Essay writing 1	○●	○●	○●	○●	○●	○●
Essay writing 2	○●	○●	○●	○●	○●	○●
Tackling coursework	○●	○●	○●	○●	○●	○●
Comparing texts	●	●	●	●	●	●
Analysing unseen texts	●	●	●	●	●	●
Final tips	○●	○●	○●	○●	○●	○●

Writing essays 1

Most of the written work you complete during the AS/A2 course will take the form of **essays**: homework essays, coursework essays and essays written in the actual examination. The principles of essay writing outlined over the next four pages are applicable to all these kinds of essay, though you'll also find later in the chapter some additional advice on **coursework** (pages 176–7) and **exam technique** (page 183).

Know your assessment objectives

Links

See pages 6–7 for more on **assessment objectives**.

If you are writing an examination or coursework essay, your mark will depend on how far you have met the **assessment objectives** for that particular text or module. For example, it is sometimes important to show an understanding of *'cultural, historical and other contextual influences'* on the text you are writing about. An essay which made little or no reference to the text's context would obviously not be given a high mark. In the case of exams, the relevant assessment objectives are always printed on the question paper, and usually stressed in the questions themselves, but you should familiarise yourself with them beforehand.

Understanding the question and answering it

With coursework essays it is sometimes possible to devise your own task (see pages 176–7), but most of the essays you write during your AS/A2 course will be in response to a set question. Here are a few tips:

Examiner's secrets

Try to link the question to the assessment objectives, and think about how your answer can address these objectives.

→ Read the question **carefully** and make sure you **understand** it. Students often misinterpret a question not because it is too difficult for them to understand but because they have read it carelessly. If you genuinely can't understand it, choose another question, or identify those parts of the question you can understand and then try to work out what the rest of it might mean. Occasionally there are questions that can be read in different ways, and explaining in your opening paragraph how you are going to approach the question can be a good idea.

→ Underline **key words and phrases** in the question, and work out how many **parts** the question has. Breaking down a question in this way helps you to understand it, and also can help in the **planning** of your answer. Imagine for example that this is the question:

How far do you agree that The Nun's Priest's Tale is a comic story which nevertheless has a serious purpose?

The key words and phrases here are *How far do you agree*, *comic* and *serious purpose*. A very broad outline for an answer which addresses these three elements might be:

1. *Is the Tale comic?*
2. *Does it also have a serious purpose?*
3. *Conclusion – how far do I agree with the view expressed in the question?*

→ When you plan your answer and when you are writing it, you should always have **the question** in the back of your mind: all of the arguments you present should be geared towards answering it. To keep on track, and to show that you are clearly answering the question, you might occasionally use words from the question in your answer. With the above example, the words *agree*, *comic* and *serious purpose* would feature in most good answers. However, you don't need to overdo this – continually repeating words and phrases can make an answer seem mechanical and tedious.

Planning and paragraphing

It is important to spend some time working out the main points you will make, and the order you'll put them in. The advantages of doing this are:

→ You're more likely to produce an essay that puts forward a **coherent, structured argument**. This will impress the examiner.
→ Your answer is more likely to remain **relevant** to the question.
→ In an exam, if you start by planning the answer you'll discover quite quickly if you've **chosen the wrong question**. There should still be time for you to switch to another one.

Here is some advice on **how to plan**:

→ As mentioned above, the **wording of the question** itself might suggest a plan for you. If the question has three or four elements in it, can these be arranged to form the main stages of an answer?
→ A standard way to plan is to make a **list of points, ideas etc.** that might be relevant to an answer. You then arrange these into three or four **groups** of linked points; these will be the main **sections** of your essay. As you are doing this, you might well find that identifying your main ideas or topics helps you to think of more points. If any points don't 'fit' they could simply be left out. Alternatively, if you really want to include them, think about how this could be done. Could they be used in the introduction or conclusion? Are they strong enough to stand on their own as another stage in the argument? Once you have decided on the main sections of the essay, work out the best **order** for the sections.
→ Each section of your answer should usually be presented as one or two **paragraphs**. This means an average exam essay is likely to have roughly six to eight paragraphs. It is difficult to be too precise about the number of paragraphs you should have, but if your essay has a lot more than this your paragraphs are almost certainly too short. On the other hand, if your essay only has two or three paragraphs they're too long (or the essay is not long enough!).

Watch out!

Although it's important to make a plan, in an examination **you shouldn't spend too long on it**. As a rough guide, if you have an hour to write an answer, you should probably aim to spend about 10 minutes on planning. Students sometimes overdo it by writing a very detailed plan and then find they don't have long enough to write the actual answer.

Take note

Remember as you plan that you're looking for points that **answer the question** and help you to meet the **assessment objectives**.

Links

For more advice on **introducing** and **concluding** an essay, see page 174.

Take note

It is helpful for paragraphs to begin with a **topic sentence**, which clearly indicates what the paragraph is going to be about. You should also try to link the paragraph to what has gone before. A sentence such as *Roderigo is another character who is easily manipulated by Iago* does both these things.

Writing essays 2

This is the second of the two sections on writing essays, with advice on beginning and ending essays, making points effectively and the importance of demonstrating a personal response to the texts you have studied.

Introductions and conclusions

The main point about both introductions and conclusions can be summed up as: **avoid waffle**. More specifically:

→ Avoid the kind of **all-purpose introduction** that could be tagged on to any essay (e.g. *Charles Dickens lived from 1812 to 1870 and wrote many famous novels*). You won't get any credit for an introduction such as this.

→ When you're **planning** your answer, don't start by trying to think of an introduction. You need an introduction that fits in with the rest of your essay, so it's more sensible (and also easier) to decide on an introduction after you've worked out what the main body of the answer will cover.

→ It's important to be on track from the very beginning, so make sure your introduction is **clearly linked to the question**. Explaining in your own words what the question means, or how you intend to answer it – or both – often makes for an effective start.

→ Another way of starting can be to refer to an **early part of the text**. For example, if you're writing about a character, how is the character first introduced to the reader or audience? If you're writing about a theme, when does the theme first appear? An advantage of this approach is that you quickly engage with the text and offer detailed analysis of it from the outset. There are dangers though: the rest of the essay is probably not best answered with a simple chronological approach (i.e. one which works through the text from start to finish), and it is easy to spend too long on the opening pages of a text – remember most essays (especially exam answers) need to show a good grasp of the text as a whole.

→ In your **conclusion** it might be appropriate to emphasise and reinforce your main points, but conclusions which simply repeat what you've already said won't get much credit. Often it is a good idea to **broaden** the argument, by offering some kind of **overview** of the text. If you've been discussing a theme, how is it linked to other themes? Above all, you need to be sure that by the end of the essay you've **answered the question**. If you were asked to respond to someone else's interpretation of the text, how far you agree with the interpretation should be clear from your conclusion.

Making and supporting points

Although it is important that an essay should not read like a simple list of points, in practice essays do usually consist of a series of points. What prevents the 'list' effect is ensuring that the points you make are properly **linked** and **developed**:

Take note

Often the first stage of your argument – i.e. your first main point – can be used as the introduction.

Examiner's secrets

It is quite common in answers for students to show a detailed knowledge of the opening pages of a text, but only a limited knowledge of the rest of it. When you're looking for evidence to support your points, try to range across the whole text.

- Many points can be developed by using the **PEA formula**: **P**oint – **E**vidence – **A**nalysis. Points constructed in this way begin with an assertion or argument: *The novel has an ambiguous ending*, *The characters in the sub-plot in many ways mirror those in the main plot* etc.
- The **evidence** that is then offered to support the point can take two main forms: **quotation** from the text, or **reference** to the text in your own words (e.g. references to what happens, or to things that are said). Whichever you choose, it is important that the evidence is **specific** – you need in answers to demonstrate a detailed knowledge of the text.
- Avoid **quotations** that are **too long**. Most quotations should be no more than two or three lines. Short quotations (a single word or a short phrase) can be very effective. Remember also to take care over how you **set out** quotations. It is unnecessary to put short quotations on a new line, but you should do this with longer quotations.
- **Analysis** of the evidence will give your answer more depth. If you have included a quotation, this is a good opportunity to comment on the author's **use of language**. For example, can you explain or comment on the use of imagery in the quotation?
- Try to ensure the points in your answer are effectively **linked**. Arranging them in a logical order is part of this. It is also helpful to use words and phrases such as *however*, *in contrast*, *another*, *a similar* etc.
- Take care over **your own style**. In particular, students can tend to be too colloquial – avoid conversational expressions such as *lots of* and *over the top*. **Proofread** what you have written (try to allow time for this in an examination), looking for errors in spelling, expression etc. Misspelling characters' names will only irritate the examiner – especially if they're correctly spelt in the question!

Personal response

There is nothing wrong with expressing personal opinions about a text, provided you can support your points with evidence. In fact, a genuine **personal response** to the literature you have studied is always seen as a strength by examiners and rewarded accordingly. Even when you are showing your knowledge of how a text has been interpreted in different ways by other readers, critics and audiences, don't forget to explain where *you* stand.

You need to prepare thoroughly for the exam, but try not to switch to 'auto pilot' when you're writing your answers. This is especially a danger if the question appears a relatively straightforward one, when you might well be putting forward arguments that you've written about before. You don't want to write an essay that seems jaded and mechanical. Try to show the examiner that you've engaged with the text on a personal level: that you've thought about it, been moved by it, have your own opinions about it – and still feel *enthusiastic* about it!

Take note

It is especially important when quoting **poetry** to observe the poet's original **line divisions** – i.e. set the quotation out as clearly separate lines of poetry.

Take note

If you're commenting on language, using relevant **terminology** in your analysis ('metaphor', 'connotations' and so on) will gain extra marks.

Tackling coursework

Most AS/A2 English Literature courses include a coursework element. Coursework essays usually involve writing about a single text or comparing two texts.

Links

The earlier sections on essay writing (pages 172–5) also contain advice and information that is relevant to coursework.

Take note

Something else you might be able to do before you start is look at some specimen coursework essays written by other students (your teacher might have access to these). Seeing how other students have approached a similar task can be helpful, and you'll also gain an insight into the kind of standard that's expected.

Before you start

Before you start, you need to make sure you have the following information:

→ The **essay title**, which you may be able to devise yourself (see below).
→ The **assessment objectives** for the unit or module. For example, it might be important in your essay to discuss different interpretations of the text(s) you are writing about. Your teacher will probably explain the relevant assessment objectives to you, or you can find out what they are from the examining board website.
→ The **word limit** for the essay.
→ The **deadline** date.

Once you know all of the above, you can draw up a **schedule** for completing your coursework. Your teacher might help you with this, for example by giving you interim dates for submitting early drafts. You need to allow time to research, plan, write the first draft and work on later drafts (including the final one). The earlier you start the better, so you can allow a sensible amount of time for each stage.

The essay title

You may be given a **set title** for your coursework assignment. Alternatively, you may be given the opportunity to **devise a title yourself**, though your teacher will probably need to approve it. If you're making up the title yourself, here are some points to bear in mind:

→ You need a title that will be suitable for **you**, and that will also enable you to gain **high marks**.
→ In creating a title that's suitable for you, you need one that reflects the areas of the text (or texts) you find **interesting**, and that will enable you to demonstrate to the full your **knowledge** and **understanding** of it.
→ You need to find the happy medium between a question that's **too broad**, and one that's **too narrow**. '*Death Of A Salesman* is a very moving play' is a title that's almost certainly too broad, while 'Discuss how Shakespeare presents Cordelia in the opening scene of *King Lear*' is too narrow. If the question is too broad, an answer that remains within the word limit is likely to be thin and superficial. If it's too narrow, you'll only be able to show a limited insight into the text.
→ You also need to find the happy medium between a question that's **too easy** for you, and one that's **too difficult**. If the title is an easy, straightforward one, it will be harder to interest and impress whoever is marking the essay. If it's too difficult, you'll obviously struggle with it. You want a question that stretches you, as this

will help you to show your analytical strengths. It will also help to develop skills that will prove useful when you take the examination – but don't be *too* ambitious.

→ Much of the above should help you to devise a question that will make it possible to gain a **high mark**. You also need to check that your title addresses the **assessment objectives** for this component of the course. Make sure you know the criteria that will be used to grade the essay, and that you'll be able to write an essay that meets the relevant objectives.

If you're answering a question that has been **set**, you need to make sure you **understand** the title. Breaking down a question into its constituent parts is a useful approach (see page 172). If any aspect of the question confuses you, ask your teacher for help.

Research and planning

In carrying out **research** for your essay, your main sources of information are likely to be your existing study notes, handouts, essays etc.; books; and the Internet. Don't spend too long on the research stage, and avoid **information overload**: you don't want to end up surrounded by piles of books and photocopied articles, wondering how you're going to put it all together. You need to be **selective**: look for material which is relevant, and of good quality (if you search the Internet, you'll probably find plenty of information, but much of it is likely to be of no real use). You also need to remember that the essay is meant to express **your** knowledge and understanding of the text(s), not somebody else's. So while your research might uncover stimulating ideas or interesting insights, these have to be **integrated** into your own arguments. For advice on **planning** essays, see page 173. You need to arrange your ideas in a **logical order**, ensuring that you address the question, support your points with evidence and meet the assessment objectives.

Drafting

Drafting is very important, so you must **allow time** to refine and improve your first attempt. If your first draft is **over the word limit**, you could try editing it down yourself, but it would probably be better to discuss this with your teacher. Often examining boards allow some flexibility with regard to word limits, and essays are allowed to go a little over. If you do need to reduce the essay, your teacher can probably suggest the best changes to make. If your first draft is **too short**, your teacher should again be able to advise you. It might be possible to broaden the question, or to add more evidence to support your arguments. When you are writing your final draft, avoid major changes unless these have been discussed with your teacher, and make sure you **proofread** the final version before handing it in.

> **Take note**
>
> Ideas and information gained from books etc. also need to be expressed in **your own words**, unless you make it clear that you are **quoting** from another source. If you do include quotations, make sure there is an **accompanying analytical point** of your own: instead of writing *X says this*, write something like *X claims this and there is evidence to support her argument*, or *X claims this but it is not true of all the characters in the play*.

> **Take note**
>
> List the main works that you make use of in a **bibliography** at the end of the essay. The convention here is to follow the order of author, title, publisher, date – as in: Terry Eagleton *The English Novel* (Blackwell, 2005).

Comparing texts

Comparative tasks are an important element in all A2 courses. This includes the comparison of longer texts (such as complete novels or plays – often for coursework), and the comparison in the examination of shorter unseen texts (such as single poems or short prose extracts). The advice given in this section applies to both kinds of task.

Understanding the task

Whether the comparison you are writing is in an examination or for a coursework assignment, it is important that you understand exactly what you are required to do:

→ What are the **assessment objectives** for this task? Remember these determine how marks are allocated, so it makes sense to know what they are. In an examination they will be listed on the question paper, but as part of your preparation you should get to know them beforehand.

→ Study the **question** carefully (if you are writing a comparison for coursework, this might actually be a question you have devised yourself). You will almost certainly find that you need to compare **specific aspects** of the texts, such as the treatment of a particular theme or the portrayal of certain characters. Focus on these elements and don't include irrelevant points or attempt to write a general, all-embracing comparison.

→ With some examining boards, one of the texts you are comparing will be the **'primary' or dominant text**, which means it should be given the most emphasis in your answer. Make sure you know if this is the case.

→ Finally, remember that comparisons involve identifying **similarities** as well as **differences** (students sometimes make the mistake of assuming the whole of the answer should be devoted to contrasting the two texts).

Planning an answer

There are two main approaches to writing a comparison between two texts. Either can be successful. Both also have possible pitfalls, but these can be avoided if you are aware of them. Here is the first of them:

1. Begin with an **introduction**, which might make some broad comparative points about the two texts and give some indication of the argument you will be developing in the rest of the essay.

2. An **analysis of the first text** ('Text A'), focusing on those aspects which are relevant to the question and which will later be shown to be in some way similar to, or different from, Text B.

3. An **analysis of Text B**, which incorporates frequent **references back** to Text A, pointing out similarities and contrasts.

4. A **conclusion**, which summarises the argument. You should avoid simply repeating what you have already said, but it can be helpful to bring together your main arguments in a condensed form.

Links

See pages 6–7 for more on **assessment objectives**.

Take note

It is not a good idea to miss out the introduction and launch straight into an analysis of Text A. If you do, it will be a long time before it becomes clear that the essay is a **comparison**.

Links

You will also find relevant advice on writing an answer in the sections on writing essays (pages 172–5).

The advantage of this approach is that it is quite straightforward and the structure of the answer is easy to follow. The main danger is that if you spend too long analysing Text A, not enough of the answer will be devoted to **comparing the texts**. For this reason, part 2 of the answer should usually be shorter than part 3, because part 3 is where you will be making the important comparative points.

This is the second approach:

1. An **introduction**, which can be broadly similar to the introduction used in the first approach.
2. In the main body of the essay, you then focus in turn on relevant **points of comparison** between the two texts. There might be three or four of these. For example, if you are writing about a theme, one point of comparison might be the way the theme is introduced in each text, and another might be the way the theme is expressed through characters.
3. A **conclusion**, which again can be on the same lines as the conclusion used in the first approach.

The advantage of this approach is that the answer is clearly **comparative**. The danger is that it is more complicated and your argument might appear fragmented and hard to follow.

Ways of comparing

Listed below are some of the aspects of texts you might consider looking at when you are writing a comparison. The relevance of each will of course very much depend on the question you are answering, but running through this checklist can stimulate ideas and help you to think of comparative points.

→ **Characters**
→ **Themes** (including ideas, attitudes and values)
→ **Plot** (Be careful here. Remember in a literary essay you should not simply 'tell the story' of a text. However, there might be relevant similarities or differences – for example, one text might have a lot of action, and another very little; both texts might have sub-plots that run parallel to the main plot.)
→ **Language and style**
→ **Form and structure** (For example, the **genres** might be different, or methods of narration might contrast.)
→ **Contexts** (The texts might have been written at different times, and this might account for some of the contrasts between them.)
→ **Interpretations** (For example, there might be ways of interpreting the texts which see them as similar, while other approaches or interpretations might consider them very different.)

Take note

Often it is a good idea in the conclusion to return to the question, ensuring you have given a clear, unambiguous answer to it. You might want to make one or two new points as well. For example, if you are comparing the presentation of a theme, do you prefer one text's treatment of the theme – if so, why? Is the theme more important in one of the texts than the other?

Take note

Some examining boards recommend an approach to the specific types of comparative task required by their syllabus – you could ask your teacher about this.

Watch out!

Here is a list of things to **avoid** when writing a comparison. The list includes some common mistakes made by students.
→ Discussing each text in isolation, with no real comparison between them.
→ Writing too much on one or other of the texts.
→ Writing a long list of short, underdeveloped points.
→ Including too much narrative paraphrase ('telling the story' of each text).

Analysing unseen texts

Links

For further advice specific to these three genres, see 'Analysing poems' (pages 40–1), 'Analysing prose extracts' (pages 72–3) and 'Analysing drama extracts' (pages 104–5).

Take note

As with all your English exam papers and questions, you should make sure you know the **assessment objectives** for the unseen task. You will be expected to show analytical skills, but depending on the examining board, knowledge of contexts and the ability to compare texts may also be important. The assessment objectives will be on the question paper, together with an explanation of how the objectives relate to specific parts of the paper. Obviously you'll be better prepared if you know all this beforehand. (See pages 6–7 for more on assessment objectives.)

Take note

Practising timed questions will give you an idea of how much time you can afford to spend reading and annotating the texts.

The analysis of unseen texts (extracts of poetry, prose or drama) usually forms part of the final synoptic A2 module. The exact format of the paper varies according to the examining board but usually there is a comparative task, which might, for example, involve comparing several unseen texts, or comparing an unseen text with a set text that you have previously studied.

Understanding the task

Always read the **question** carefully. It may give you useful background information about the unseen text, and will also probably ask you to focus on particular aspects of the text when you analyse it.

Reading the text

Depending on the length of the text, you should read it **at least twice** (you may find that the question paper advises you to read each unseen text 'several times'). This includes a **first reading** and subsequent **closer readings**:

→ **First reading** Try to get a **general understanding** of what the text is about. Try also to identify, in broad terms, such aspects as genre and period (the question might help you here).

→ **Closer readings** Read the text more closely, annotating the text as you go along (see 'What to look for' below). Have the question in mind, and concentrate on aspects of the text that relate to it. Try to arrive at a deeper understanding of what the text is 'about' – what ideas, attitudes, feelings etc. are being expressed? If you have to compare the text to others, look also for similarities and contrasts with the other text or texts. Identify **good quotations** you can use – especially significant words, lines or phrases, either because of their meaning or because they have stylistic features that you can comment on.

What to look for

The question will point you in particular directions, but here is a list of those aspects of an unseen text which are usually worth mentioning in an answer.

→ **Themes and ideas** What, ultimately, is the text 'about'? What is it trying to 'say'? What attitudes are expressed within the text?

→ **Settings and characters** If a text has these, how are they presented?

→ **Language and style** This is very important. You need to show understanding of how writers use language, and you need to use relevant terminology when you do this – referring, for example, to the connotations of particular words, or to a writer's use of similes and metaphors.

→ **Form and structure** This includes the genre of the text: for example, it might be a poem, and make use of poetic techniques such as rhythm and rhyme. It also includes the overall structure – the division into verses or paragraphs, and the effect that this has.

→ **Contexts** i.e. factors such as the historical and social background to a text. With some specifications, this is included in the assessment objectives and is therefore especially important.

→ **Interpretations** Are differing interpretations of the text possible? Are parts of it ambiguous? What is your own response to it?

Links

See pages 148–59 for more on **contexts**.

Links

See pages 160–5 for more on **interpretations**.

Links

The sections on 'Writing essays' (pages 172–5) also contain relevant advice.

Writing an answer

Questions on unseen texts may involve a **comparative** element: you are likely to have to compare the unseen text with one or more other texts, which may also be unseen or which you may have previously studied. The advice on structuring a comparison essay (see pages 178–9) is therefore relevant here. You might well look at each text in turn, but it is not usually a good idea to give a 'chronological' account of each text, in which you work through the text from beginning to end, making points as you go along. This is partly because you would almost certainly run out of time, but also because it is better to have a structured argument which focuses clearly on the question. This means you need to organise your key points in a logical order, picking out those elements of the text which are important and relevant.

In framing your points, the **PEA formula** (see page 175) is usually appropriate: **P**oint – **E**vidence – **A**nalysis. Make sure your points are supported by evidence (usually quotations), and develop your points by explaining them more fully, and perhaps by commenting on the use of language in the quotations.

Common mistakes

You are also likely to write a better answer if you know what you should **not** do. These are some of the mistakes commonly made by students:

→ **Misinterpreting texts** This is forgivable if it occurs after a genuine attempt to understand the text, but often it happens because of careless reading, or because information included in the question has been ignored. Remember also that you don't need to refer to every single word of the text, so if parts of it are unclear to you the simplest solution might just be to leave them out of your answer.

→ **Too much narrative paraphrase** This means 'telling the story' of the text – i.e. giving a simple account of its surface meaning.

→ **Feature spotting** It is important to use relevant terminology, but only refer to stylistic features if you can comment on their significance or effect. Avoid baldly stating *There is a simile in line 3* or *There is alliteration in line 12*.

→ **Spending too long on one text** This is especially a danger if you adopt a 'chronological' approach to the analysis (see above).

Final tips

Here is some final advice to help you succeed.

Know what you have to do

Try to make sure that from the outset of the course you have a clear idea of what lies ahead of you. You need to know which examining board **specification** you're taking, how many examinations you'll be sitting and when you'll be taking them, whether you'll be doing **coursework**, what **set texts** you'll be studying and so on. Your teacher will probably give you much of this information; make sure you keep it in your file and remember where it is for future reference. The complete specification can usually be downloaded free of charge from the relevant examining board website.

Making use of past papers

Some boards also have **past papers** which you can download free of charge. Alternatively, all examining boards have publications departments which can supply copies of past exam papers. You can telephone them for more details or order from their online catalogues.

Past papers are very useful. Try to get recent ones in case there have been any changes in the format of the paper or the style of the questions. Use them to familiarise yourself with the structure of the paper: check how many sections there are, how many questions you have to answer, whether there is a choice of questions, the allocation of marks for each question and so on.

Practise for the examination by planning some answers, or by writing some complete timed answers (this may be unnecessary if you get plenty of exam practice at your school or college).

Studying set texts

When you are studying a set text for an examination, you need to know whether it is for an **open book** or a **closed book** exam. 'Open book' means you can take the book into the examination with you, 'closed book' means you can't.

If it is an open book exam, you are usually allowed to **annotate** the book with handwritten notes. Be careful here. The examining boards usually stipulate that annotation should be brief, and notes rather than continuous prose. In any case, excessive annotation can lead to confusion in the examination itself. You should have a detailed set of notes which you use for revision purposes, and the book then only needs to contain key words, highlighted passages etc. to remind you of these more detailed arguments.

In an open book exam you should be careful to avoid the temptation to include overlong quotations, and should not copy out passages from any critical material (such as an introduction) provided in the book itself (examiners can always spot this). Although you will have the book with you, **you still need to know it thoroughly**. You do not want to waste time in the examination hunting down quotations.

> **Take note**
>
> It's also important to know the **assessment objectives** for each component of the course. See pages 6–7.

> **Take note**
>
> Don't leave all the annotation until the last minute – students who do this often find they haven't enough time and wish they'd annotated the book while they were studying it.

If it is a closed book exam, part of your revision will involve memorising key **quotations**. When you learn the quotation, always revise at the same time the point that the quotation illustrates.

Coursework

There should be no excuse for students under-achieving on **coursework** modules, though many do. The reason is often that the work has been completed in a rush and as a result does not reflect the student's true ability. You need to give yourself plenty of time to complete the assignment, and it is important to keep to deadlines. The deadline for the first draft is often the most crucial. Meeting this gives your teacher time to look at your work, and you time to act on your teacher's advice.

Grade A students have not always achieved the top grade in every examination. Instead, through conscientious effort, they have gained a very high coursework mark and this has offset lower marks in one or more of the exam modules. On the other hand, if you get a low coursework mark you will be facing an uphill battle to achieve a high overall grade when you sit the examinations.

Exam revision

Many books have been written about **revision techniques**, and you will certainly be given advice by your school or college. Most experts would agree that you should do the following:

→ Start early.
→ Be organised. Work out what you're going to revise and when you're going to revise it.
→ Don't draw up a revision schedule that's over-ambitious. Allow for breaks and days off.
→ Find a revision method that works for you (this might involve a bit of experimentation!).

Exam technique

As part of your preparation for the examination you should familiarise yourself with the format of the exam paper. Even so, in the real examination it is still important to **look over the paper carefully**, checking how many questions you need to answer and how many marks are allocated to each question (the way you divide your time in the examination should reflect this). You should also **read the questions very carefully**. Underline key words and make sure you know exactly what the question wants you to do. There may be valuable advice on how to approach the question. Often questions also contain important background information about unseen texts.

Above all, **be positive**: if you've prepared well, you should be able to look forward to the examination as an opportunity to impress the examiner with the depth of your knowledge and understanding. Good luck!

Take note

Quotations that might be useful in answering a number of possible questions (because they can be used to illustrate several different points or arguments) are especially worth remembering.

Take note

Obviously the first step in passing the examination is actually turning up for it! Every year some students miss morning examinations because they thought they were in the afternoon. Make sure you know the correct dates and times for all of your examinations.

Glossary

Abstract vocabulary

Vocabulary which refers to things that do not physically exist (ideas, feelings etc.).

Adjective

A word used to describe a noun.

Adverb

Usually a word that gives more information about a verb. Many adverbs end in -ly (e.g. *slowly*, *carefully*).

Allegory

A story with at least two levels of meaning, often involving the use of human characters to represent ideas.

Alliteration

When two or more words begin with the same sound.

Ambiguity

Having more than one possible meaning.

Anapaestic metre

Within poetry, a metre in which two unstressed syllables are followed by a stressed syllable.

Anglo-Saxon

See **Old English**.

Antithesis

When words, ideas etc. are directly opposite in meaning.

Archaism

A word or expression that has fallen out of use.

Aside

In drama, a brief piece of speech heard by the audience but not by the other characters.

Assessment objective

One of the criteria used to allocate marks in AS/A2 assessment.

Assonance

The rhyming of vowel sounds within two or more words.

Asyndetic listing

A list which does not use conjunctions.

Auditory imagery

Imagery which appeals to our sense of hearing.

Augustan period

The first half of the 18th century.

Ballad

A poem that tells a story in simple, everyday language.

Bildungsroman

A German term for a novel that charts the growth of a character from early years to maturity.

Blank verse

Unrhymed poetry based on the **iambic pentameter**.

Caesura

A pause in a line of poetry – usually in the middle of the line, and usually shown by a punctuation mark.

Comparative

An adjective which makes a comparison, such as *bigger*, *worse*, *better*.

Colloquial language

The language of everyday conversation.

Conceit

An elaborate, extended metaphor based on an unexpected comparison between dissimilar objects.

Concrete vocabulary

Vocabulary which refers to things that physically exist.

Conjunction

A word that joins together parts of a sentence (e.g. *and*, *but*).

Connotations

The associations that a word has.

Contexts

The background influences on a text or part of a text.

Couplet

A pair of rhymed lines.

Courtly love

A set of conventions related to the presentation in literature of romantic love. Especially influential in the Middle Ages.

Criticism

Comment on, or analysis of, a text (not necessarily unfavourable).

Dactylic metre

Within poetry, when each stressed syllable is followed by two unstressed syllables.

Denotation

The straightforward, objective dictionary meaning of a word.

Dialect

A form of language with distinctive features of vocabulary, grammar etc. Usually the term refers to **regional dialect** (e.g. Geordie, Cockney).

Dissonance

When the sounds of words are so different that they clash with each other, creating a discordant effect.

Dramatic irony

In drama, when something said by a character has an additional meaning or significance, apparent to the audience but not to the character.

Dramatic monologue

An extended piece of speech by an imaginary character.

Elegy

A poem that mourns someone's death. The term is also sometimes applied more generally to solemn, contemplative poems.

Elision

The omission of a sound or syllable (e.g. *o'er* instead of *over*).

Emotive language

Language intended to produce an emotional response in the reader or listener.

End-focus

When emphasis is placed on the end of a sentence.

End-stopped line

When the end of a line of poetry coincides with a grammatical pause, which is usually indicated by a punctuation mark.

Enjambement

In poetry, when the sense of one line continues into the next, and the end of the first line has no punctuation mark.

Epic poetry

Long poems, often about mythical heroes and with grand, impressive settings.

Epistolary novel

A novel in the form of letters written by the main characters.

Extended metaphor

A metaphor which is continued and developed over several lines (or more) of a text.

Fable

A story with a clear moral or message, often with animals as characters.

Figurative language

Language that is not to be taken literally.

First person

Use of first person pronouns such as *I, me, we, us*.

Foot

A group of two or three syllables forming a unit within the metre of a poem (e.g. a line based on the iambic pentameter has five feet because there are five pairs of syllables).

Foregrounding

Using word order to highlight part of a sentence.

Foreshadowing

See **prefiguring**.

Form

The overall shape or pattern of a text. Sometimes used to mean the same as **genre**.

Formal language

The opposite of **informal** language; language that is not casual or conversational.

Genre

A type of text (e.g. short story, newspaper article).

Gothic novel

A type of horror story, especially associated with 18th and 19th century English literature.

Grammar

A broad term for the rules that govern how we form words and combine them into sentences.

Gustatory imagery

Imagery which appeals to our sense of taste.

Half-rhyme

When a rhyme is not quite complete; usually the consonants in the rhyming words match but the vowels do not. Also known as **pararhyme**.

Heroic couplet

In poetry, a pair of rhymed **iambic pentameter** lines of verse.

Hyperbole

Intentional exaggeration.

Iambic pentameter

A poetic metre in which a line has five pairs of syllables, with the stress falling on the second syllable in each pair.

Idiolect

The way language is used by a particular individual.

Imagery

Any aspect of a text that appeals to the reader's senses. Also used more specifically to refer to the use in literature of **similes** and **metaphors**.

Informal language

Language that is casual, conversational; the opposite of **formal**.

Internal rhyme

Occurs when words rhyme within a line of poetry.

Intonation

Tone of voice.

Inversion (or **Inverted syntax**)

Reversal of the normal order of words in a phrase or sentence.

Irony

Saying the opposite of what is meant. Can also refer to an event having consequences which are the opposite of those expected or intended. See also **dramatic irony**.

Kitchen sink drama

A movement within British drama mainly associated with the 1950s, in which there was a strong emphasis on domestic realism.

Lyric poetry

Poetry which expresses an individual's thoughts and feelings (most poetry can be described as lyric poetry).

Magic realism

Writing which is a blend of realism and fantasy.

Metaphor

A comparison which is not literally true because it refers to something as if it were something else.

Metaphysical poetry

A term used to describe the work of a group of 17th century poets, including John Donne and George Herbert.

Metre

The pattern of stressed and unstressed syllables within a poem.

Middle English

The version of English spoken and written from (approximately) 1150–1450. It was a mixture of **Old English** and French.

Modernist poetry

A term used for the work of some poets in the first half of the 20th century, which deliberately rejected traditional forms and conventions.

Monologue

An extended utterance spoken by one person.

Monosyllabic

Having one syllable.

Motif

An element such as an image, phrase or action which occurs repeatedly in a work of literature.

Narrative poetry

Poetry that tells a story.

Naturalistic dialogue

Dialogue which resembles natural conversation.

Neologism

A new word or expression.

Noun

A word which names an object, person, feeling etc.

Novella

A short novel.

Ode

A lengthy poem addressed to a person, object or abstract idea.

Old English

The version of English spoken and written from (approximately) the fifth century to 1150. Also known as **Anglo-Saxon**.

Olfactory imagery

Imagery which appeals to our sense of smell.

Omniscient narrator

In prose fiction, an 'all seeing, all knowing' narrator.

Onomatopoeia

When words imitate the sounds they describe (e.g. *splash*, *buzz*).

Paradox

A statement or situation which appears to contradict itself but which is nevertheless true.

Parallelism

When parts of sentences (or complete sentences) have a similar pattern or structure.

Pararhyme

See **half-rhyme**.

Parody

A humorous imitation of another work.

Passive voice

Using a verb in a way that emphasises the object of an action rather than the person or thing performing the action (e.g. *The man was questioned by the police* instead of *The police questioned the man*).

Pastoral

Literature associated with rural life.

Pathetic fallacy

A literary technique which uses natural elements (such as the weather) to reflect human moods and emotions.

Persona

In a literary work, a narrator who is a character created by the author.

Personification

When something not human is described as if it were.

Polysyllabic

Having three or more syllables.

Postcolonial literature

A term used for literature from, or about, Britain's former colonies.

Prefiguring

Occurs when something in a text anticipates (or **foreshadows**) a later part of the text.

Preposition

A word that indicates how one thing is related to something else (e.g. *The book is on the table*).

Pronoun

A word that takes the place of a noun (e.g. *he*, *it*).

Protagonist

The central character in a play.

Pun

A humorous play on words, dependent on a word or phrase having a double meaning.

Quatrain

A four-line stanza, usually with a regular rhyme scheme.

Renaissance

A term used for the resurgence of art and literature that occurred in the 15th and 16th centuries.

Restoration period

The period of English history immediately following the restoration of the monarchy in 1660.

Rhetorical features

Traditional devices and techniques used to make speech or writing more powerful and persuasive.

Rhetorical question

A question which does not require an answer.

Rhyme scheme

The pattern of rhymes within a poem.

Romantic poetry

A term used to describe the work of a group of poets from the late 18th and early 19th centuries.

Satire

A literary work which uses humour and ridicule to make a serious point.

Second person

Use of second person pronouns such as *you* and *your*.

Sibilance

The repetition of 's', soft 'c', 'sh' and 'z' sounds.

Simile

A comparison which uses the words *like* or *as*.

Soliloquy

In drama, an extended speech by a character, heard by the audience but not by the other characters.

Sonnet

A poem of 14 lines, usually with a traditional rhyme scheme and a rhythm based on the iambic pentameter.

Spondaic metre

Within poetry, when there are two successive stressed syllables.

Standard English

The 'standard', formally correct variety of English, used in most written texts and taught in schools.

Stanza

A separate section of a poem consisting of several lines (also sometimes known as a **verse**).

Stream of consciousness

Writing which aims to capture as accurately as possible an individual's flow of thoughts; in doing this, conventional punctuation and sentence construction are sometimes abandoned.

Stress

Within poetry, emphasis on a syllable that is required by the poem's **metre**.

Structure

Similar to **form**, but a broader term which also covers the sequence of ideas in a text.

Subplot

A secondary plot running alongside the main plot of a play or a novel.

Superlative

An adjective meaning 'the most' of something (e.g. *biggest, worst, best*).

Symbol

Something (often a physical object) used in a literary text to represent something else.

Syndetic listing

A list with one or more conjunctions.

Syntax

An aspect of grammar, referring to the ways in which words are put together to form sentences.

Taboo language

Words that are avoided because they are considered offensive or obscene.

Tactile imagery

Imagery which appeals to our sense of touch.

Theatre of the Absurd

Within drama, a movement that emerged in the 1950s. It sought to reflect the absurdity of existence by deliberately rejecting conventional approaches to plot and dialogue.

Third person

Grammatical constructions which do not use the **first** or **second person**. This may involve nouns (e.g. *The house is a ruin*) or third person pronouns (e.g. *It is a ruin*).

Trochaic metre

Within poetry, when the first syllable in every pair of syllables is stressed.

Unseen texts

In the examination, texts set for analysis which you are unlikely to have seen or studied before.

Verb

A word that refers to a physical or mental action (e.g. *run, think*) or to a 'state' (e.g. *seems, is*).

Visual imagery

Imagery which involves an appeal to our sense of sight.

Vocabulary

A writer's choice of words.

Index